Uncommon Voyage

*Parenting a Special Needs Child
in the World of Alternative Medicine*

Laura Shapiro Kramer

Foreword by
Seth Kramer

FABER & FABER
BOSTON · LONDON

First published in the United States in 1996 by
Faber and Faber, Inc., 53 Shore Road, Winchester, MA 01890

Copyright ©1996 by Laura Shapiro Kramer

Library of Congress Cataloging-in-Publication Data

Kramer, Laura Shapiro.
   Uncommon voyage : parenting a special needs child in the world of
alternative medicine / by Laura Shapiro Kramer.
      p. cm.
   ISBN 0-571-19887-2 (hardcover)
   1. Cerebral palsy—Alternative treatment.   2. Developmentally
disabled children—Medical care.   I. Title.
RJ496.C4K73   1996
618.92′836—dc20   95-40161
                                                                              CIP

Jacket design by Darlene Barbaria
Printed in the United States of America

Some names, identifying characteristics,
and other details have been changed.

For Jay
because you are everything

Contents

FOREWORD

❖

My Name Is Seth

❖

MY NAME IS SETH. I am twelve years old. I have a disability called cerebral palsy. It isn't curable, but it feels fixable. I have it, and I have learned to live with it. Sometimes I think it makes me special. For one thing, I've met many interesting people like scientists, doctors, scholars. My disability has taken me all over the world. I don't actually feel that I would change having cerebral palsy because I wouldn't be me if I didn't have it.

When I watch people I think of things that other people wouldn't think about. I look at how people act, how they move. Sometimes I do more watching because I can't participate. Also I like to think a lot. When I first see people, I think about whether when they meet me they will think I'm strange or how they will react to me. I think about what to do if they think I'm strange, so I'm ready for them. Little kids ask me why I am the way I am, and I respond according to their age. Sometimes I just walk away, or sometimes I ask back, "Why do you dress like that?" or "Why do you have that accent?" If they're older, I try to explain myself, but really older kids don't ask me much because they're more mature.

You need hope if you are a parent who has a child with cerebral palsy. Hope helps you. You need hope to live on. I know my parents had hope, and that's how I progressed. They believed in me and what they could do for me. You need to feel what your child is feeling. What motivates me is my family and how much my parents care about me and are interested in getting help for me. My sister, Haya, has always been great through all of this.

My friends and teachers also motivate me. My doctors help me believe in myself. They tell me I'm lucky that I don't have worse things wrong with me. They help me do things I thought I could never do. Today I go biking on a tandem bike. I learned to swim. A baseball player taught me how to swing a bat and climb on monkey bars. These were some of the things I didn't think I would ever do. There are things I worry about for the future, but I'm trying not to think about them now. I think I will be able to learn to drive a car. I hope so.

My mom makes me feel she understands me because she's my mother and she reassures me especially in new situations with new people. She did lots of research. She talked to the doctors and read their reports. She knows what my situation is because she has personal knowledge. In my case, I needed to be pushed sometimes, too. I didn't always like the doctors, but my mom insisted that I go.

I know other people have cerebral palsy and their lives are harder than mine. I still think they and their parents should have hope. They won't die from cerebral palsy.

A few of my friends really understand me. Like Evan and Matt, who don't think it's a joke that I have disabilities. They asked me once about it, and then we never talked about it again. They're the kind of friends who will wait for me to say what I want to say about how I feel being me. They include me and make me feel as if I can do everything they can do. I try to do everything they do, but there are some things I may not be able to do ever.

Then there are my friends who watch out for me even though we've never had big conversations about what is wrong with me. Maybe I tell them why I can't do something. This depends on the situation. To some people I say I have a disability. To other people I maybe say I will get hurt. When we go to the park my friends try to help me even if I never told them anything.

There are people who just don't understand anything about me and think my disability is a joke. They giggle and sometimes they make fun of me. When I was smaller I got used to all this, so now I don't say anything. I just ignore them. But if someone asks me, I explain myself to them. I say why I have it, but that happens very, very rarely. In my life a stranger has never asked me anything about why I am the way I am. Sometimes I see they are wondering, though. The most important thing is I don't want pity. Don't pity me. It may take me more time to do some things. But I will do them if I have time, so don't pity me.

When I was in the first grade I knew I was different for the first time I guess. Evan, who is now my best friend, asked me why I was in California and going to Dr. Frymann. First I said I didn't know. Then I asked my mom. She told me about when she was pregnant with me and how I was born. Whatever she told me made me feel astonished, but not astonished. I was too young to be afraid or worried. I think I was too young to understand much about what it all meant. Later, between third and fourth grade, I started to worry. When I saw other children doing sports and activities I couldn't do, I thought they would be leaving me behind.

As I get older, I use my brain to help me be with other children, not my physical body. Not many kids ask me what's wrong with me, and not many kids tease me. I've been so long in one school until now that everyone knows me. I am going to a new school next year. I visited there already once or twice. I saw another boy who is very small. I don't know if he's a dwarf. But no one is the same. The world is full of people with differences.

If I knew someone with cerebral palsy, I would tell them to speak to my mom or dad, who know a lot about medicine and doctors. They found out about alternative medicine when I was two years old. My mom had a back problem and finally had an operation. She went to a woman who taught her breathing work. Carola taught my mom things to do with me. Then I went to Anat. She had a big studio with a plant in it. She did exercises with me that I didn't like. The positions she put me in hurt. I was too little to know that the exercises were going to help me.

I think it's great that this treatment my mom has me do and the whole family uses works using nature and the mind and body. I love nature, and when I do this work I can see how much nature is helping me. I like technology, especially computers, but sometimes technology does not exactly fall into place. The new machines, all the antibiotics, they sometimes don't work for you. I don't think anything gets much better than this, I mean the body and mind that God gave us.

When I go to a doctor or therapist I know if they really want to help or if they're just doing it for the money. I can tell by the way it feels. I just know by the way they treat me. There was a time in my life when I was sick of having people touch me. I did not want to go to any doctors. There were too many doctors, too many hands on me, too many diagnoses. They would put their hands on me, do their thing, spend half an hour with my parents, give a diagnosis, and then on another day, a totally different doctor. Maybe this wasn't exactly reality, but this is how it felt. Now I have three to four main doctors that I feel are really my friends. They know how to help me and want to because they really believe in helping. They're not like the other doctors I saw who see me, get paid, and go on to another patient.

Dr. Frymann makes me feel more loose. I feel relaxed, tired, and very ready for action all at the same time when I see Dr. Frymann. I hate the music. It's not my type of music. I like rock-and-roll and rap, and she only plays classical. But Dr. Frymann definitely makes me more relaxed and loosens my body.

All that I am saying is that none of this makes the disability go away. But it makes it easier to live with. Maybe this book will help other people have an easier life, too. I hope so.

I told my mom when I started writing this chapter that I wanted to mention some people who help me to be more comfortable in my body and to breathe better. They are Dr. Frymann, Dr. Masiello, Dr. Stough, and Dr. Springall. Kirsten DeBear is someone I worked with for a short time who taught me small tricks for everyday living, things like cutting my own food, tying my shoes, and buttoning my buttons. She made me feel I had a real friend in her.

My teachers at the Stephen Gaynor School—Mr. Jacobson, Miss Kennedy, Mr. O'Hare, and the school itself—have helped me know I was always normal. The teachers at the Beth Israel Day School in California let me come to their classes and be a part of things even though I didn't live there all the time. They also made me know I was normal. Especially Mrs. Solomon, my first-grade teacher in California, who knew I could read when not everyone else thought I could. I love these people and think about them a lot.

PREFACE

◆

The Landscape

◆

I HAVE WRITTEN THIS BOOK in response to the letters and phone calls I constantly receive from parents who have children like my son, Seth. They ask me what to do, what I know, and how I found out what I needed for my child, for me, and for our family. They want to talk and to cry. They want hope. Encouragement. My own need for hope returns again and again. Sharing helps me lend dignity to my personal battle.

Any praise I receive for what I have accomplished, I weigh against the fact that I am guilty of looking to heal myself through my son's circumstances. My search for a meaningful career was resolved by my son. It is the reason I finally became a writer and gave up a long career in the entertainment industry. My confrontation with God—why my child, why my family, why me—forced my own spiritual awakening. And I have a confession: serendipity has been the biggest player; I have been remarkably lucky. I have been accused of using my son and his circumstances, of exploiting them. This is true. It is this combination of great good fortune and manipulation (a pestering advocacy, very assertive at times) that has propelled me forward. And defined me.

All parents of "special" children experience confusion, fear, sadness, and frustration. I wish to give universal voice to our heartfelt struggle, to offer encouragement and information. My story belongs to me, but in sharing it I reach out to embrace our mutual experience, so all of us will be less alone. I want to be an example, to help galvanize others to think, to act, to create the passport to their children's potential. The Chinese word for "crisis" has two characters: one is a symbol for danger; the other is a symbol for opportunity.

When a child is diagnosed as "special"—learning or hearing impaired, asthmatic, blind, autistic, diabetic, allergic, and on and on—confusion marks a traumatic period; heartbreak best describes the emotional reaction. It is difficult enough to latch on to a rudder, an even keel in our emotions, never mind to the empirical information. It is difficult to know what to believe about anything, especially the orthodox medical establishment, educational and physical rehabilitation options, prognosis and expectations, special programs, immunizations. To do this at a critical, demanding time when important decisions and immediate resolutions are needed is taxing. We are off balance, unsettled. Everything is unfamiliar, yet critical assessment and evaluations are mandatory.

Sorting out feelings, our own and those of the people around us, is daunting—and continual. Loved ones, the siblings of our child, in-laws, spouses, all are a central ongoing part of the equation. The feelings are recurring, not static. To this day I have not found collected in one place a cohesive perspective, relevant personal experience, practical information, and resources. I am frustrated by the truth: there are no answers, only the right questions. I cannot tell you what to do. No one told me. I can relate what I did and what I felt along the way and hope that it will help others make decisions.

When our son was diagnosed with "mild cerebral palsy" at ten months old—I had to insist on, even beg for, a diagnosis—no one professional helped me or gave me an overview or guidelines to navigate the maze that suddenly confronted me and my family. When the neurologist told us that Seth had mild cerebral palsy, I asked, "What does that mean?" The picture we had in our minds was of kids in special vans, in wheelchairs, who couldn't hold their heads up, whose speech was slurred. Did it mean he would not walk for a long time and would never walk "normally"? I got vague, incomprehensible answers. (I was surrounded by top medical professionals, yet no one ever mentioned speech. It would be months before I looked "cerebral palsy" up in the dictionary and realized, yikes! there's more!)

I asked, "What about physical therapy?" and the doctor answered that I could try. But I didn't know much about it or where to look. And he offered no suggestions. I didn't know how many kinds of physical therapy existed or how to evaluate a physical therapist or a physical rehabilitation program. (In the moment of the diagnosis I could barely swallow, never mind collect my thoughts to ask important questions.)

Once I knew what Seth's circumstances were, I had an agenda: defy the pessimistic diagnosis and the defeatist prescriptions of the orthodox medical establishment and uncover all information required to help our son realize his full potential, not knowing what that potential was.

Blindly, I plunged into an ocean I had never swum in before, believing that I could make right all the wrongs. It would be years before I knew anything and years before Seth walked. But today I am familiar with all conventional therapies, gait trainers and orthotic and orthopedic remedies, as well as neurodevelopmental treatment (NDT) and the Bobath method. My voyage took me around the world of mainstream, orthodox medicine and delivered me into a completely other world, a world of "alternative" therapies—osteopathy, cranial-sacral work, the Feldenkrais method, sensorimotor work, homeopathy, Yoga, and more. A multitude of other concepts, alternatives, and possibilities are now part of my lore. I still find nothing about these options in books about cerebral palsy. I built networks and support systems. I uncovered resources and guides in the world and within myself. I became educated. I learned to advocate. I became a communicator, an expert, and a pioneer. I became a resource for others.

My world became something it was not before. My perspective on life was profoundly altered. And I suffered feelings of abandonment and guilt. There are still storms of confusion and shock. The horizon is always within view, but I have never stopped wishing I could lie back and sail to a place where all would be well, that FINALLY the right course would be established. Weary from the demands to be vigilant, exploratory, constantly attentive, on guard, I intermittently allow myself to sink into lethargy, to fall into a stupor. It's not worthy, even though it happens.

Three years after the diagnosis, my channel of memory opened. Out of nowhere I recollected youthful summer experiences and presentiments of my past. The only curiosity is that it took so long for me to remember. My husband and I had started vacationing on Cape Cod the summer of Seth's first birthday. We believed the Cape's unique environment offered stimulation and potential for Seth; it has, but in many different ways than we ever imagined. It was during our fourth summer on the Cape that the prescience of my early years seeped into my consciousness. There was a flood of recognition and feelings and shock. Was I telepathic? Had I had some inkling of my destiny? Had I invented my son to satisfy a youthful fantasy? These emotions challenged my equilibrium. I felt off balance.

Recently I shared this experience with Seth. We were discussing the differences between the doctor who had attended me with his sister's birth and the doctor who had attended me with his. It was not a discussion long on details, as I have yet to thoroughly describe to him what specifically occurred. But he knows there were anomalies surrounding the labor and delivery. He asked me which doctor was better, knowing I would answer that his sister's was superior.

"Anyway," I said, looking into both of his radiant and knowing blue eyes, "I invented you."

"Oh, Mom," he responded, laying his head across my chest and letting me embrace him.

We are linked, each of us fulfilling our destiny. Was it preordained? Whatever our fate, Seth and I are now joined by a common exigency. I have a job, a mission. I need to educate myself about everything available for Seth and be sure he gets what he needs so he can realize his potential. At the same time, Seth's circumstances have presented me with the opportunity for my own self-improvement. Only by evolving psychologically could I set an example and inspire him to be all that he can be.

There is no hand wringing. While I do not deny that I have recurring feelings of rage, disappointment, and sorrow for him and for our family, I support the integrity of Seth's experience by not confusing it with my reaction to it. I try to manage my feelings and keep them distinct from Seth's and from the feelings of Haya, our daughter. Unearthing the meaning in this experience encourages my own inner growth. Coping brings me closer to my family and loved ones. It means summoning all my personal resources.

Seth's presence fills me with joy. He helps me discover the capacity to love and to nurture, to open my heart and my soul; to offer what is gleaned there to others, patiently, gladly.

We all became the people we are because Seth is our son, our brother, our grandchild, our cousin, our neighbor, our friend. There is a life-long tension between trying to intervene and make the disability go away and accepting the person our son is. There is stigma and frustration, and anger, but there is also purpose and meaning.

I have covered the surface of the earth in search of solutions, help, aid, understanding, hope. Often I am in conflict. There came a time when my husband and I instigated a lawsuit because of the circumstances surrounding our son's birth, a trauma I had blotted out. I was forced to undergo a painful psychological self-examination. It meant confronting my own ignorance and a pattern of self-delusion that was difficult to admit. The process highlighted how little I knew because I didn't want to know more. I continue to struggle with this syndrome, with decisions, with conflict, with lethargy. Once I agonized over whether to teach Seth sign language. Then we had to decide about surgery. Sometimes the battles are obvious, and sometimes they are hidden.

I hope my book will be good company for you on your singular journeys. At the countless and inevitable crossroads we encounter, perhaps because of this book you will know more about how to interpret the guides and read the indicators, how to clarify situations, how to be tuned in to intuitions and instinct. I have only one absolute word of advice: bring a notebook and pen to record the trek. Memory is the best marker. To safeguard it, write everything down.

Acknowledgments

I WISH TO THANK Dr. Viola Frymann and Mary Helen and the office staff at the Osteopathic Center for Children; Dr. Domenick Masiello and his secretary Bibi; Dr. Carl Stough; Dr. Peter Springall, Valerie Cimino; Karen Gantz; and Liz Pennisi in Dr. Yale's office; Alan Mann for making me computer literate and then some; George and Greg Johnson for organizing me during the summer; Michele Parker for being the best wife any person could have and making possible the summer I needed; Helen Reilly and Betty Medina for keeping me and my family fed and organized; Rosemarie Whitelaw for every kind of administrative help and otherwise; Bob Eastwood for the space for me to write that he found in Woods Hole; Judy Dimon for the incredible example to me of all that is good and worthwhile; Claire Roderick Keerl for being there every day; my dear friends in the BJ community who support and nourish me, especially Myriam, Aviva, Marta, and Matt and Millie, Laurie Baum and Roly, as well as others too numerous to mention; Sherry Suib Cohen for her unflagging encouragement; Maureen Baron for making the difference.

Haya, the daughter every mother dreams about, who gave me a chance to be the mother I wished to be.

Seth Jeremy Kramer, my inspiration and love.

Uncommon Voyage

1

◆

Origins

◆

JUNE 16, 1984, was a perfect early summer day: warm, but not yet hot like July. The sky was pure blue, the blue of Seth's sparkling eyes. The air was imbued with hints of summer's fragrances. Our family was gathered in our rented summer house in the Berkshires to celebrate Seth's first birthday. It was a Sunday. My parents were visiting for the weekend. Aunt Edna and Uncle Irving had driven up from Boston for the day. Everyone wanted to be part of the festivities for their beloved grandchild and their favorite grandnephew. He had captured everyone's heart.

My mother was busy with Seth's favorite dessert: strawberry shortcake. She stood in the yellow country kitchen and whipped the cream with an old electric beater. My father entertained Seth by working to disentangle the line of his fishing rod. Daddy already doted on his only grandson. Seth's dad, my husband Jay, arranged the presents while I decorated the table with typical birthday ornaments. Aunt Edna and Uncle Irv hung streamers, chattering incessantly about their affection for their grandnephew. Seth's dazzling smile and bright blue eyes eclipsed even the grandeur of the hills we could see out our windows.

Seth's enthusiasm was contagious. At one year old he knew how to use his incredible charm. He engaged everyone, even strangers, with his eyes, which radiated a knowing twinkle. It made everyone feel he was special. From the very beginning Seth drew people into his world and connected them to himself. We already knew he was a rare individual.

An easy baby with immense charisma, he had been sleeping through the night since he was three weeks old. He loved his baby swing. He sat cheerfully with adults in his table seat, one of those contraptions that fastens to the side of the table. In restaurants, in his stroller, at the shops and in the streets, people always stopped to admire him; how handsome he was, how attractive, how charming. He never complained about anything. He basked in all the admiration.

When the cake was finished, adorned with a crown of huge luscious ruby red strawberries and appropriately engulfed by whipped cream, I carried it to the table, singing "Happy Birthday" in full voice. Seth glowed. He blew out his candles and ate his cake with gusto. Sounds of joy and pleasure emanated from all of us. The snapshots depict him laughing heartily, whipped cream everywhere.

But earlier that morning, I had gone down to the basement of the house, where the washer and dryer were. Alone with the laundry, standing in the dim light, I spilled the tears I had yet to cry. I hung my head, then shook my fist toward heaven, questioning. Inwardly, silently, I hollered my determination. But I was afraid of the future. Seth had been diagnosed with cerebral palsy only eight weeks before. What could I hope for now? What could I expect? How could this be true? What would it mean? The only sureness I had was that my life was inalterably changed. Nothing would ever be the same again.

When Seth was born, in 1983, Jay and I had been married for five years. Jay is an attorney with a passion for baseball. At the time of our marriage, Jay decided to go into business for himself as a sole practitioner. At the same time he supported my effort to try independent producing. Both of these quests required huge leaps of faith and even bigger financial risks. For that reason we had postponed parenting.

When I was thirty-five and enjoying a small professional success and Jay's practice was stabilized, we decided to have a baby. When we first learned I was pregnant, baby books were scattered all over the house. Once we confirmed that we were expecting a child, I thought I remembered the instant the baby had been conceived. I was blissful. I would be the very model of a healthy contemporary woman, working and remaining physically active throughout my pregnancy. I didn't smoke, and I planned to continue my regime of swimming and taking exercise classes. Although I was not as slim as I once had been or hoped to be again, I intended to stay active.

I was also at the peak of my professional life. Our child was conceived in the Berkshires, where I was producing a play at the Berkshire Theater Festival. I had just returned from Santa Fe, New Mexico, where I had produced a new musical with Madeline Kahn, and I was in the midst of casting a Broadway show.

Looking back at the books I read at the time, I realize they were more about babies than about pregnancy. That was before the publication of *What to Expect When You're Expecting.* Years later I told the Eisenbergs, the authors of that invaluable book, how much I wish I had had their book to read when I was pregnant the first time.

My doctor was handsome and cavalier. He took a nonchalant attitude toward my pregnancy, and I let him. Jay and I did go for genetic counseling to determine the risk, the possibilities, and probabilities that our child could have genetic anomalies that might result from age, ethnic background, family history. The genetic counselor asked us a lot of questions to ascertain what we should be tested for based on our genetic history. One suggestion was that we go for a Tay-Sachs screening.

Tay-Sachs is a genetic disorder, usually found in people of Eastern European descent, especially Jews, that has serious consequences for a developing fetus. It causes severe mental retardation and some physical limitations. Babies with Tay-Sachs usually live only three to five years. The screening is accomplished by testing the blood of both parents, since both parents have to carry the gene in order for the baby to have a 25 percent probability of getting the disease. Our Tay-Sachs screening was negative.

I was Rh-negative, and Jay's blood type was positive. This combination concerned the doctor. It meant that there was a chance that the fetus would be Rh-positive, and I could build antibodies to his or her blood. Therefore, I was administered Rhogam, which is an immunoglobulin. I received the Rhogam at twenty-eight weeks, after the amniocentesis, and again after the birth. In the case of Rh-negative mothers, anytime there is the possibility of maternal-fetal blood contamination, Rhogam is administered.

Twenty-eight weeks into the pregnancy I also had a test for gestational diabetes. At twenty-eight weeks the placenta begins to secrete a hormone that interferes with the mother's metabolism of sugar. The glucose tolerance test determines how the mother is metabolizing sugar over a period of time. There are various ranges of normal. While the test was unpleasant, I was glad when the results showed my metabolism of sugar was normal. Except for a few sarcastic remarks about my increasing size (ultimately I gained forty pounds), the doctor had no other concerns. And neither did I.

The doctor prescribed a multivitamin with iron that made me nauseous and constipated. I opted not to take it. In the first three months I experienced severe headaches. The doctor told me to take as much aspirin as I needed. I took two, sometimes more, during the day if I needed them. What are the implications of the aspirin I took so easily? Today no one in our family takes aspirin casually. Mostly we rely on other remedies.

In preparation for my amniocentesis at twenty-eight weeks, which I remember vividly, I received my first Rhogam injection. The doctor monitored the insertion of the needle with ultrasound, so I observed the fetus on the monitor. I thought I wanted a girl baby, but the moment I saw the image of the child within me on the video monitor, I knew it was a boy. I was ecstatic. Technology captured our unborn child with his little hand going to his mouth to suck. A few weeks later the hospital confirmed the male sex of our child. Our son was due June 2.

I got fat even though I continued to swim every day. I was working hard to get my show produced on Broadway, and we were in the midst of rehearsals. The show was opening at the end of March.

During the second trimester I felt fine. I had no headaches, and my only two concerns continued to be my weight and the future episiotomy. Something I had read made me feel almost "political" about not having the episiotomy. My doctor took an unconditional stance, suggesting that an early hysterectomy was inevitable if I didn't have the procedure.

Around this time Jay and I went for a tour of the hospital and began attending a natural childbirth class. My doctor took a skeptical view of natural childbirth. I was experiencing misgivings about my doctor. Jay and I went to visit him together to talk, but not specifically about my doubts. Those I continued to keep to myself. I criticized myself for not feeling more confident. After all, the doctor had a successful practice. He had delivered many babies. That was my attitude toward doctors until I recognized that I was being passive, and then I changed. But it was already too late.

In the third trimester I was waking every morning about 5:00, often experiencing a severe headache. After an hour or so I'd take two aspirin, and at 7:00 I'd usually fall back to sleep for an hour. I was tired during the day, and I liked to lie down for an hour's nap in the afternoon. When I awoke again, often I would have another severe headache. On the doctor's advice, I'd take two more aspirin.

Jay and I moved into a large duplex apartment, and I was excited and pleased by our new surroundings. After my show opened on Broadway, my attention shifted to the anticipation of our baby's arrival. Everything felt right except the headaches and early-morning waking. I dreamt that my son weighed seven pounds. My due date of June 2 came and went. I felt no change, but I began paying close attention to every shift and motion. I continued swimming daily and going to the office, but I got a later, less energized start each day. My afternoon naps continued. At the end of the day my husband and I often would go to the movies or to the theater if only for distraction. Producing a Broadway show had made me eligible to be a Tony voter, so every Broadway producer was inviting me to his or her show that spring.

Monday evening, June 13, we went out for dinner and a movie. I ate seafood. The movie was *Blue Thunder*. The following morning I awoke feeling that there was a consistency and a regularity to my contractions, though they were mild. Jay remained at home with me throughout the morning, but nothing changed dramatically. We telephoned the doctor. He recommended that we go about our business for the day.

That night, again, I felt consistent, though mild, contractions. Discomfort, anxiety, excitement kept me awake. By Wednesday morning I was exhausted. My bag for the hospital was packed and near the front door, but though regular, the contractions were quiet. The doctor recommended that I come to his office for an examination. After examining me, he said that my cervix was dilated only slightly.

"It will be at least twenty-four hours," he pronounced. "Here is a prescription for Secanol. Fill it and go home and get some sleep. You'll need it." Again, I never questioned or argued with his attitude, which in this instance included the casual administration of a powerful narcotic. I even recall that when I went to the pharmacy to fill the prescription, I had to fill out a state form because Secanol is a controlled substance.

The doctor was matter of fact, unconcerned, and so sure of himself that it never occurred to me to mistrust him. And I was ignorant. If I'd known better, I could have asked for a stress test or queried whether this was prodromal labor—a precursory stage before the onset of labor—but since I didn't know, I was inclined to rely on the expert.

Our friendly UPS man woke me in the late afternoon, totally apologetic for disturbing my sleep, but bearing a gift for my yet-unborn son. My husband came home for a light dinner, and about nine in the evening we went to the hospital. Not much had changed, but some of the contractions were stronger, and by then we persuaded ourselves it was time. The baby was two weeks late. We were impatient.

After my admission, my doctor arrived, examined me, and nonchalantly pronounced that it would be quite some time, so he was going to get some sleep. A nurse and a doctor, both women, attended me. I wore no fetal monitor. Around 11:00 that night my waters broke. I was in a private labor room with a private bathroom and alone when the waters burst. No one fetched the waters or examined them. Had they done so, the first signs of trouble would have been apparent. It is customary to check the mother's waters for signs of meconium, a dark green fecal material that accumulates in the fetal intestines and is discharged at or near the time of birth. If meconium is aspirated by the infant, there are many consequences, some of which we discovered later.

After my waters broke, things got difficult. The contractions were stronger and more painful. I asked for something to ease the pain and was given Demerol orally. I was writhing around, trying to find a comfortable position, summoning all I could remember from the natural childbirth classes, the ones my doctor had summarily dismissed.

Soon the nurses began to monitor the baby and insisted that I not lie in the fetal position or on all fours, the only two positions in which I felt somewhat at ease. The nurse worried that the baby was not getting enough oxygen and prodded me to alter my pose. This went on for some hours. She kept after me insistently and grew increasingly concerned, finally leaving to get the resident doctor. My cervix was still not dilated completely, and I was screaming to have the attendants "get him out of me." I wanted a cesarean.

Around 5:00 in the morning my doctor poked in and suggested that I be given an epidural. I was moved to another labor room. The epidural was not effective. I could not get comfortable. The epidural was administered again. This occurred several times. Through the haze of my fatigue, pain, and the vaguely numbing effect of the epidural, I was able to feel the contractions originating and building. I announced them to my husband, who somewhere along the way had cloaked himself in a green hospital gown. He remained with me throughout.

My obstetrician came and went, but the anesthesiologist remained in the room with me. My doctor asked the anesthesiologist to administer Pitocin. I remembered reading about Pitocin and how it speeds up contractions, but I also knew that there was some controversy regarding its use. I was too disoriented to care. I was given Pitocin. Then I was given more Pitocin.

My doctor left to scrub up. The anesthesiologist, who was left alone in the room with my husband and me, asked, "Does the doctor know the baby is crowning?" My husband and I had no response. The anesthesiologist summoned a nurse. "Does the doctor know the baby is crowning?" he inquired. Suddenly I was wheeled out of the room and into the hallway toward the delivery room.

Halfway down the corridor, from the source of my primal self, from my origins, I felt the rush and presence I knew was our baby. I announced, "Here he comes."

Out came our son, an icy blue color. He lay there between my legs on the labor table in the hallway. The clock on the wall above showed 7:00 on the dot. I was quickly shuttled into the delivery room.

Alarms sounded. A team of other doctors, with green masks and gowns, my own not among them, arrived instantly. The baby was taken from me as the cord was cut. I can't remember who performed that procedure, but my baby was whisked from the room.

"I want to see him for a minute. Show him to me. Let me touch him," I cried out.

I was allowed a cursory look as the doctors rushed out with him. "He'll be all right," reassured my doctor, who had miraculously materialized from somewhere. "He's fine. He's breathing, and he simply aspirated some meconium."

Maybe I had heard the term "meconium" before, but it didn't register at that moment of chaos and anxiety. I was scared, not knowing really what was happening or what anything meant.

I was delirious with anxiety, wild. But I required a lot of stitching, having been badly torn when our child came bursting out onto the labor table. In the end, the episiotomy I had never wanted and so dreaded was never performed. There wasn't time.

I was moved to the recovery room. It was 8:00 in the morning, one hour after our baby's arrival. Around 8:30 my doctor visited me briefly and told me that our son would be fine and that he weighed 8 pounds, 2 ounces. He said that Seth was in the neonatal intensive care unit (NICU) as a precautionary measure and that I would be able to see him shortly. All the fantasies and expectations I'd had of holding my newborn child were dashed. The dream that I would nurse him on the delivery table, cuddle him, lessen the separation for both of us between his presence in the womb and his emergence into the light of day, evaporated. I only wanted to know when I would see him. The doctor seemed remote and unconcerned, again very cavalier.

A social worker visited me. She wanted to prepare me for what I would see in the neonatal unit. She said that Seth was hooked up to a lot of tubes that were necessary for monitoring and feeding him. I resisted her professional concern. I felt patronized, and I was angry. When she said she would be available to me for further support, I mentally dismissed her, denying any possibility that my son would be less than perfect.

Soon I was escorted to the NICU to see Seth for the first time. I broke down and began to cry when I saw the incubator and my infant boy child, tubes emerging from him like the tentacles of an octopus. Exhaustion engulfed me, though there was no way I would succumb to sleep. I pulled up a stool and sat down next to the incubator, determined to see everything through to a happy ending. I wanted to nurse him and directed someone to see if I could get a breast pump in my room so I would be prepared when the first opportunity presented itself. I identified the most sympathetic nurse in the NICU and enlisted her help. I nicknamed her "The White Rabbit." Jay, looking ashen and frightened, joined me by our baby's side.

At some point my doctor passed through the NICU to perform a procedure on another infant. He barely looked at us, never mind our baby. In the meantime, Jay and I got permission for the pediatrician we intended to use after Seth's birth to make a special trip to the hospital. Early the following morning Dr. Lee, after seeing Seth in the NICU, visited me in my room where I was frantically pumping my milk. She was very reassuring, very upbeat.

My hospital room was two floors away from the NICU, and the hospital procedure dictated that a staff member escort me there from my room. Once at the NICU, there were several procedures required before entering. All visitors, including my husband and me, had to scrub with a special soap and don a green hospital gown and gloves.

By the end of the day following Seth's birth, I informed anyone who dared to question my presence at any place in the hospital corridors or elevators, in no uncertain terms, that I was not waiting for a hospital staff member to take me to the NICU. I was going to go whenever I wanted to see my son. In the little time I spent away from the NICU and in my room, I worked desperately at the breast pump. The stitches in my torn perineum were uncomfortable when I sat. During the night I went to the NICU several times, instinctively talking to my new baby with soothing, constant words of love.

The White Rabbit was sympathetic. She allowed me to perform all of the essential tasks such as changing Seth's diaper, feeding him, and doing other maternal chores. I accomplished these ministrations through the small porthole of the incubator. When I returned to my room to pump milk, I remember walking uncomfortably through hallways, seeing and hearing other babies safely ensconced in their mothers' rooms in their mothers' arms, and feeling terribly sad.

The morning after Seth's traumatic birth, all of the tubes attached to him were removed. The White Rabbit helped me try to breast-feed. Seth was unresponsive. Because he was receiving an antibiotic, it was necessary to feed him regularly. He was already used to the bottle and the formula, and, although I was providing some breast milk, the amount was not sufficient for his feedings. So the feedings were being supplemented with formula milk. After all, he was a big baby, I told myself. I wasn't going to give up, though. Throughout the day I made one attempt after another to nurse. In between I kept pumping milk so that my milk would go into the bottle he got. The White Rabbit went off duty, and the other nurses were too busy and unconcerned to help, but I kept at it.

Seth was the most beautiful baby in the NICU, probably the healthiest, biggest, handsomest infant that unit had ever seen. One of the nurses remarked about his startling good looks. The nurses nicknamed him Don Juan and discussed how much the girls would love him. After all, he wasn't a preemie, and ostensibly after the initial scare, there was nothing seriously wrong with him. The doctors wanted to observe him for a few days to be sure that no infection developed because of the meconium fluid he had aspirated during his birth. Otherwise, not one doctor told us that there was anything to be concerned about. Seth looked 100 percent healthy. The fact that he demonstrated so little sucking motivation during my continual efforts to nurse didn't give anyone a clue about what was to come.

My attempts to breast-feed continued, as did my constant vigilance in the NICU. By the third day I was part of the surroundings, and the personnel simply expected to see me. On Saturday night, almost seventy-two hours after Seth's arrival, I made one more attempt to nurse him. The White Rabbit coaxed me into getting comfortable holding him like a football. I was at the point of desperation. I would be going home the next morning, and I was uncertain about whether he was going to be staying behind for a few more days of observation. It felt like my last chance for the bonding I craved. At 2:00 in the morning, he finally began sucking milk from my breast. Sometime around dawn I dozed with him at my bosom and later awoke to the changing shift and my nursing child.

When the resident doctor appeared, I remarked what a champ Seth was. He was thriving and handsome and functioning 100 percent without any support systems. The doctor agreed and suggested that the NICU staff would consider sending him home with me later in the morning. I was ecstatic. It was a hot muggy day, Father's Day and my mother's birthday. I prepared to dress Seth in the very same clothes I had worn home from the hospital on a July morning thirty-five years earlier.

My husband and new baby and I went home together. Seeing the waiting rocking chair and white crib, the nursery festooned with the typical accoutrements, my recollection of the nightmare I had experienced only days before was obliterated. My preoccupation with my new baby was absolute. Every aspect of his care delighted me. Changing his diapers, nursing him, holding him and talking to him gave me inconceivable delight. My joy buried all recollection of the recent trauma.

Seth was so good, always smiling, handsome, and easy, it never occurred to me to worry about the events surrounding his birth. In fact I was eager to forget them. I was not alerted by any of the hints a worried mother might have seized upon as evidence for concern.

2

◆

Discovery

◆

THERE WAS A LOT OF EXCITEMENT and enthusiasm about Seth after his birth. He was handsome and big and constantly smiling. He ate well and was alert, making marvelous eye contact from the very beginning. There seemed not a flicker of anything wrong. I wanted to show him off everywhere. I especially wanted to display him to all my friends at the Y, where I had been swimming every day during my pregnancy, where the women had been witnesses to my increasing size, to his unseen development.

Throughout the last months of my pregnancy I had had a massage once a week. The massage therapist who worked at the Y was an immigrant from Russia, where she had worked as a masseuse in a hospital for sick children. In Russia the medical community relies on massage as a legitimate treatment for disabled and suffering children. Of course I wanted her to massage Seth. Massaging your child was very au courant at the time, and the subject of numerous videotapes and books. It was encouraged as a path to bonding and promoting physical and psychological development. I wanted to take advantage of the current thinking about handling babies.

With a new baby in the house, schedules were difficult to coordinate, so Seth's first massage appointment didn't happen for a few weeks. By that time I was delirious with excitement over my child, madly, passionately in love with him. I went to the Y full of myself, bursting with pride about my beautiful son.

Seth reveled in all the attention of my friends at the Y. To this day he unabashedly enjoys being the star attraction. Anya, the masseuse, was excited to see him. We prepared him for the massage table by undressing him and playing with him. For the most part he seemed to like being handled, although he did complain some.

When Anya was finished, she startled me by saying, "He's very stiff, and you must stroke his head a lot." She demonstrated a caressing motion across the top of his skull away from his forehead.

I asked, "What do you mean?"

"He is very stiff. You must stroke his head a lot," she repeated with emphasis.

Anger engulfed me. What a stupid, horrible woman, I thought. I must be insane to entrust my son to her, a backward Russian whose use of the English language was primitive. I shut down. Seething inside from the insult, the gall that anyone would dare to diminish my son's obvious perfection, I dressed Seth and went away.

Years later, after many long searches finally led us to the rehabilitation method known as cranial osteopathy, I recalled Anya's advice about stroking Seth's skull. I watched a world-renowned doctor do just that in an effort to create motion and circulation inside Seth's head, and I wished I had understood what Anya had told me years before.

I had met my friend Beth at the Y. We came from similar backgrounds: we were both Jewish, middle-class, suburban women who had come of age in the sixties. But we had very divergent experiences: she had married an Israeli man after knowing him only a short time and had gotten pregnant immediately; I had married Jay after a long courtship and had waited five years to get pregnant. Beth and I had been pregnant at the same time, and we had each been swimming every day at the Y. We became even closer friends over those nine months that we carried our sons, sharing our hopes and dreams and our anxieties for our unborn children every day. Our boys were born one week apart.

Getting together with our newborns was an emotional reunion. Jonathan was big like Seth, but huskier. During the afternoon of our visit, I was surprised to learn that shortly after he was born Jonathan had required therapeutic attention. In utero he had not periodically altered the position of his head and neck. I vaguely recalled reading that this was a fairly common occurrence. Evidently the doctor recognized the anomaly and prescribed early intervention. Beth engaged a physical therapist for regular rehabilitative sessions.

To rectify the problem, the therapist told Beth, the most important thing was to change the direction of Jonathan's head when he was lying down or sleeping to be certain that he faced in either direction at some point. Beth was almost nonchalant and unconcerned. She was sure that by addressing it early, the problem would disappear.

We had a pleasant afternoon, chatting and comparing notes. I can still picture the two infant boys, about five weeks old, in their respective infant seats, happily enveloped by the surrounding friendly talk of their loving and doting mothers. Then Jonathan reached out and grabbed one of the toys dangling above him and deliberately put it into his mouth. This was hand-eye, hand-mouth coordination exemplified; executed with aplomb.

Seth had not yet demonstrated anything approaching this developmental stage. Jonathan's action surprised me. An immense surge of anxiety welled up from the pit of my stomach. Then I suppressed it. Literally, my heart had skipped a beat. I retreated to a safe inner refuge and blotted out my intuition, vague though it was, that I had witnessed a prophetic episode. I was luxuriating in new motherhood. For the moment, the intimations of our destiny, the foreshadowing, went fleeting by. A week later our family, Seth, his dad and I, left for our summer in the Berkshires.

My clear and distinct recollection of Seth that summer is of him lying on his back, arching up as though he were looking behind himself or preparing to do a backbend. My mother also noticed this remarkably frequent act. By September, after a summer of perfect baby bliss, Seth was holding his head up, smiling constantly, sleeping regularly, and eating well. But he always held his left hand clenched in a fist. It is typical of babies to have small clenched fists at birth, but at three or four months old it didn't seem appropriate. Playfully I would smack his tiny left hand and ask, "What is this fist?" and he would laugh hesitantly.

Later in the autumn, Seth and I flew to Boston to visit my grandmother, my "Honey Nana." In my photograph album there is a testimony to the day. Seth lying on his belly, commando style, on a blanket atop Nana's carpet; Seth sitting supported in an infant chair with the ubiquitous offering of Cheerios before him. There is Nana beaming nearby. But her look is accompanied by an undercurrent of concern regarding Seth's inability, or limited ability, to grasp things, a topic she discussed with me briefly.

Four weeks after Seth was born I had hired Mayra Amaya to come and live with us and help me care for Seth. She was twenty years old and came from El Salvador. Mayra had been in the United States for less than six months and was living with an aunt whose apartment was not far from ours. She agreed to live in our home from Monday morning to Friday evening, returning to her aunt on the weekends. We employed Mayra at the time when I was slowly beginning to return to work. Still nursing a few times a day, I now began pumping my milk to store in a bottle for those feedings that took place when I was absent. The pump went with me to the office. Mayra became an important member of our household for the next four and a half years. Her relationship with Seth and with the therapists we eventually engaged became integral to our family's unfolding experience.

There are a lot of pictures of Seth in Mayra's arms, his left hand still mostly in a fist, or of Seth placed standing by the side of his crib and smiling. Always smiling. But not on all fours, not sitting independently, not even trying. At that time, Seth's routine checkups with the pediatrician took place without so much as a whisper that anything was wrong. The pediatrician continued to give Seth high marks. By December I was concerned that he wasn't sitting up by himself. I interrogated everyone—other mothers, the housekeeper, Mayra. I began consulting baby books obsessively. I instructed Mayra to surround Seth with cushions in an effort to encourage him to sit. The pediatrician's reassurances were still unequivocal. Some babies sit at four months, and many not until ten months. All children develop at a different pace. That was her message.

On a Thursday evening in early January, on my sixth wedding anniversary, I was nursing Seth in the white rocking chair in his room. My concern about his not sitting persisted. It was becoming an almost full-time mental distraction. During the feeding, as I gazed down lovingly, adoringly upon my son, he took himself away from the breast, looked me full in the face, and said, "Mama."

A tremor of gladness coursed through me. The sound of his voice saying an actual word was thrilling. I was smitten. The anxiety of the last weeks was obliterated by the deep connection I felt to him. He recognized me. He knew who I was, and he knew my name. I decided then and there that his motor delays were directly attributable to his cognitive development. He couldn't be growing in both realms simultaneously, and his verbal capacity, his obvious mental accomplishments, far overshadowed the motor deficiencies. Over the next weeks his words were more frequent and more varied. I relaxed.

Later in January, when Seth was well past the six-month mark, nursing changed and became difficult. He'd start out sucking fine and then would let out a wail, pulling away violently from the breast. I agonized, did some research, and decided that maybe he was teething. Nothing I did to try to accommodate him changed his extreme behavior. Very reluctantly I gave up nursing.

It was a long time before I correlated Seth's initial difficulties of sucking and the violent alterations in nursing with the neurological anomalies associated with his condition. Eventually I did acquire the knowledge to make this connection. I learned from the physician who offered Seth his greatest rehabilitative possibilities that the first question she asks the mother of any child is "How did your baby suck?"

In February, when Seth was going on eight months, Jay and I discussed enrolling him in day care at least part-time. I wanted Seth to interact with other children. Otherwise he was almost always one-on-one with me or Jay or Mayra. Jay and I visited the Bank Street program near Columbia University. We were encouraged by what we saw. There were building blocks and toys and climbing apparatuses.

On the particular morning when we visited, there were children of various ages present, but only one other child Seth's age. That boy was pulling himself to a standing position and climbing over huge building blocks meant as obstacles to reaching other areas of the room. I was surprised by his advanced motor skills.

As Jay and I rode downtown in the cab afterward, I kept asking him whether he'd seen what that other child was able to do. Fear gripped me. I had witnessed a child Seth's same age moving and handling himself in ways completely unlike what Seth was capable of doing. The child had demonstrated an ease and flexibility and ability I had never observed in Seth. At that point Seth could only stand if we put him in what we called a "walker." It was a small circular structure on wheels that allowed him to scoot about in an erect position. Eventually, this walker would become a source of controversy, but at the time it was a source of immense joy for Seth.

After our visit to the day-care center, my obsession with Seth's inability to sit, supported or unsupported, returned full force. He was due shortly for another checkup with our pediatrician, so when the time came, I went armed with a list of questions and concerns. Dr. Lee was fairly nonchalant in her responses. She said that his reflexes were good, which was a good sign. As far as sitting was concerned, she thought we should wait until he was a year old to judge. But I couldn't wait, not one more second.

My friendship with Beth had continued. The needs of our infants and our other domestic and professional concerns kept us from getting together, but I spoke to her every few days by telephone. I knew Jonathan was sitting, but I didn't get to see him, so I was unaware of what else he was now capable of doing. When I told Beth about my concerns, she was very sympathetic and suggested that I consult the physical therapist she had used for Jonathan after his birth, when he'd had the head-position anomaly. The therapist's name was Amy, and Beth gave me her number.

Amy Katz came to see us on a Saturday afternoon two weeks after Seth's most recent routine checkup with Dr. Lee. It was March. Seth was an easy and happy child, so after twenty minutes of letting him get acquainted with Amy, I left the two of them alone surrounded by his toys. After an hour Amy summoned Jay and me to Seth's room. She remarked about what a wonderful, happy, and amenable child Seth was, and that he had a lot of good movement in him.

"A lot of good movement. What does that mean?" I asked.

Amy encouraged us to have our physician recommend a specialist. She thought Seth would benefit from a physical-therapy program. That was all she would say.

I wanted Amy to tell us more, to elaborate. I wanted her to come back the next day and the next week, and every day until she thought Seth was doing what he should be doing. As soon as she left, I called my pediatrician. It was Saturday, but I wanted to speak to her. When Dr. Lee returned my call sometime in the early evening, I told her about Amy and what she had said.

The doctor gave me the name of a neurologist to call for an appointment. "We may as well get a baseline," she said. "After all, he was a meconium baby."

That was the first hint that she or anyone else had ever given me that meconium and the circumstances of Seth's birth might be a factor in his delayed development. By this time I had a vague knowledge of what meconium was, having asked about it shortly after Seth's birth. The truth is, though, I had no idea about what exactly a neurologist does. I just made the call on the following Monday morning to Dr. Chutorian, the neurologist Dr. Lee had recommended.

The morning of the appointment, in mid-April, Jay and I were coming from separate places so we met at the neurologist's office in the hospital. Mayra met us there with Seth. Dr. Chutorian interviewed Jay and me before examining Seth. He asked a lot of questions about my pregnancy and delivery. Dr. Chutorian's questions spiked my memory. As I answered him, I remembered for the first time all the headaches I had had early in my pregnancy. The actual delivery was blurred, and I skimmed over it, not even mentioning the meconium Seth had aspirated. About the night of difficult labor I said nothing. I had completely suppressed most recollection of Seth's birth. The neurologist inquired about the milestones in Seth's development, like rolling over and crawling. I told him about my concern that Seth was not sitting. We used this opportunity to describe Seth's wonderful demeanor, his easy personality.

The doctor examined Seth with me standing nearby. He took only about twenty minutes. Then he asked Jay and me to step into his consultation room. I asked Mayra to dress Seth.

Right away, the doctor said, "Your son will live a normal life. He will walk and talk and feed himself and dress himself. But he will never walk normally, and he will not walk for a long time. Your son has mild cerebral palsy." We were floored, overwhelmed. I had to catch my breath.

"What do you mean 'he will never walk normally?'"

"When you see people on the street, look at them and see how they walk. He will never walk like them. Later on we can discuss learning difficulties."

I was so overcome with panic and questions that I didn't know the first thing to ask.

"There must be something we can do. Some kind of rehabilitation or physical therapy."

"You can try whatever you want, but I don't think anything will help. However, feel free."

"Will he go to normal schools? Will he swim and play tennis?"

"I can't answer these questions," the doctor replied. "This is a developmental disability. I am not going to order any invasive tests, though. The case is mild enough not to warrant CAT scans and so forth now. As things develop we will reconsider."

What is a developmental disability? I wanted to ask. What is this disability? What will it mean? Give me answers. Give me a crystal ball.

I emerged from the consultation room shaking, drawing a smile on my face, almost in a trance, as I glided over to Seth. He was sitting in his stroller, smiling his ever-present smile, eating apple slices. Even then I knew that I would never look at him the same way again. The pit in my stomach was monstrous. I felt sick and anxious. I sent Mayra and Seth on their way, and Jay and I went looking through the hospital for Dr. Lee, the pediatrician.

Nothing had prepared me for this revelation. None of my prior anxiety or musings had ever led me to this level of alarm or consternation. Although I had been worried for some time, it had never occurred to me that anything was so seriously wrong. And I didn't know the first thing to ask, to think, or to do.

In a flash I knew there was only one clear mandate. I had to do everything possible to make my son's life as good as it could be. Family members would need to know a certain amount, schooling would have to be investigated differently, home care might need to be reconsidered.

I had very little idea what cerebral palsy meant generally, and certainly not in Seth's case specifically. The neurologist's belief that nothing could help, that there was no course of intervention, I dismissed as hogwash. My intensely optimistic nature and my action-prone personality took over. I was scared and confused, but I mustered my energy. I would find ways of helping him. Intuitively I knew I was the starting point.

What I didn't recognize was that an altered life, a new destiny, a changed set of values, was set in motion on that April day. The diagnosis was the beginning of immense challenges—and opportunities. I struggled, failed, grew, hid, fooled myself. And through serendipity, perseverance, and the ability to risk I mostly came through for my son—and for my husband and family. Luck is really the angel of my experience. I always think of how much worse it could have been. The truth is that time assisted me in this attitude. Time and good fortune. Seth's "developmental" condition took me years to fully comprehend. Only time revealed the requirements and necessary adaptations. Time taught me the interweaving of information and circumstance. Time continues to be my master.

3

◆

Embarkation

◆

I ENTERED ADULTHOOD the day when Seth was diagnosed with cerebral palsy. I was stunned, unable to move normally. I couldn't feel
anything. I had no idea where to begin. Jay and I wandered the halls
of the hospital in search of Dr. Lee. We knew that she was on rounds
that morning. Finally, standing in her small hospital office, we told her
the news. She was shocked, truly surprised. I began cross-examining
her, pleading for answers, for a forecast. My craving for answers was
like an adolescent's. I wanted reassurance, predictions, to know how
it would turn out. She was reassuring, which endeared her to me for a
long time afterward. She told us, I remember exactly, that you can tell
some people have cerebral palsy only by turning over their shoe and
seeing the anomaly of their gait in the imprint of its sole.

While we were talking, Dr. Chutorian strolled by. Dr. Lee invited
him in to join our discussion and then quizzed him in our presence. My
overriding hunger was for a prediction. "Developmental" was the word
I kept hearing. What did "developmental" mean? It meant that we
wouldn't know what was in store, how great the challenges would be,
until they developed. What did I know about a child's normal development, though? How would I gauge the dimensions of the problem
as they manifested? Mothering was new. I felt a chord of primal fear.

I was scared, but the look on Jay's face gave real meaning to the
word "devastation." Later, as we went down in the hospital elevator, I
reassured him that it would all come out right. I was responding to my
innate optimism, sure that things couldn't be as bad as they sounded.
Somewhere deep down I also believed that if I said it would be all right

enough times, it would be true or come true. By telling Jay, I was really telling myself. Thus began the first phase of being a mother of a special needs child. The struggle for me was to find the fine line between trying to will things to be all better and being realistic. The struggle has never ceased.

We went to our offices in a taxi. During the ride I kept asking Jay what he thought, how he felt, as though his answers could change everything. At the same time I recognized my immediate responsibility to my son, my husband, and my family. There was no time for me. I had to bolster everyone around me. True to my nature, I wanted to do everything I could, to take charge and defy the odds. My first task was to be the informer.

At the office I sat at my desk taking deep breaths, and then I called my father. At first I couldn't tell him that the diagnosis was cerebral palsy. I skirted around the words, describing instead the expectations as presented by the doctor. I told him I couldn't answer empirically what the neurologist had used for the diagnosis. Finally, I confessed. Yes, the label the neurologist had used was cerebral palsy. I begged Daddy not to repeat it. It was a label. And I had no real understanding of its meaning.

As much as I wanted to lay my head down and cry, I knew it would be too alarming for our family. I felt fear. I felt anxious and sick. But I knew I couldn't show it. I think this was the moment I recognized my responsibilities as an adult. My husband's family, my family, and close family friends, all needed to be told, each in a particular way. Each would have reactions I had to be prepared for. I was still reeling, but I had to discipline myself.

After speaking to my father and getting my bearings, I phoned the physical therapist, Amy, who had encouraged us to seek the neurological diagnosis. She was unable for personal reasons to take over Seth's case, but she recommended a therapist she had worked with during her hospital years. The therapist, Susan Scheer, Amy warned me, was hard to get, busy, and much in demand.

I also phoned Annie Black, a friend who had also been my physical therapist. Over the years, episodes of lower-back pain had forced me to consult several therapists for myself. Annie's open-minded, all-embracing attitude to my treatment had convinced me of her worth. When I told her what we had learned that morning, she agreed to use all her resources to get the best recommendation for a therapist. Without consciously knowing it, I was already becoming resourceful and preparing to advocate for Seth.

So began one of the most significant aspects of my relationship to Seth's needs: the diary of my own experience and the discoveries that what I need for my own body's health illuminates the path to take for Seth. I have become a clearinghouse and a preview. I am the subject upon whom all experiments are first judged. Inevitably, my physical circumstances take me on searches for innovative solutions for myself. When the results are significant or meaningful, I am excited about the possibilities for Seth.

Annie Black's investigation also led to Susan Scheer. By the afternoon of the day of the diagnosis I had left a message for her. I was still stung by disbelief and anxiety, but I wasn't paralyzed. And I was going to be sure that my son would not be either. Not that I didn't have feelings; I just didn't have time to indulge them.

At the same time that Annie gave me Susan's name, she also mentioned the Feldenkrais method. She was training in this method of body work and suggested that it had proved very successful in treating people who had sustained insults to the nervous system. Whenever she started talking about "alternative" therapy, I listened halfheartedly, feeling vaguely resistant to anything New Age, wanting to latch on to only the old tried and true.

Meanwhile Jay's parents had to be told something, but not "cerebral palsy." Planning our approach to them was paramount. In the case of my own mother, I knew she would be calling me as soon as my father spoke to her. On the one hand, I wanted to lay my head on her shoulder and weep and beg for reassurance about the future. Realistically, I knew she would be wringing her hands and needing me to alleviate her anxiety. Reassuring everyone else and bracing everyone with "think how much worse it could be," went a long way to prop me up. The attitude I adopted for everyone else's benefit came to be my own salvation. Repeating the phrase like a mantra rescued me from self-pity then and still does today.

Hearing the words of the neurologist on that April day had set my head spinning. I had gone to the consultation not really knowing what a neurologist was and not expecting to hear anything like what he told us. Even though I had been anxious for months owing to intuition and ultimately Amy Katz's observations, I never thought that cerebral palsy would be my reality. Maybe I should have been better prepared to ask questions. But about what? Until that moment, my child was the most perfect child in the universe.

Where to begin? Everyone's style is different, but mine necessitates action. Others may need to explore first, or go to a library, or call experts. I needed to act. While I investigated getting a second opinion, the most important thing was to get Susan Scheer into the house as soon as possible. I wanted to "fix it," and she was the person who would know how. I needed an expert with tools.

Susan Scheer became the primary caretaker of Seth's rehabilitation and my principal point of reference for the next twenty months. After doing an initial evaluation, she came to the house three times a week for one-hour sessions with Seth. Susan was trained in the "neurodevelopmental" method of physical therapy (or NDT), also known as the Bobath method. This method is the one most commonly used for infants and children with cerebral palsy in the United States. It was introduced in the 1950s by Karl and Berta Bobath, a husband and wife from England, and it is considered very mainstream.

The NDT approach helps prepare the child's posture and movement to permit the development of "functional skills" or those skills needed for feeding, dressing, and bathing, the skills that are basic to living independently. Treatment focuses on encouraging the child to use normal rather than abnormal movement patterns and on preventing deformities or muscle patterns that make developing movement skills more difficult.

Susan was very positive about Seth's prognosis. She was always upbeat and balanced in our home, enchanted by Seth, while remaining professional. At the same time, she could throw me off balance completely because instantly and unconsciously I made her the authority and the barometer of Seth's future. Anything she said was loaded for me.

For a long time after the diagnosis, the overriding sensation was of being out of control and depending on others: other people's information, other people's predictions, other people's experience, other people's abilities. It was not a comfortable position to be in. Nobody was ever so reassuring that I was able to calm my anxiety. No one offered an overview, precise answers, or specific solutions. I could not depend on anyone to follow through the way I would. My problems were my problems, and there was no professional or friend who would take them as seriously as I did. At the same time, I was not an expert. I did not have the tools to do without anyone's help. Of course, that happens to all parents of children with problems. We are dependent on so many other people besides ourselves. We have to be. They are the experts. They have experience in the realms that affect our children, and they know what can make a difference in our children's lives.

Our relationships with these people are complex. We need them. We desperately hope that they will succeed. Maybe we also believe that if they like us—the parents—they will help our children more or be able to achieve more. We want miracles, magic. And these professionals hold the promise of those miracles. We make them into gods.

In my case, Susan could make the most casual, offhand comment and it would either encourage me for days or devastate me to the point of obsession. Her most frequent statement was that she was working for "quality." That was reassuring. I wanted Seth to have quality, and nothing persuaded me he wouldn't. Of course, quality was integral to the Bobath philosophy.

Susan demonstrated patterns or activities she wanted us to practice with Seth. I had Mayra observe the therapy sessions and carry out all Susan's instructions, as well as practice with and encourage Seth as much as possible. Mayra was much better at it than I was. At the end of my day, I wanted to come home and simply love my baby. I didn't want to do physical therapy with him. I barely wanted to worry about his situation, even though I did to the point of mania at times. Watching Mayra, I learned how to encourage better movements for Seth. I continued to have faith that things would be all right. But I kept asking Susan about things like tennis and downhill skiing, as though she would be able to tell me everything I wanted to know about the future.

In June we traveled to Boston, to the Children's Hospital to consult with a celebrated neurologist, Dr. Michael Bresnan, and get a second opinion. My parents live in Boston, and Dr. Bresnan had been recommended to us through my mother's contacts in the hospital world. My father accompanied Jay and Seth and me to the interview. Dr. Bresnan characterized Seth's problem as "moderate" as opposed to "mild." I asked which was worse. "Moderate" was worse.

Dr. Bresnan illustrated what he predicted Seth's gait would be by walking across the room with a perceptible scissoring action, knees knocking together, his legs dragged forward by swaying his hips one at a time. We were stunned. I looked across the room at my father and knew in his forlorn gaze that he was desolate. I vowed then and there to do all the interpreting of any firsthand observations. From then on everyone would get their information only through me.

Needless to say, we did not feel cheered by Dr. Bresnan's diagnosis. We spent that afternoon with my grandmother, my "Honey Nana," before returning to New York. Nana kept telling me not to worry. "He has a good head on him," she repeated many times that afternoon. She told me that every time I spoke to her until she died eighteen months later. I knew what she meant.

When I looked into Seth's eyes, I knew how smart he was. I knew he had mental acuity, and that this was one of his strengths. And I knew this capacity would get stronger because of the challenge in his life. That intuition came more and more into focus. Go with the strengths. Develop them and use them to support and improve what's not as strong.

We spent much of the summer in the Berkshires. Our small, rented French-style farmhouse, with its large, leaded bay window, was our family's first weekend home. Friday afternoons Seth and Jay and I would pile into our two-door compact car. Waving good-bye to Mayra, the three of us would then travel the two and a half hours to West Stockbridge, singing songs or conversing in baby talk. Seth never complained on long car rides. He amused himself or us, giving us an early glimpse into his amenable nature. He was an incredibly cooperative and happy infant. The pain of his circumstances had not yet become entwined with his psyche.

To the outside world Seth seemed like any other one-year-old. Nothing was obviously amiss to the casual observer. On close observation, though, many prophetic movements and postures were already in play. As I have mentioned, Seth continually held his left hand in a small, tight fist. There are many photographs of him being held by one of us, and his left fist is in this characteristic ball. I used to playfully slap his fist and ask him why he did it. Not too many years later I learned the value of stimulating his fist in this way. So while intuition already governed many of my responses, learning to trust my instincts was another matter.

The way Seth liked to lie on his back, arching as though to look behind him, always drew a comment from my mother. Later I learned that this tendency, too, is characteristic of the kind of cerebral palsy Seth has. Ironically, the photograph I treasure most from this summer is one of Seth in a red, one-piece short-sleeved cotton suit lying in this exact pose on the sofa under the bay window in the living room of the farmhouse. Had I had experience with another child, I might have known right from the beginning that Seth's tendency to lie in this position was a major indication of his neurological condition. It wasn't until four years later, when I handled my infant daughter, that I recognized the extreme stiffness, the almost brittle nature, of Seth's body.

That summer of 1984 was a summer of continual consultations and interviews. It was a time of engagement. My whole life focused on Seth and his care. Susan Scheer was a new entity in our family life. Mayra was probably present more of the time during Susan's sessions than I was. Her interpretation of each of Seth's sessions was of great importance for me.

Mayra adored Seth, as did Susan. The same appeal that was apparent in the NICU hours after he was born was at work for Seth already. It continues to serve him today. His innate intelligence and charm assisted him then as now and is a strength he draws upon.

Susan Scheer recommended that we get a pediatric orthopedist to evaluate Seth. She said that the growth of his bones needed monitoring. When I consulted our pediatrician, Dr. Lee, she concurred. The "best" as far as Dr. Lee was concerned was the same doctor Susan Scheer wanted us to use: Dr. Alfred Grant, chief pediatric orthopedist at the Hospital for Special Surgery, a very reputable institution. We made an appointment.

What vaguely disturbed and unsettled me, even at this early juncture, was my increasing awareness that I was doing all the initiating. No one was giving us an overview, especially not our pediatrician. Dr. Lee had been casual about Seth's progress. I had consulted Amy Katz without the pediatrician's encouragement. I was the one who had gone to the doctor and said that we wanted more information based on Amy Katz's observations. Only then had Dr. Lee suggested a neurological consultation. I couldn't determine whether it was because she felt sanguine about Seth's prognosis or whether she didn't know much more than I did.

Here I was, initiating again, asking for another doctor. What if Susan Scheer hadn't suggested such a consultation? I asked myself. Who was there to guide me? Dr. Chutorian had said that I could try physical therapy for Seth if I wanted to, but he hadn't suggested anyone, and he certainly hadn't provided any explanation of the different kinds of therapy, and neither had Dr. Lee. I felt I was floundering. The happenstance, random nature of acquiring information troubled me. There never has been anyone to help me chart an overall course of treatment for Seth. Different professionals offered various prognoses and insights, but none of them helped me map out steps and goals. When I realized no one was going to help me in this task, I felt abandoned and alone. Coping with this isolation burdened me with a sense of responsibility that at times felt very scary.

When I finally dared to look in the dictionary for a definition of "cerebral palsy," I got another jolt. I read, "a disability resulting from damage to the brain before or during birth and outwardly manifested by muscular incoordination and speech disturbances." Speech! No one had said a word about speech, I realized. Muscular incoordination seemed benign. But speech, an entirely new sphere, loomed. I felt exactly as I had on the day when Dr. Chutorian had stated his diagnosis and as I would each time I encountered a new piece of information: lost in the unknown, flailing and spinning, asking myself, what now?

A few days later Susan Scheer agreed that we should definitely consult a speech therapist. She recommended Phyllis Fabricant. I knew a woman who was a speech pathologist, and she recommended that before doing anything else I should get Seth's hearing tested. So I had two upcoming appointments: the orthopedist, Dr. Grant at the Hospital for Special Surgery, and Jane Madell, Ph.D., at the New York League for the Hard of Hearing. Coincidentally, the League for the Hard of Hearing was located in the same building as United Cerebral Palsy (UCP), a place I was never directed to.

How do I remember all of this, all the names, the chronology, the results? Because it is all written down in journal after journal. Although not too much had occurred in Seth's care up to this point, we had had the neurological consultations and diagnoses. We had Susan Scheer. So I decided to keep a diary of Seth's progress and record information as I received it. Keeping this record has been one of the most significant aspects of my experience as a mother of a child with special needs; it is a helpful practice with any child, for that matter. To this day I also keep a journal about my daughter and all her medical visits and school conferences. I record random thoughts and observations about both children as well as all their little illnesses. How did this happen? True, I am a writer. But this particular diligence was suggested by someone else.

A friend had told me about her recent health problems. She said that in her search for a remedy, she had had to consult many specialists and inform them accurately about her condition. The only way she was able to keep everything straight, to remember everything, was to keep a detailed diary. She recorded her own health status as well as everything the doctors told her. Listening to her, I knew I needed to do the same for Seth.

July 3, 1984, was our appointment with the orthopedist. Seth was not even thirteen months old. I remember waiting for Dr. Grant for an inordinate amount of time in a waiting room full of cigarette smoke. I was angry about being treated as though I had nothing else to do in life but wait for a doctor. Furthermore all of us in that waiting room, a pediatric environment, a room full of parents and children, were breathing air full of cigarette smoke.

From my notes, I see that I learned more about cerebral palsy from Dr. Grant than I had up until that point, although I might have availed myself of even more information had I tried. He said that cerebral palsy is a perceptible motor problem.

Medical professionals hesitate to use the term "cerebral palsy" when first diagnosing the condition because it implies a prognosis. Because of the "plasticity" of a child's central nervous system, there is always the possibility that a child will recover after an injury. The brains of infants and young children repair themselves more frequently than do those of older children. As the nervous system organizes over time, motor abilities are affected differently. If a brain injury occurs early, the undamaged areas of a child's brain can sometimes take over some of the functions of the damaged areas. As Seth's treatments evolved, we certainly subscribed more and more to this theory of the brain's capacity.

Dr. Grant gave us a definition of Seth's kind of cerebral palsy: static encephalopathy. While the phrase had appeared in the reports of both neurologists, I had read them very cursorily and with great resistance. The book *Children with Cerebral Palsy: A Parents' Guide,* explains the term "static encephalopathy" to mean an abnormal brain function that is not getting worse. Other terms used in this context are "motor delay"; "neuromotor dysfunction," or delay in the maturation of the nervous system; "motor disability," indicating a long-term movement problem; "central nervous system dysfunction," which is a very general term to indicate improper functioning of the brain.

But *Children with Cerebral Palsy* had not been published when Seth was small, and I had not consulted any books except the dictionary after Seth was diagnosed. What Dr. Grant was telling us was all new information, and it was specifically about Seth's condition. He repeated something Dr. Lee had told us the day of the initial diagnosis when we stood in her consulting room at the hospital. She had said that "cerebral palsy" is a "wastebasket" term, a broad label that encompasses many different disorders of movement and posture. Later I also learned that all such disorders are caused by a brain injury that occurs before birth, during birth, or within the first few years after birth. There are pregnancy risk factors, delivery risk factors, and neonatal risk factors. The causes of cerebral palsy are unknown in 20 percent of the cases. The injury does not damage the child's muscles or the nerves connecting the muscles to the spinal cord, only the brain's ability to control the muscles.

When used as a label, "cerebral palsy" refers to a disorder of movement and posture that is attributable to a nonprogressive abnormality of the brain. The basic distinctions of cerebral palsy are the age of onset and the lack of progression. This static nature of cerebral palsy, its lack of progression, means that the disability itself does not worsen. One of the chief diagnostic signs of cerebral palsy is the persistence of primitive reflexes. However, even a child with the mildest form of cerebral palsy has difficulty performing the continuous changes in muscle tone that are required for normal walking.

Depending on its location and severity, the brain injury that causes a child's movement disorders may also cause other problems, including mental retardation, seizures, language disorders, learning disabilities, and vision and hearing problems. The parts of the body in which the child experiences abnormal muscle tone depends upon where the brain damage has occurred. The one common denominator is that all children with cerebral palsy have damage to the area of the brain that controls muscle tone.

Children with *increased* muscle tone are said to have *high tone,* *hypertonia,* or *spasticity.* Because their muscles are tight, movement is tight and awkward. These children love to stand on their legs, but they stand on their toes or scissor their legs. Scissoring, which is the most common gait disturbance, occurs because of the increased tightness in the muscles that control adduction and internal rotation of the hips. Children with increased tone can be identified by the ways they arch their backs and roll over. At first I thought that Seth fell into this group. But all children with cerebral palsy have problems with movement and posture.

Children with low tone or *decreased* tone are said to have *low tone, hypotonia,* or *floppiness.* It is difficult for children with low tone to remain upright against the pull of gravity. Sitting, for instance, is difficult. Low tone also influences a child's ability to keep his trunk stable enough so that he can use his arms to reach and to grasp. When low tone affects a child's abdominal and respiratory muscles, it can hinder the development of speech. Seth seemed to fit into this category too, but as I learned more I found that there was a third classification.

Fluctuating or *variable muscle tone* describes children who have a combination of high and low tone. For instance, Seth has low tone while at rest but high tone with activity. Increased tone helps to stabilize a position such as sitting or standing, but it may end up making other movements difficult or impossible because it may cause the tightening of muscle groups in other parts of the body.

My resentment about waiting for Dr. Grant was ameliorated when the doctor suggested that although one can't make accurate predictions, there were predictors, and they looked good for Seth. At best, the doctor said he wouldn't even rule out downhill skiing. (He was wrong.) He said that Seth would need either surgery, inhibitory casts, or braces. He X-rayed Seth's hips and said that there was only the slightest flaring. All the bones were okay. Because he was so positive and seemed to appreciate Seth's personality and humor, we liked Dr. Grant very much.

It's strange, looking back, that someone who prides herself as much as I do on thoroughness and action took such a passive stance regarding my son's devastating diagnosis. I relied wholly on the professionals— the neurologist, my pediatrician, Susan Scheer, and Dr. Grant. I would bounce along from one expert to the next, heeding their advice for some time to come. I did no research. I barely read the neurological reports, and when I did, I skimmed. I never contacted United Cerebral Palsy. I didn't go to the library. I was too scared. I wanted to believe Seth's condition was so mild that the early intervention I was orchestrating would be enough to ensure his normal development. The thought of something more severe was out of reach. And I wanted to keep it that way.

"Muscle tone" was a term I heard repeatedly. I had recognized early in Seth's development that Seth's body was different than other children's, but I hadn't known enough to identify these "tone" characteristics as indicators that anything was wrong.

Why wasn't I paying attention? What was I avoiding? I was what psychologists call "in denial." All the parents I've met and interviewed say that they responded as I did during some phase of coming to terms with their child's special needs. We cannot blame ourselves. Who wants to hear that your child is not perfect, never mind possibly impaired, ill, or in danger? Such concepts are so difficult to grasp and to live with. To say nothing of explaining them to others!

It took several years before I was able to open the channel of memory, but I finally did have a startling recollection of a childhood experience with two disabled children. There are many layers of feeling when I think back on these two central figures in the landscape of my childhood summers on Cape Cod. My best friend Patty's youngest sister was "mongoloid"—we call it Down's syndrome today—and our neighbors had a young son, Jimmy, who had severe cerebral palsy.

I spent long days at the beach playing "mother" to Patty's sister or to Jimmy. My friend's sister was with me almost daily, and I seized every opportunity to be with her. She came from a large family of ten children, so I slipped in easily. We had long, varied days together swimming, building sandcastles, and taking walks.

Jimmy was wheelchair bound and on the beach infrequently, and he visited only briefly. So my time with Jimmy was more specific. Jimmy was severely impaired. He was unable to support even his head. It drooped over to one side, his chin grazing his collarbone. He drooled, and his speech was slurred and unintelligible. There were no motor functions he performed himself. But he was sweet and smiled, and I loved him. Jimmy visited his mother in the summer only for a few weeks. Afterward he returned to the Fernald School for the Handicapped, a state institution in the Boston area, close to our winter home.

Jimmy's mother, Mrs. Townsend, was my parents' good friend and neighbor. She had her hands full. Because of a congenital condition, her husband, Jimmy's father, was also confined to a wheelchair. Most of the time he was in a constant-care facility, but Mrs. Townsend had him visit accompanied by a nurse's aide while their son was visiting home, too. It was work for her to care for two extremely needy individuals simultaneously. Consequently, Mrs. Townsend was delighted by my doting on Jimmy.

Tending to Jimmy, keeping him entertained, occupied, fed was my occupation for two weeks every summer. Jimmy's intelligence was limited, but I saw that he knew me and responded to my care. I felt important and capable. I patted myself on the back for loving someone seemingly so discarded. After all, his parents had no place for him at home, and society was certainly not welcoming him into its midst.

For many years, while I was eight and nine, ten, and eleven, my summers included the company of these two "retarded" children. I had many other friends and activities, but Patty's sister was a consistent companion, at least during the day, every summer. Jimmy's visit was a centerpiece each July. It felt natural to be nurturing, patient, and understanding. I liked it. Did I have an inkling of my future? Were these clues?

When I was growing up in the 1950s, words such as "retarded," "mongoloid," and "handicapped" were commonplace. The child with Down's syndrome was identifiable by certain unmistakable characteristics. I remember a doctor friend of our family visiting us and instantly noticing the little girl on the beach. I watched him come up to her, look curiously, take her hands in his, and turn them over to examine her palms.

In the months between September and June, I gave only fleeting thoughts to my two favorite summer companions. Until I was twelve. That winter, at Christmas time, Mrs. Townsend came to visit us. The plan was for me to go to her home for an overnight and bake Christmas cookies. En route, she spontaneously suggested that we stop at the Fernald School and make an unannounced visit to Jimmy.

The school had a policy of not allowing children under sixteen in to visit, but I looked very mature. We walked into Jimmy's ward. I was confounded by what I saw. A room the size of a gymnasium was full of severely disabled young boys. There were children with hydrocephalus, their heads the size of watermelons and their bodies like midgets; there were boys with cerebral palsy in wheelchairs; boys with Down's syndrome; autistic boys lying on beds looking vacant or encased in straitjackets. The spectacle was devastating.

Presumably, I handled the visit well—I didn't break down or run away. But afterward I obsessed about people who had overcome great obstacles. Helen Keller was one individual who intrigued me. I read obsessively about her and others who had surmounted difficult odds. People who were disadvantaged, but nevertheless realized notable achievements fascinated me. And I read voraciously about their mothers; about parents of children with special needs. I remember the shelf where I parked myself in our town's public library to pore over these books.

My parents barely spoke to Mrs. Townsend again, angry that she was so careless and exposed me, a child, to the vastness of the physically disabled, engendering in me an inner world of dark anxiety. Like many little girls, I was forever thinking about babies and being a mother. Now I worried intensely that I would have a child with cerebral palsy. I wrote about it in my diary, wrote stories about it.

Eventually my parents moved to another summer home in another neighborhood, and I don't remember the last time we saw "Mrs. T." My concerns faded as I grew into adolescence. Elvis, the Beatles, the Vietnam War occupied me. I went to college thinking I wanted to study anthropology or psychology, and instead I was absorbed by the arts, by theater, dance, film, art history, literature. I moved to California to study and to work. I was distracted by and immersed in new aims and interests. Somewhere along the way, I recall being told that Jimmy or his father or both had died. By then I rarely thought about Jimmy or my friend Patty's little sister.

Three years following Seth's diagnosis, when my passage to this memory opened from nowhere, the only curiosity was that it had taken so long. I was still in an early stage of coming to terms with Seth's disability. Looking back now I realize that I was doing my best just to get the help I needed, to overcome the lack of direction from the primary-care physicians. Yet, I must admit, this denial, this tendency to acquiesce in the presence of "authorities," had led me to stick it out with my ob-gyn during my pregnancy even though I had doubts. It had led me to postpone earlier intervention in Seth's care even though I intuited that something was not right. The understandable tendency to accept the status quo would come into play significantly again and again in my responses to various situations along the way.

4

◆

At Sea

◆

AS THE SUMMER WANED and fall became intoxicating, we spent more time in the city on weekends. Our neighbors had an adopted Korean daughter, Kara, and they were expecting to adopt another little girl from Korea any day. Kara was six years older than Seth, and the two played together all the time, Kara delightfully acting the part of older sister. It was a warm September, so the children were often in bathing suits splashing in a small inflatable swimming pool.

Seth's inability to ambulate is the story told in the photographs from that autumn. Kara is busy propping him up or tending to him much as I must have tended to Jimmy and to Patty's sister years earlier. Seth is full of smiles, obviously content to be waited on and assisted like a little prince. The twinkle in his eyes never diminished, and the bond between Kara and Seth was so strong that even Lia's arrival a few months later did little to fray it.

In September of 1984, on the front cover of my first journal, a blue-and-white hardback diary, I affixed a typed list of the specialists involved with Seth's care, their addresses and phone numbers. Looking at it today evokes an ocean of memory.

The list begins with Dr. Lee, the pediatrician. Today she no longer treats Seth or my daughter, Haya, but it took a lot of time before we let go. (As I recall, her casual attitude toward my initial concerns in the early months, her failure to educate me about the risks of immunizing Seth, her inability to offer anything but empty praise, I am shocked that it took me so much time to decide to stop seeing her.)

Since Dr. Lee constantly applauded my efforts on Seth's behalf, it was hard to resist her. I gloried in all I was doing for Seth, and all the recognition she gave me. Many years of ongoing self-examination have helped me to realize my shortcomings in this regard, but also to see that I was responding in a very human way.

Praise is a wonderful feeling. I was on a perpetual quest for love, the result of a childhood not always emotionally happy. Dr. Lee's admiration bonded me to her. But it clouded my ability to decipher good advice or to feel entitled to aggressively question her or other professionals. As I gained insight into my psychological needs, I was more able to separate myself from this yearning for love. I recognized my need for affirmation, but I stopped it from interfering with my getting information or results. It remains an ongoing battle, though.

The second name on the list is the neurologist, Dr. Chutorian, who provided the initial diagnosis. We went back to him only one more time. Although a third neurologist besides Drs. Chutorian and Bresnan would examine Seth the following year, it would be five years before Seth got a complete neurological work up, in 1989, at the Spitz clinic in Philadelphia.

Dr. Alfred Grant, the orthopedist, is the third name. Three or four more consultations over the next two years made us reconsider Dr. Grant's suggestions.

The three therapists who were treating Seth every week were Susan Scheer, who came three times a week; Peggy Smith, an occupational therapist who came twice a week; and the speech therapist, Phyllis Fabricant, who treated Seth every Friday. Phyllis's sessions were sometimes conducted with Susan Scheer's participation. I have a file full of these therapists' intermittent reports, requested by me or by the various doctors. Phyllis also wrote a short weekly report, which she left with me every Friday. It greeted me when I arrived home at the end of the week and influenced my state of mind every weekend. I have an abundance of recollections and feelings about each of these people. So does Seth. They dominated our lives.

Susan Scheer was definitely the "captain," although Peggy Smith's outlook and approach predominate to this day because Peggy was extremely prescient. She did many things that later came to be encouraged in the more unconventional treatments. She rolled Seth around playfully and hung him by his ankles. She stimulated him with various modalities and games, using shaving cream, applesauce (which would play a big part later on), and water. Peggy mentioned the Feldenkrais method occasionally during the first few months, as Annie Black had, but I didn't investigate it. It sounded too "far out," and I was hanging on for dear life to what I thought was tried and true.

Peggy discussed stimulating Seth's lung power, getting him to scream and sing and make loud noises, an insight that proved prophetic. Today his care vis-à-vis his speech issues is handled by a voice/breathing teacher very successfully. Peggy's sessions were vibrant, comprehensive encounters unlike anything else in Seth's life at the time.

Seth's life was one long therapy session when we factored in Mayra's participation. Everyone was working at his rehabilitation. I was reassured, believing in the power of these influences to make everything all right. We purchased a therapeutic bolster and a huge ball for Seth's sessions with Susan and Peggy. Phyllis also used the bolster to position Seth during some of her work with him. To this day we are on the mailing list of the company that sold us the equipment. The catalog arrives three or four times a year. Its cover always depicts a child either in a wheelchair or using other orthopedic devices, reminding me of what I haven't had to face. Our whole family uses the bolster for one thing or another, and I still encourage Seth to sit on it whenever he can.

In sharp contrast to Peggy's sessions, according to Phyllis Fabricant's accounts, her sessions with Seth were nettlesome, and that state of affairs only escalated over time. Although, as I look over Phyllis's reports, I see that she often wrote, "Seth did well," it always felt as if there was some qualification. In one report she wrote, "Seth had an excellent session. I hear a variety of sounds. He imitates many words. Try to continue to have him say a word before he gets what he wants. He is a great pointer, and we don't want that to be his main mode of communication. I asked Mayra to put out his clothes in the morning, and he must say each piece before it is put on."

But most of Phyllis's reports were not so upbeat. Seth didn't like the sessions with her. He especially resisted when she tried to work in his mouth with a little stimulus tool, and his reaction would upset Phyllis. At the time, I didn't make the link between the discomfort he had had when nursing months earlier and his difficulties in his mouth. Phyllis encouraged Mayra to use a toothbrush in his mouth, too. He hated it, and I think Phyllis almost hated him for his adversity. Years later, when another professional asked me why Seth had so much reluctance and sensitivity to overcome in his mouth, I knew why instantly.

Like many people with cerebral palsy, Seth's sensory experience is different than mine or Jay's or Haya's or most people's. One place he experiences increased sensitivity is in and around his mouth and tongue. As my awareness and knowledge expanded, I learned that the tongue is often at the center of function, especially movement. The tongue is a fleshy, movable, muscular organ. It attaches in us to the floor of the mouth. It is the principal organ of taste, an aid in chewing and swallowing, and our primary organ of speech. The movements involved in every action of ourselves affect every other aspect of our organism. Our sympathetic nervous system consists of two large nerves on either side of the vertebral column. All these nerves have their roots coming out of the thoracic and lumbar regions of the spinal cord. Here the tongue has genuine power and influence, and these dimensions are only partially recognized. All of Phyllis's prodding and pushing in his mouth increased Seth's anxiety and resistance. As Thomas Hanna wrote in one of his numerous and lucid essays, we must think of ourselves as being controlled not from without but from within. What is more within than the tongue? Movement is the best clue to life. In Mr. Hanna's view we have from birth until death a loop of four elements: skeleton, muscles, nervous system, and environment. I believe the tongue links all of these elements.

Soon after Phyllis began treating him, and when Seth was only fifteen months old, she said she wanted to teach him sign language. Susan Scheer concurred. I was shocked. What! Did that mean that he was not going to talk? Would we all be signing? How could they know at fifteen months? Was he expected to make words fully comprehensible already? Frantically I began consulting baby books about normal sound production and the expectations regarding speech development. Since I had no point of reference, I was in a complete dither. When I asked Dr. Lee, she felt that it was premature to make an assessment, but she was uncertain. Jay was unalterably opposed to Seth learning to sign.

I felt I was in charge, that I was being very capable and responsive, but I also had little gnawing doubts, nagging anxieties. The debate over teaching Seth sign language, as well as my level of anxiety, persuaded me to search for a pediatrician who specialized in developmental disabilities. I thought that such a person could educate us, provide some perspective and an overview on Seth's condition, and give us some guidance in making decisions. Coinciding with the conundrum about teaching Seth to sign and the beginning of our search for this pediatric expert, Susan Scheer persuaded us to consult Dr. Larry Price, a podiatrist, about Seth's feet.

Susan Scheer wanted us to consult Dr. Price because of Seth's poor feet and ankle alignment. She believed that an orthotic device would preserve the bony alignment of his feet and the integrity of his joints. She thought that the orthotic adjustment would mean a stable base for his feet while weight bearing, distributing the pressure more evenly over the surface of the heel and border of the foot. She communicated this to us directly and by letter to Dr. Grant, a letter which I kept in my file. In her letter to Dr. Grant she wrote that there was no need for an extension of the orthotic apparatus over the ankle. We were all thinking in terms of a device that would fit easily into Seth's shoe. However, when it came time to stand by that assessment, Susan backed down.

Seth was not standing independently and was not pulling himself to a standing position, although he loved being placed in a standing position. He adored his "walker." There are a multitude of pictures of Seth in this contraption. In every picture he is wearing a broad smile. The walker gave him mobility, allowing him to move about from place to place just like the other children of his age who were already walking and getting about independently.

I was vaguely aware of some disagreement about the advisability of walkers. I knew that Peggy believed, for instance, that a child should stand only when development allowed for standing and not before, otherwise the feet would be compromised. On the other hand, it was Dr. Lee who had first recommended the walker and pooh-poohed the criticism of its efficacy. Susan Scheer had had no objections to it.

The walker made life easier for us. It helped Seth get from place to place more quickly and independently. He was fifteen months old, the age when most children begin to walk, and he was getting heavier to carry. He would get much heavier before he could walk independently. In the meantime, for better or worse—and later we learned that it was for worse, much worse—we let him use the walker and have the joy of getting about as though he were walking. We were about to make another ill-advised decision as well.

In my diary I noted that the office visit to Dr. Price was the beginning of a pattern of my having to rehash the very painful events surrounding Seth's birth. The nurse received Jay and me, and, while Seth played nearby, we had to answer many questions regarding my pregnancy and delivery. I still did not link Seth's condition with the nightmare of the delivery. Was I sleeping? I became emotional when I recounted the events of Seth's birth, but I was too absorbed by his daily care and his future care to make connections. Later, when I did let it all register, it was because it was necessary to face myself, too—a difficult thing to do. The same qualities that prevented me from getting rid of my ob-gyn and getting rid of Dr. Lee also prevented me from making those links. The lesson I've learned is that you need to be aware so that you can take responsibility. And the mandate is to keep the doctors and professionals human, not to elevate them. This means giving constant, ongoing attention to health-care providers in both the mainstream and the alternative worlds of medicine.

Dr. Larry Price, the podiatrist, advised us to put Seth into "inhibitory casts." These were removable plaster casts that covered his entire foot and ran up to his knees. He wanted Seth to wear the casts most of the day and always while he was in a standing position. Unlike Susan Scheer, Dr. Price thought that an orthotic device was an "under treatment." He was glad that Seth could get his heel on the ground when standing. He felt that we could experiment with helping Seth while he was still an infant by putting him in the inhibitory casts.

Dr. Price believed the casts were better than braces because the braces increase "tone" and diminish the sensory experience of the foot on the ground. He said that the inhibitory cast would decrease tone, as for instance a hiking boot does, keeping the alignment of the foot neutral. "Tone" was becoming a familiar word. But while the doctor was talking about decreasing tone, I wasn't thinking about whether these inhibitory casts would influence Seth's sensory experience. Insecurity, a sense of having to deal constantly with the unknown yet having to make important decisions, was becoming a familiar circumstance, though not a comfortable one.

Later the question of sensory experience would become paramount, radically altering the whole course of Seth's therapy. Eventually we realized that only the contact of Seth's foot on the ground could be considered a sensory experience; casts, braces, and orthotic devices interfered with the tactile experience. But I didn't have this information then. I had to discover it as part of my own education. For the time being, I relied on Dr. Grant for guidance in making the decision about the casts.

Dr. Grant said that the issue of inhibitory casts was still being debated. There were those who believed that the casts decreased tone and those who said that they did nothing. He told us that he was in the middle. Although the casts occasionally helped to decrease tone, neither he nor his colleagues believed that the devices eliminated or reduced the need to cut the Achilles tendon. He insisted that we were still going to face surgery. (I couldn't begin to contemplate that possibility for the moment.)

At fifteen months Seth was not a candidate for surgery anyway, so the casts couldn't hurt him, Dr. Grant said. He insisted, twice, that in his experience a time would come for surgery, that the physical therapist would object, and that we could get twenty-five other opinions and still have a painful decision to make. But he went along with putting Seth into the casts. In the meantime, eleven years have passed, and surgery has not come yet.

Encountering conflict, confusing information, mixed messages, and differences of opinion, forecasting the future, having to decipher and choose: this was my life. I spent my time following through, checking everything, trying to filter all the information. In the meantime, Dr. Grant also urged us to use his clinic for Seth's rehabilitation. I wanted to stick with the status quo. It was familiar when everything else wasn't. The therapists in Dr. Grant's clinic were not trained in the neurodevelomental treatment (NDT) method of the Bobaths. I told Dr. Grant that I objected to making a change in the kind of therapy Seth was receiving. I wanted to continue using therapists trained in this Bobath method. He told me that he had had enough of the NDT people. They were coming out of his ears, and he objected to my insistence on this kind of therapy.

At the same time, Annie Black was urging me to make an appointment with a Feldenkrais teacher in our neighborhood, Charles Bonner. Afraid of offending her and alienating someone who might be a potential source of information or a valuable link, I agreed and scheduled the appointment. We were on a voyage to heal, to care, calling on all doctors, spending all our money, searching everywhere, everyone, searching each other.

My time alone with Seth had sanctity beyond anything I had previously known. Aside from my husband, I had never adored anyone so completely as I did my son. I felt close to him in a sacred way. My instinct to nurture was aroused tangibly. Sometimes I would look into Seth's twinkling blue eyes, feel the contact of our two souls, and say aloud, "Seth, my darling boy, my love, my life, I need guidance in making the right decisions for you." He would smile. I felt that he answered me with complete trust. His look gave me the faith that I was making the right decisions.

Seth had a busy calendar. In September we had him fitted for his casts. That involved an appointment where he had to be mildly sedated; the prospect caused me no end of anxiety. I scheduled the time to meet with Charles Bonner, the Feldenkrais practitioner. There were also routine checkups with the orthopedist and the pediatrician. We finally located a developmental disabilities expert, a pediatrician at New York Hospital/Cornell Medical Center, Dr. Daniel Kessler, and scheduled a series of interviews with him. The three therapists were coming for a combination of seven visits every week. We were also considering some kind of day-care environment where Seth would be exposed to other children. We needed to set up interviews and visits to make that happen.

Thinking back, I ask myself, what if I hadn't been self-employed? What do the parents of other special needs children do about time away from work? How do their employers treat them? What allowances are made? I was also lucky to have Mayra. Her assistance was invaluable. Mayra absorbed the therapists' messages and kept up what I never could have done, providing Seth with constant, vigilant intervention. I always felt that she was my greatest hope. Her continued optimism and devotion to Seth was a bulwark.

We could barely afford all the medical care and consultations. The insurance company lagged in reimbursing us for the therapists and doctors, all of whom wanted to be paid immediately. They resisted paying for any speech therapy, so that cost was our responsibility entirely. The issue of a preexisting condition was about to arise with the insurance company. We eventually resolved the issue of the preexisting condition, but in the meantime bills began to mount up. Self-employment was fine for the latitude it allowed in the way of time, but I had to generate business. Travel loomed. I was going to have to be away in Los Angeles for ten days every month. I was developing several literary properties for the motion picture studios and television networks, and the meetings with writers and administrative personnel took place exclusively in Los Angeles. I arranged ten days each month to be in L.A. to accomplish what I could in one fell swoop. Mayra's presence took on a new dimension.

In October Seth's hearing test proved he had no substantial auditory difficulties. He responded well to low frequencies, which include people's voices. Dr. Jane Madell at the New York League for the Hard of Hearing observed that only high-frequency sounds had to be significantly louder in order for Seth to respond. This was not unusual in children with cerebral palsy, she said. Although there was no significant hearing problem, a loss of high frequency meant that the fricatives—*f*'s, *sh*'s, *th*'s, and *z*'s—would be harder to hear.

What I couldn't know then was that the fricatives would also be harder for Seth to say. Saying his very name, "Seth," would become one of my son's daily struggles. Announcing himself by name—whether it be on the telephone when he calls a friend, when he walks into a new situation, a new classroom, when he is asked, as we all are so often, who is calling—is his everyday chore. It is the constant reminder of who he is and how he struggles.

The hearing test was very important. An estimated twenty one million Americans have some degree of hearing impairment. Hearing affects a wide range of skills, including the development of language and learning abilities. We were glad to learn that Seth's hearing was intact.

In early October we were on our way to consult with Dr. Daniel Kessler. As with so many other things in our experience, serendipity played a major role in our finding Dr. Kessler. One chance encounter had led to another, as we wended our way along circuitous paths to a suite of offices in an attic in New York Hospital. These "random" instances of good fortune combined with my dogged determination and tenacity often brought results. Yet there was much more I could have investigated, and this is still a continuing theme I play out in my mind. Vigilance is the watchword of parenting a child with special needs, but it's tiring work.

Dr. Daniel Kessler was a protégé of Dr. T. Berry Brazelton, the Dr. Spock for my generation of parents. When I was pregnant, it was Dr. Brazelton's books I thumbed most often. After Seth was born and before he was diagnosed, Dr. Brazelton's books seemed to offer the clearest guidance. Dr. Kessler was our dream doctor. He was a pediatrician with a small group practice whose specialty was children with developmental disabilities. Not only did he pick up the phone and talk to me at length the first time I called; he was willing to consult with another doctor on either a short- or a long-term basis. He had no clinic, so there was no agenda about using his physical therapists. Eventually he offered the most comprehensive perspective. His competence in the field prompted me to consider using him as Seth's primary-care physician, a decision over which we agonized for months. In the end, we decided to use him only as a consultant.

The testing Dr. Kessler wanted to do was not scheduled until late November. But before our first face-to-face meeting in October, he read the existing neurological reports and discussed with us by phone the importance of environmental influences and current assessments regarding Seth's cognitive problem-solving abilities. I asked him many questions about casts, the orthopedic versus physical therapy conflicts, the issue of the urgency of Seth beginning to learn sign language. I also had questions about play groups.

New psychological questions were cropping up, for instance, how much to let Seth struggle and how much to help him (another recurring theme). Dr. Kessler's responses were very helpful. I liked his unsanctimonious perspective on his own medical profession. He struck me as extremely instinctive, exceptionally bright, a promising beacon of insight.

In the meantime, because of Annie Black, I took Seth to see Charles Bonner, the Feldenkrais practitioner who worked down the street from where we lived. Mayra went with us. Charles Bonner asked a few preliminary questions and then spent an hour handling Seth. Seth seemed to love him and didn't object to being handled. (This changed later.)

Afterward, Bonner was very reassuring. He specifically said that all of Seth's functions would come in, and he was convinced that Seth would be fine. Bonner thought that Seth was very strong and that Seth's favoring one side over another was normal, and that Seth's flexion was good. He did not think that Seth would have difficulty walking. He said that his "fantasy" was that Seth would have absolutely no perceptible difficulties. He said that Susan Scheer was doing everything he himself would do, and that if he took on Seth as a patient, his work would be overlapping with what she was doing.

Naturally, I wanted to believe everything Charles Bonner said. I was buoyed by what I heard, and he immediately endeared himself to me with his positive outlook. Bonner also said that if Seth's feet developed okay, there would be no hip problems. That prediction helped me counteract the image the neurologist, Dr. Bresnan, had given the prior spring when he demonstrated what he imagined Seth's gait would be. Bonner thought that Seth would follow his own distinct patterns, which would parallel normal patterns. The one thing that caused Bonner alarm was Seth's failure to realize when he was at risk of falling. Bonner believed that Seth's biggest teacher in the end would be gravity.

The prospect that Seth could be injured in a fall brought up the issue of helmets and protective headgear. The brochure for the company from which we had bought the bolster illustrated children in different kinds of headgear. By this time I knew that Seth's falling was due to his lack of a reflexive action to protect himself rather than the result of a lack of balance. The nagging theme of how much to protect him, when to intervene, when to leave him alone, raised its head once again. That was not the last time we thought about helmets.

How can I tell you now how prescient Charles Bonner's insights were? After years of practicing Yoga and other body work, and from what I have gleaned from the doctors who have worked with us over the last seven years, I am now aware of many things about the development of bones, the differences for all of us in our two sides of the body, and the master part that gravity plays in all our lives. But I didn't know then what I know now. I only reacted to the positive sense Bonner gave me, at least in the beginning.

The reality and the ordeal of being a first-time parent of a child with special needs induces paralysis and confusion. I've cried out so often the refrain, "if only I had known." This desire for hindsight hits all of us at different times in our lives. With this particular kind of parenting challenge, the words take on new significance. Our children are diagnosed, but we aren't offered much besides the labels. If we only had access to more information and greater perspective, we could make wiser choices, if not more informed ones. Our relationships to the professional and medical communities are fostered in a narrow and dependent atmosphere. We don't trust ourselves to question, probe, challenge, and investigate.

It had never occurred to me, for instance, that I should question whether or not Seth should be immunized. How could I have known to even ask such questions when Seth was getting his first diphtheria-pertussis-tetanus (DPT) shots? Years later, when I met other parents of children with developmental disabilities, I learned about the vast studies that discourage the immunization of children with any neurological anomalies.

Now, because I have read *A Shot in the Dark* by Harris L. Coulter and Barbara Loe Fisher, I know that in large field trials conducted by Britain's Medical Research Council to assess the efficacy of the pertussis vaccine in children from six to eighteen months old, children with any personal or family history of convulsions, epilepsy, hydrocephalus, mental defect, as well as any child who had been recently sick, were excluded. The authors and others have recommended that the pertussis vaccine be withheld from patients with any neurodevelopmental defect, because they are considered a high-risk group.

Coulter and Fisher report that in 1981 the National Childhood Encephalopathy Study conducted in Britain gave the following contraindications to pertussis vaccination: "a personal or family history of epilepsy or other neurological disorders, evidence of developmental neurological defects," and so on. Most doctors have been taught very little in medical school about reactions, contraindications, or the permanent neurological damage that can be caused by the pertussis vaccine. I remember the old adage, There are no answers, only the right questions. How does one begin formulating these questions? How many American parents are aware that their child could die or become brain damaged after a serious reaction to a DPT shot?

I was ushered out of the darkness by a guest on Oprah Winfrey's TV show. This woman's son had gone to the pediatrician a happy, healthy child and gotten a DPT shot. He began to have convulsions and seizures within hours of receiving the shot. The child is now permanently brain damaged, living part of each day on life-support systems, in and out of the hospital for treatments. Very few Americans know that some Western European countries have stopped recommending mass immunization with the pertussis vaccine because they have decided that the risk of vaccine damage is greater than the risks of catching the milder form of whooping cough that is prevalent in developed nations today. Certainly we should have been informed of the vaccine's potential hazard and controversy before Seth received the pertussis vaccine.

Our knowledge about risks and options is limited by a powerful orthodox medical society that shields us from exposure to possibilities outside the conventional. But there is a huge alternative world out there that includes mainstream, sometimes nonorthodox, medicine, alternative therapies, as well as the practice of various Eastern disciplines such as massage, Yoga, acupuncture, and Ayurvedic medicine.

For instance, the *Reader's Digest Family Guide to Natural Medicine* says that Ayurvedic medicine, which arose in India at least 2,500 years ago, is considered the first organized approach to health care based on natural phenomena as opposed to magic and superstition. Its emphasis is on preventive health care. It prescribes an individually designed diet and a unique daily routine and activities that will help each individual maintain balance. Texts dating back several centuries attest to the skill of Ayurvedic practitioners in a variety of major and minor surgery procedures. Those familiar with traditional Chinese medicine can trace the lineage of pulse diagnosis and the importance of keeping energy forces in balance to Ayurvedic medicine.

The Reader's Digest guide points out that along with many other holistic health practices, Ayurvedic medicine contrasts sharply with the simple (and perhaps simplistic) cause-and-effect thinking of modern orthodox medicine known as allopathic medicine. For instance, the Indian medicine deals in an integrated way with body and mind. Although Ayurveda and Yoga come from the same ancient roots, they have for some time been considered distinct. Nowadays there is a trend toward bringing the two back together. Patients who learn specific Yoga postures, meditation, relaxation, and breathing are able to maintain their health and manage themselves using these tailor-made combinations.

The guide also suggests that the Ayurvedic philosophy of medicine may be an excellent integrating perspective for bringing together different holistic therapies. It is perhaps the oldest system in use today and easily accommodates therapies and treatments as diverse as homeopathy, osteopathy, antibiotics, surgery, nutrition, massage, meditation, and acupuncture.

But most of us are scared about seeking out alternative treatments. What do we know compared to the experts and specialists? We want to do right by our children, to help them in every possible way. How can we go about discovering a method of thinking so that these alternatives are at least considered? We need to share information amongst ourselves. There are many networks for accessing information, but trying out one group or another may feel like just another thing to do, another responsibility. Where does one start looking? Who has time? From my current vantage point I believe I have much to tell others about what I know. Yet I often find that when I offer my experience, my divergent view is not well received, even by parents who are searching for answers.

We have lots to do in our own lives as well as in the lives of our children. With Seth I didn't even have many of the problems that other parents have. He was not as impaired as many other children are. He wasn't terminally ill or hooked up to life-support systems. He wouldn't need a wheelchair or other functional help (such as help with toileting). When he was still small we didn't have another child to worry and care about yet. I had much to be grateful for and much more time than others to explore. And still I didn't do everything I could have. I wasn't in touch with United Cerebral Palsy, because I was still avoiding reality. I didn't spend all my spare time reading up on cerebral palsy or therapeutic responses. I hadn't written to any organizations or contacted any of the networking opportunities that existed.

Instead I kept thinking about how much I was doing. And I heard it from everybody else too. I can't count the number of times that other parents or friends or total strangers said something about what a good mother I was and how much I was doing for Seth, how lucky he was. I tried to demur and be graceful. After all, what else would I do?

As Pearl S. Buck writes so eloquently in *The Child Who Never Grew*: "Driven by the conviction that there must be someone who can cure, we take our children over the surface of the whole earth, seeking the one who can heal. We spend all the money we have and we borrow until there is no one else to lend. We go to doctors good and bad, to anyone, for only a wisp of hope. We are gouged by unscrupulous men who make money from our terror, but now and again we meet those saints who, seeing the terror and guessing the empty purse, will take nothing for their advice, since they cannot heal." Or even when they can, they refuse money from those who cannot really afford it. We eventually met healers who did this.

Growing up in China, Pearl S. Buck was exposed to people with many deformities and challenges. Chinese society openly accepted people as they were, believing that any affliction was part of one's destiny, ordained by heaven. Yet Ms. Buck hid her mentally impaired child from the world even as her own fame grew and more about this great writer's personal life became known. There was shame and embarrassment. People were cruel.

I have been a witness to this in Seth's life. By now he has more than a dim knowledge that he is not like others. He and I have learned a lexicon of responses when questions are put to one or both of us. I recognize the unkind glances of others, their overt and implied ridicule, and I fear for my son. He is managing, although there are dimensions that have not yet been revealed and experiences yet to occur that we cannot yet imagine.

I always have to think about how lucky I am, too. I was surrounded by excellent professionals who were both accessible and affordable, and I had the good sense and an inclination to use them. I was fortunate to live in a city where there was a wealth of talent to choose from. I myself was the product of a positive upbringing that had offered many opportunities, fine education, and had fostered in me a belief that I could influence my circumstances. My husband was supportive and encouraging and continues to be. Although he needed reassurance, Jay still never got depressed or stopped being a helpmate.

Looking over all my notes and diary entries, I see that Charles Bonner's appointment with Seth occurred before Seth began wearing the inhibitory casts. We met with Dr. Kessler in early October, but his testing was not completed until the end of November. Meanwhile the two therapists, Susan and Phyllis, were keeping up the pressure on me to teach Seth sign language. I investigated alternative therapy settings. The information I gathered continued to be haphazard and conflicting. I talked extensively with someone at the Developmental Disabilities Clinic at Roosevelt Hospital where there was a school program. In the course of that conversation I was informed that the staff physiatrist was inalterably opposed to inhibitory shoes.

In the meantime, Seth visited Dr. Lee a few times because he had a persistent rash. At every visit she told me that Seth was gorgeous and that whatever I was doing was working wonderfully. I also took Seth to see Dr. Grant, the orthopedist, for a routine follow-up visit. Dr. Grant told me that Seth's neurological ability was improving, that he was making great strides, but that his hip cords and ankle cords were a little tight. He told me he thought that the anticipated inhibitory casts would help decrease tone, but that if the muscles were going to be tight, they'd remain tight anyway.

The doctor kept saying that the question we needed to ask was what we should do after the casts. (We hadn't even gotten the casts yet, but we were already having to be worried about what to do after them!) He said that we ought to be thinking about clear plastic braces since Seth would have to have braces for stability. He also kept saying that bone surgery was probable between the ages of four and eight, and that Seth would need to wear casts until his growth was complete, probably at fourteen.

Soon after this visit with Dr. Grant, we went for the tests at Dr. Kessler's clinic. Dr. Kessler's office was in an attic, but his clinic was in the basement of New York Hospital, and I noted in my diary that it was rather an unpleasant place. Seth was not thrilled to see Dr. Kessler, especially his white coat, so the doctor removed it right away. The staff wanted to weigh and measure Seth but, seeing Seth's anxiety, I discouraged them, and in the end they forgot all together.

The conclusion of the tests matched my instincts. Except for the gross motor achievements such as walking, Seth was considered "age appropriate," though he was on the "low" end of the sound-production scale. His cognitive and small motor achievements fell in the normal age range. The staff told us to relax and enjoy him, that he would absolutely be in the mainstream and would go to school with other "normal" children. They did observe, however, that Seth was an appealing child and how eager everyone was to eliminate frustration for him. They cautioned that we should let him be a little frustrated, that frustration stimulates learning.

The ramifications of their suggestion would thread their way through the rest of Seth's life, my life, and this book. Questions about when to intervene and when to leave well-enough alone occur on every level. Just seeing Seth struggle with his shoelaces makes me want to jump up and tie them for him. Just hearing a question put to him about why he talks the way he does, prompts me to answer.

By the end of 1984, eighteen-month-old Seth had seen two neurologists and was being treated by three physical therapists for a total of seven sessions per week. A pediatric orthopedic specialist was following him with routine visits and series of X rays. A pediatric podiatrist was treating him, and he was wearing plaster inhibitory leg casts. A developmental disabilities expert, a hearing specialist, and a Feldenkrais teacher had all diagnosed him. He was going for routine pediatric checkups as well as visits for minor pediatric ailments.

It took me years to recognize the extraordinary number of people who were examining, handling, and diagnosing Seth. Together we were on a voyage to heal, to cure, calling on all doctors, rehabilitators, spending our money, searching, searching each other and other's experiences, looking into the faces of the healers and facilitators for a glimpse of the future.

One big issue that loomed was the one of speech versus sign language. As Dr. Kessler explained to us, children at about eighteen months begin to make logical connections between two ideas. Articulation problems don't become a concern until three years of age. The question for us was: Would sign language give Seth greater independence? Children are capable of learning several languages. How could it hurt him? Seth already seemed to have developed his own sign language. How would this option affect his motivation?

Peggy Smith always remarked how wonderful Seth's motivation was. She said that he had no perceptual deficit and a strong automatic desire to use both hands together despite the disability. As his occupational therapist, she was pleased with the changes in Seth's shoulders, where he was initially very sensitive around the neck. She thought his hands would change, although it would take time because he was beginning to sit up. She had complete confidence in him.

When she, or others, used words and phrases such as "perceptual deficit," it was hard for me to ask what she meant. It's part of my personality not to want to seem ignorant. But I was ignorant. In this case, she was referring to a deficit in visual perception, not the ability to connect two ideas.

The question of intervening, of either helping Seth or allowing him to remain frustrated, seemed part of the equation in the dilemma about signing. If we taught him sign language, would he ever learn to talk, or would we have eliminated a motivating frustration? Dr. Kessler, whom I trusted so much, supported Phyllis the speech therapist, while Dr. Lee and Jay were opposed to the sign language. I called Dr. Madell at the New York League for the Hard of Hearing, and she, too, was opposed to the signing.

We entered January 1985 with a full appointment book and an immense mixture of anxiety and hope, two emotions that seem to go together in all our experiences with Seth. They are joined to pride and joy these days, but the anxiety and hope are never absent, the fingers of these two powerful emotions endlessly intertwined with each other.

During a routine visit to Dr. Price, the podiatrist, we learned that the tone in Seth's legs was "dramatically reduced," and that he was standing beautifully. Dr. Price built up the inhibitory casts so they fit better. We went back for a reevaluation at Dr. Kessler's clinic in March. The report was good. Although Seth continued to have some difficulties in gross motor function, there had been marked improvement in recent months.

In the personal-social area, Seth was capable of imitating house-work, was able to remove at least one garment, but he was still unable to put on any items of clothing. Dressing him was very frustrating for me at this time. Mayra took over during the week, and I tried to grow into it on the weekends, but often I left it to Jay, who continues to be his fashion consultant-valet to this day. Seth could scribble sponta-neously, build a tower of two cubes, and was capable of dumping a raisin from two bottles simultaneously. He was functioning near an age-appropriate level. His vocabulary consisted of approximately thirty words, and he was capable of expressing two wants.

It was less than a year after the initial diagnosis, and I was confident and hopeful some days and nervous on others. I still didn't know what to expect. Seth wasn't walking, so I knew I couldn't consider a con-ventional kindergarten. A long-time member of the Health and Fitness Center at the 92nd Street Y, I was aware of parents coming and going on the elevators to the nursery school three floors above the gym. There were certain weeks during the year when the school conducted inter-views of prospective candidates for this much sought after school and parents would be weighing their children's options for kindergarten after "graduating." I overheard the anxious talk of mothers, mostly as they contemplated aloud the odds for their children being accepted into the program.

Dual emotions snaked through me while I listened to such talk. My perspective on the priorities of life was shifting. While these parents worried about the status of their children's early education, I was think-ing about whether Seth would ever walk at all. Repeatedly, I was re-minded that my agenda was different, and that theirs possessed rami-fications I never expected to confront. Surprisingly, I was also relieved. At least I was spared the excruciating anxiety over the position and rank of Seth's schools. He had cerebral palsy. What I was looking for had nothing to do with prestige or reputation. Of course, years later when our daughter, Haya, was getting ready for kindergarten, my thinking changed once again.

Then in April an unforeseen circumstance inaugurated a new phase in Seth's care. The events of the next six months had more to do with me than with Seth, but ultimately the course of all our lives was changed.

5

◆

New Horizons

◆

By EARLY 1985 my back pain, which had begun five years earlier, became unbearable. I tried everything. Always active, swimming, practicing Yoga, dancing, I was open to any path to fitness, but nothing seemed to relieve my discomfort.

One of the women at my gym recommended the group of physical therapists where Annie Black worked. When Seth was diagnosed, I had turned to her for resources, and she had been a great help. Annie had a good touch, and we talked often during my sessions with her. She described a wide gamut of physical rehabilitation methods that interested her. She talked about cranial-sacral therapy, the Feldenkrais method, and other unconventional methods. She wasn't encouraged to use these alternatives in the group practice, but she described them. I listened a little. Then I began listening a little more. I recognized the resistance most of the medical culture had to the kind of therapies Annie was describing. I was resistant myself.

Annie's work helped, but I got to the point where I could no longer get comfortable, and I was always in pain, sharp pain. Annie wanted me to try Robbie Ofir, a therapist who was a Feldenkrais practitioner as well as a physical therapist. She had met him the summer before when both of them were participating in a Feldenkrais "training" in Canada. He could come to my house. She thought I should give him a try because I wasn't getting better. Her insistence about the benefits of the Feldenkrais method had led me to take Seth to Charles Bonner the previous fall. She often mentioned a Feldenkrais practitioner, a woman

53

named Anat Baniel, and wished out loud that Anat was available to see Seth.

In her book *The Magic of Touch*, Sherry Suib Cohen, discussing the Feldenkrais method, reports that the violinist Yehudi Menuhin, the theatrical director Peter Brook, the anthropologist Margaret Mead, Karl Pribram, director of the Neuropsychology Laboratories of Stanford University, and even the basketball star Dr. J—Julius Irving—have revered Feldenkrais and his methods. The Feldenkrais method is an almost impossible to describe neuromuscular education and reorganization program designed to promote better posture through self-awareness of stance and movement.

Moshe Feldenkrais was a Russian-born Israeli scientist with a black belt in Judo, (the first European to hold the black belt), an electrical and mechanical engineer, and a mathematician. He also worked as a researcher on the French atomic bomb program. Having watched his videotapes and encountered his students and disciples, I believe he must have been a difficult, contentious person. Be that as it may, he believed that one can break age-old self-destructive patterns of movement, influence the brain to change hurtful body movements, and improve one's quality of life and functioning through body movement awareness and skill. Feldenkrais believed that the emotional and nervous systems can be "taught" to heal the physical person. This process is known as "sensory reeducation."

All of these ends are accomplished with special exercises that reorganize and stimulate parts of the brain and initiate new learning. Students learn from their own sensorimotor experience by using the process of "childhood organic learning." Learning comes from doing and is greatly dependent on the unconscious functioning of the nervous system. Learning itself is seen as a powerful therapeutic and self-actualizing force.

The Feldenkrais method is an educational system, not a therapeutic system. The exercises are designed to improve function rather than correct it. Learning is engendered not through moving, but through awareness of the *process* of moving. Feldenkrais believed that nervous structures look for order, that movement is the most efficient means for achieving this order in the mobile, changing world. Repetition is necessary to facilitate learning.

There are two aspects to the learning. One phase is known as functional integration. It is accomplished by a one-on-one relationship between the therapist and the student. The therapist gets the student to repeat ordered, prescribed body movements and manipulations, using his or her hands to skillfully influence, pace, and suggest possibilities to the student. Specific exercises open the nervous system to new potential. An intimate relationship develops, similar to the one between a physical therapist and patient. The technique is basically nonverbal and hands-on, geared to those students requiring individual attention.

The other aspect to the learning, taught in groups, is called Awareness through Movement (ATM). ATM is a learning process that makes self-direction easier. In both methods the student *learns to learn* how to attend to his or her particular movements with greater awareness. The student learns to refine the details of his or her actions.

Eventually, I benefited from both aspects of the teaching. I discovered old habits and explored previously unused muscles and patterns of movement, and in the process I developed greater balance, more control.

Robbie Ofir, the Feldenkrais practitioner/physical therapist Annie recommended, came to see me in early March. Amused, he watched me as I demonstrated a panoply of exercises I had learned over the years for relieving my back pain. I showed him the movements that bothered me now. Then he asked me to lie on my back and close my eyes. He gently, very gently, manipulated my head and then my legs in small, imperceptible ways. Maybe I breathed more deeply. I know that when I got up after the treatment, I felt changed.

So a new therapist was now added to the parade, except this one was for me. I scheduled Robbie's treatments on the afternoons when Seth wasn't having his sessions. From the beginning Robbie was interested in Seth, his diagnosis and his current prognosis. Robbie encouraged me to read the Feldenkrais literature and bragged about the incredible success Feldenkrais had had with children with cerebral palsy. One especially well-known book in Feldenkrais circles is *The Case of Nora,* about the challenging case of a young girl whom Feldenkrais had treated. I read this book and saw videotapes of Feldenkrais working with children. The tapes eventually persuaded me to teach Seth how to ride a horse. But more on that later.

Like Annie Black, Robbie also spoke often about Anat Baniel, Mr. Feldenkrais's protégé, an Israeli woman known for her exceptional talent for rehabilitating children. Before his death, Moshe Feldenkrais had led many large seminars and demonstrations all over the world, and Anat, then a young woman, had assisted him. She was his last personal disciple and pupil, and apparently Feldenkrais had passed on much of his knowledge to Anat before he died.

Anat was at the forefront of the Feldenkrais "trainings" that were currently being offered throughout the world. The seminars were lengthy, sometimes running for six weeks, and were held several times a year. It took over three to four years to train in the Feldenkrais work. Up until the 1970s only thirteen people had been trained to practice functional integration. Then in 1975 Feldenkrais accepted an invitation to establish a three-year training program in San Francisco for some sixty-five students. With the completion of the program, the Feldenkrais Guild was formed, representing the more than seventy-five people then capable of practicing functional integration.

The Feldenkrais therapy was very helpful to me. I was always better after the treatments. Not only was I without pain immediately following the sessions, I was acquiring a new sense of my physical self. I was gaining awareness of my breathing and patterns of movement, and this influenced how I felt. But I was impatient. In the long term I felt frustrated by my back's limitations and discouraged that the pain recurred when I engaged in my regular daily routines.

Robbie wanted me to give things more time. He began treating me in March, but by early April I was restless and eager to resume my old activities. My quest for a "fix" urged me to seek help within the "establishment." On the recommendation of my personal physician, I consulted an orthopedic surgeon. After a CAT scan and examination, the doctor recommended that I have a spinal fusion. In April I went into the hospital to have my third and fourth lumbar vertebrae fused. This was a very serious surgery, and in my typical way I didn't ask many questions. It seems remarkable that I passed through this momentous surgery with no idea of its importance. I was in the hospital almost four weeks. Again, I wish I'd known there were other alternatives to the surgery. But I didn't. I still believed in the Feldenkrais work, however, and wanted to integrate it into my rehabilitation.

Seth was going to be two years old in June, and he was wearing the casts on his legs most of the time during the day. He loved the fact that they allowed him to stand with some apparent stability, although not independently. He would stand next to something like his crib or a table, where he could hold on, grinning widely, thrilled by his vertical stance.

He did, however, prefer his sneakers for crawling. He would loudly insist upon wearing his Keds or his L.A. Gear sneakers if we were going to be anywhere that didn't have apparatus to help him stand. In February, when Dr. Price built up the inhibitory casts so they fit better, he also fit Seth for an orthotic, which Seth could wear in his sneakers while crawling. Dr. Price believed that Seth would need to wear the casts until he was "cruising." "Cruising" describes what children do when they are beginning to walk and need to "cruise" from one support to another until they are more secure. Cruising was something Seth never did.

We were still struggling with the issue of Seth's speech and whether to teach him sign language. We took Seth for a reevaluation with Dr. Kessler, the developmental disabilities expert. Dr. Kessler and his staff were impressed and encouraged by Seth's progress. They reiterated that he seemed "age appropriate" except for his motor skills. As far as Seth's speech was concerned, they thought he was following the normal development of a child who combines gestures prior to speech. They didn't push the sign language.

We were relieved to hear everything the experts had to say, since, as you can imagine, every appointment for Seth was loaded with anxiety for us. The outcome dictated our mood and outlook. At this juncture I felt relieved about the prospect of not having to keep Seth in a bubble. I experienced an expectation of normalcy. Of course, over time the shades of normalcy graduated into many different hues.

In the interim, my back situation absorbed me. I left the hospital April 30 and immediately resumed the Feldenkrais sessions with Robbie Ofir. He came to the house twice a week. He continued to have an ongoing interest in Seth and often wanted to see him when he came to treat me. Just after surgery I was very limited in my activities, although this did not in any way affect my therapy. Although there was residual pain from the surgery, after my sessions I felt completely comfortable and at ease. I was learning a great deal about myself.

Does it sound fatuous to describe getting in touch with my breathing, my capacity to concentrate and differentiate small movements so that when I lifted a glass of water to my mouth, I learned not to lift my shoulders too? I was increasingly aware of the power of touch, of the effects of one person's hands on me with a "light" but significant pressure. I began listening to Robbie when he said how much this Feldenkrais work could help Seth. I began thinking about touching Seth myself.

We took Seth to see Dr. Grant, the pediatric orthopedist, in June. Seth was almost two years old and long overdue for X rays. The doctor thought the left "boot," the plaster cast, was taking on the shape of Seth's foot, but he also thought that Seth's hips looked better than they had a year earlier. He observed that Seth was making strides with "balancing reactions," which was important because stability is essential, especially at the beginning. He repeated the questions about inhibitory casts and whether they eliminate the need for surgery later. He mentioned the clear plastic braces again. He asked us to consider a future operation to cut the Achilles tendons on Seth's feet.

Then Dr. Grant said something that has continued to whisper through my entire experience with Seth, especially in recent years. He emphasized that the twenty-one-year-olds, and the young adults he has treated, whether they walked or not, had told him that they valued speech and upper-extremity dexterity and ability more than anything else. Today his words echo significantly as I witness Seth's fine motor skills. At the time I didn't know if he was indirectly addressing our conundrum about Seth's speech. Now I understand the truth of his message fully. Today Seth's frustrations center on his inability to easily execute fine motor tasks like buttoning his clothes, tying his shoes, cutting his food, using a key. Seth's speech and fine motor difficulties present the most significant challenges. But I wasn't able to imagine what Grant meant at the time. I was only worried about whether Seth would walk independently.

Peggy Smith and Susan Scheer both wrote reports about Seth during this time. I asked Peggy to describe to me how she saw Seth.

"Oh, he's wonderful," she said. "So bright and attentive. He has real self-motivation. Self-direction. You are very lucky he is so bright. I expect his own motivation will see him through wonderfully."

"But will he do everything other children can do?" I asked her, as I asked everyone constantly, as I asked myself invariably. "I mean, will he be like other children? I mean, I know, not exactly. I know all children are different, but will he seem different in a major way?" I was holding my breath.

She said, "We are doing many tasks designed to develop motor co-ordination skills, and he's come a long way."

But I saw there was still extreme deviation on the left side of Seth's body. He held his left arm, left hand, left shoulder, left leg, and left side of his trunk differently than the right side of his body. The actions on the left side of his body were less precise and more spastic.

When he played, he needed to stabilize his shoulders and trunk for building with blocks or fitting the pieces of a puzzle together. The increased tone in his neck decreased his ability to vocalize. The volume of his voice diminished. Any major effort for Seth put a strain on his lung power, on his diaphragm.

We could see that while playing rudimentary games like tossing the ball he was tense through the neck where the vocal cords reside. He drooled excessively. While he worked to remain stable and upright, even when doing simple tasks like pushing a small toy, the tension in his upper trunk put further strain on his body. We could see the exertion on his face by the involuntary actions around his nose and mouth. He made funny expressions like a little chipmunk, but of course they weren't deliberate.

Most important to us were his diminished body-righting reactions. The slightest jarring or unfamiliar noise would cause him to fall over. We were constantly worried about this, and it became a greater concern when he started his schooling. Playgrounds can be dangerous places. I knew that helmets were often a consideration for children with cerebral palsy. Years later the extent of the threat of this problem was graphically illustrated one evening when we were standing on a corner in the West Village with pizza to take home for dinner from our favorite New York pizza parlor. I was holding the boxes, and Seth was standing beside me on the curb while we tried to get a taxi. It was dusk. Suddenly a mammoth truck passed by and honked its horn. Seth fell right over, completely prone, onto the street. The loudness and suddenness of the noise had caused him to lose his balance.

Peggy wrote in her report that Seth had good basic perceptual awareness and had shown a tremendous increase in tolerance over the last weeks. He was more willing to allow Peggy to handle him. She said that he possessed a wonderful memory, especially when it came to their created play. Seth was beginning to "bunny hop" crawl; whereas up until then he had only "commando" crawled. The focus of the therapy was to change his motor patterns and alignment and to develop motor control that supported skill acquisition.

Seth demonstrated continued improvement in most areas of gross motor development. He was able to sit up on the floor by himself. Unfortunately, he preferred W sitting, which means sitting with the knees forward along the floor in front of the trunk and the feet behind the buttocks. Although the W sitting allowed him the greatest degree of trunk stability and freed his arms for play, it reinforced the already strong abnormal pattern of his hips and feet. I heard myself and others—Mayra, Jay, the therapists—say, "Seth, don't sit like that." I still issue this order to this day.

By summer Seth was creeping independently on both hands and knees as his primary mode of locomotion. During creeping, his left hand often remained in a tight fist; while the right-hand fingers were only slightly flexed, but flexed nonetheless. He was also "kneel standing." He was beginning to kneel walk, a mode of ambulating that would see us through the next few years. (We never could use his pants for hand-me-downs; they were always worn out in the knees.)

The summer of 1985 brought a significant demarcation, however. The Feldenkrais work was becoming a powerful influence for me, and I embarked on two explorations that changed me even more. I met and began working with Carola Speads, and in June I enrolled in a seminar with Anat Baniel.

When I had first taken Seth to consult with Charles Bonner the previous fall, Bonner had mentioned Carola Speads. Carola was a woman in her late eighties who taught "Physical Reeducation and Movement" on the Upper West Side of Manhattan. Born in Germany, Carola had begun her professional career in Berlin, where she later had her own school. Carola had taught for many years with the pioneering movement teacher Elsa Gindler. Since 1940, Carola had been teaching her techniques to groups and individuals in New York and in workshops throughout Europe and the United States. The benefits of Carola's instruction program of gentle exercises, or "experiments," as she called them, were incalculable.

Singers, dancers, other performing artists, body workers, psychoanalysts and their patients, victims of multiple sclerosis, asthma, arthritis, among others, were her students. She had worked in the fifties with Fritz Perls, the psychoanalyst, and she considered physical re-education to be like psychoanalysis: you had to live through it. Like Feldenkrais, she believed that the emotional life and the physical life of a person could not be separated and were greatly influenced by the nervous system. Whereas in the Feldenkrais method the work was accomplished with exercises and through one-on-one contact; Carola's work was accomplished by breathing.

Breathing! Admittedly, I was skeptical, but I was in the mood to explore. My surgery had confined me to home, and I had more time on my hands than usual. I was wearing a large plastic brace, which surrounded my entire torso. I couldn't sit comfortably, which is typical for people who suffer back pain, but it was a condition I wanted to remedy as soon as possible. I recalled Charles Bonner responding to my concerns about Seth's sitting by mentioning Carola and some of her techniques.

Jay, Seth, and I would be spending most of the summer on Cape Cod, and Mayra was going with us. I was concerned about my progress and Seth's development. Before we departed I wanted to investigate some of what I had been hearing about. At the same time, I was aware of how dependent we were on others. I wanted to expand my role in Seth's rehabilitation, to be more directly, more differently, involved with Seth's care and to be more in charge. Although my new self was still unformed, I was getting in touch with a new dimension in my self.

Robbie Ofir also knew about Carola Speads. He had read her book, *Breathing: the ABC's* (now titled *Ways to Better Breathing*) and was curious for me to find out more. During the summer, Robbie was planning to participate in the last session of a Feldenkrais training in Canada as part of his official Feldenkrais certification. Susan Scheer had planned a vacation, and both Peggy and Phyllis would not be as available during the summer months. My anxiety about being on my own propelled me to act. I called Charles to get Carola's address. It turned out that her classes were being held near our New York apartment.

Nothing in my experience prepared me for Carola and the environment of her teaching. In my high-powered, fast-track, superdisciplined life, I never imagined that in the middle of the day, in the middle of New York City, in a light, airy apartment, anywhere from ten to twenty people could be assembled for "experiments" in breathing. The students constituted almost a new breed of people who paced themselves in their lives with different priorities. There was Carola sitting lithely on the windowsill. Piled in the corner of the room was a collection of mats, poles, juggling pins, balls, wooden hoops, straws, Japanese tappers, and rolling pins. Every "lesson" would begin with Carola saying, "Now, be very open-minded. Let the changes come through."

Over the years I became a serious student of Carola's. I grew aware of the quality of my breathing, the state of my inadequate respiration. I achieved an increase in circulation, a lessening of tension, and I realized the "manifold interdependencies between breathing and the various organs of the body." But that evolution took time and many classes over many years. Later I even went to class twice a week. For the time being, however, I benefited from a half-dozen lessons before we went away for the summer.

I was completely unaware that opportunities for self-discovery in both the mental and physical realms even existed in this context. This unfolding took place within me and outside of me. I felt different after each class, although it took me time to develop the patience and concentration for the work. There was a variety of sensations related to breathing in the experiments. I recognized my "unawareness" of my poor breathing. My back pain began disappearing even though I was sitting for long periods on the floor. There were no set routines because breathing is so individual. But through the experiments I began to see an immense variety of approaches to successful breathing. I learned the importance of breathing and how it is part of the religions of many diverse cultures. I realized that among my own ancestors, the Hebrews, the word for "wind," or "breath," was the same as the word for "soul."

The other significant event at this time was that Anat Baniel was visiting New York from the West Coast. She was teaching a two-week seminar for people unfamiliar with Awareness through Movement (ATM). I knew I had to go. Again my eyes were opened wide to another universe. In a large room, during ten early-summer evenings, up to 250 people gathered to try the movements Anat directed. We began by lying on the floor, eyes closed, doing a body scan. How did each part of our bodies feel? the skull? the rib cage? the shoulders? spine? pelvis? legs? arms? We initiated a range of motions. We did head rolls and eye rolls. We did arm circles. We lay on our stomachs. We lay on our backs and sides. We moved with our legs, hips, feet. We stood, walked, bent, swayed.

How many of us feel our feet on the floor, how our toes are resting when we stand? Even in this moment as you read my words or I write them, do either of us have any sense of our breathing, where our sit bones are placed, how our sternum is positioned? Too New Age? Try again. Are we breathing into our side ribs? Are our shoulders resting on our torsos? When we reach for the telephone, step on the escalator, answer the door, are we breathing? Can we feel ourselves? Are our legs really under us when we stand? Where is our head and chin? My awarenesses grew. My body was different, though not entirely comfortable. I often felt—and sometimes still do after intense sessions of any kind of body work—as if I were wearing new clothes that didn't quite fit.

The few classes I'd taken with Carola that spring and Anat's seminar revealed a radically different range of possibilities. It never occurred to me that there were so many people involved in these studies. I felt I was part of a new culture, exploring new terrain. I was making new contacts, new friends. I was in a fantastic new orbit of experience. Seth's cerebral palsy and my recent surgery were measured and received in an unprecedented manner. We left for the Cape as I was awakening to this new world. I was committed to use the little I had already learned. And I felt I wanted to experiment with Seth and see whether I could help him as well as myself.

Seth was in his casts all summer, and I was in my brace. I tried to practice daily a little of what I had learned from Carola's few classes, what I had gleaned during my seminar with Anat, and what I had been learning in my sessions with Robbie. I made great strides in my rehabilitation. I was healing very fast. By early July, only eight weeks after the surgery, I was able to swim small distances in the ocean. I was walking on the beach, began driving again, and took up most daily routines quite freely. When I went to the surgeon for my checkup, he was genuinely amazed by my progress.

Mayra, Jay, and I were vigilant with Seth all summer. We encouraged the movements Susan and Peggy had taught us. We created play that invited him to develop more motor control. On the beach I had Mayra bring buckets and sand toys. She helped me haul buckets of water, which I encouraged him to dump on the dry sand and then pat the wet sand into shapes. I could see his fingers working, especially the ones on his left hand, which were always held so tightly. On rainy days I made cookie dough, and he helped me roll it out. Together we cut out the cookie shapes. These activities encouraged him to coordinate hand and eye movements.

Mayra and I constantly intervened when we observed him W sitting.

I initiated small touches, and he liked them. On the beach, while he was barefoot, I played with his toes and the soles of his feet. I rubbed his hands gently in the sand. If he was lying on his back at any time, I played with him to mimic the movements we had tried in Anat's seminar. "Let's roll from side to side, Seth. Let's shake our legs in the air. We'll lie on our tummys and crawl like animals; turn our heads from side to side looking for our prey. We can roll our eyes all different ways. Touch our left foot with our right hand and our right foot with our left hand. Breathe, sweetheart, breathe. Don't hold your breath."

Whenever I could, I touched him around his diaphragm and rib cage as I had learned to touch myself in Carola's lessons. I easily observed the changes in his respiration and the increased ease and softness that occurred in his body when I touched him in this way. I began looking at him differently. The little I had already learned helped me assess him and react to him with entirely new responses, new awareness.

In September, when we returned to New York, Seth could still barely pull himself up to stand. His legs were not capable of bearing his weight without help from his arms. He could be helped into standing from half-kneeling, and he could be placed in a half-kneeling position, but he could not assume the position himself. He was able to kneel walk, but his balance and tone were very poor. When he stood without the inhibitory boots or without the shoes with orthotic devices, his pelvis locked, and he showed excessive hip and knee extension. There was terrible rotation of his ankles inward and downward; while at the same time he was "fixing" in the shoulders; they were taut and rigid. He had no balance. I was appalled.

Seth's upper body was well developed, but his left hand lacked discrete control, and his shoulders were often involved in keeping him stabilized. We noticed that his drooling was even more extreme, and it was more pronounced when he tried harder at new things that were difficult. He had many more words, but he was still frustrated when he was unable to communicate his wants and needs. Nevertheless, he demonstrated above-average receptivity to language.

As explained in *Children with Disabilities* by Mark L. Batshaw and Yvonne M. Perret, if speech is the act of producing words, language implies having something to say. A usual consequence of early brain damage is a developmental delay in language, rather than a language disorder. Children with a "receptive language disorder" have difficulty understanding what they hear; it's not that they can't hear. When there is a receptive language disorder, there are also accompanying cognitive deficits, problems with social interactions, and a lot of difficulty with communication skills. Fortunately, we were not encountering any of this in Seth.

We were thinking about expanding Seth's environments and started to explore play school or preschool settings. This new step presented real challenges in our emotional life. We faced a new reality, new concerns, new fears.

A year earlier, in September, Susan Scheer had encouraged us to find "socializing" environments for Seth. She wanted a teacher or trained professional involved—to encourage his cognitive skills, to help him learn how to influence his environment. Looking back, I think she probably had so much hope for Seth, such confidence in Seth, and was so excited by the possibilities of his development that she was pushing ahead prematurely.

A year earlier, Susan had asked me to explore a preschool setting called Basic Trust. The school focused on bringing the child into the mainstream. Jay and I went to look at it. Basic Trust consisted of two large rooms with bars on the windows in the basement of a rundown brownstone on the West Side of Manhattan. It wasn't at all what we had in our minds or in our dreams for our firstborn child. We decided our own time with him, the ongoing care Mayra provided, and getting him to the park where there were other children was enough for the moment. I also looked into Red Yellow Blue & Glue, an art program at the 92nd Street Y, but he was still too young. We waited.

New York City is a unique place. The competition and drive that exists in the city is so great, so all-encompassing, that it is easy to lose perspective. Parents of two- and three-year-olds are well into the quest for the best preschools that will move their children into the best nursery schools that will ensure the children entrance into the best elementary schools and so on to college. I admit I was relieved to miss this experience. For the time being I kept a quiet distance whenever those discussions occurred, which was often. My thoughts still centered on whether my child was going to walk, or even go to school with other "normal" children.

Seth was over two years old and couldn't walk or stand independently. Many of his upper-body movements were unusual or not well accomplished. He always needed someone with him. He was toilet trained, but he needed assistance with his clothes. He ate independently, for the most part, using regular utensils and glasses, but his motions were more than clumsy. Aside from involuntary action, he could not handle many aspects of feeding. Dressing and undressing, toileting, eating, these were the daily routines for which he required constant help.

We needed surroundings where the constant presence of someone else with him would be accepted. We didn't want to underscore his differences by sending him to a place where he alone would have a caregiver. We were confident that he would ultimately learn to walk, but in the meantime he was still in his stroller. We never used the word "wheelchair," but his stroller functioned much like one. He was getting too big to carry, and the casts were a factor as well. We were facing our son's disability with new perspective.

We were interested in a Jewish school, so we went to talk to the director of the nursery program at our synagogue. It made the most sense to explore possible alternatives for Seth within our own faith. The school had a very fine reputation. I remember the interview very well. We toured the facility, which was large and impressive and housed many classes. We described Seth's limitations, and the director asked us why we didn't consider a wheelchair. I was mute. My son was going to walk one day, maybe not normally, but independently. We decided to wait on nursery school.

In the meantime, I returned to Carola's classes and resumed my therapy with Robbie Ofir. My brace was removed, months earlier than expected. The progress of my rehabilitation produced great awe in my surgeon's office. After I told him about my course of therapy, though, his reaction was different. As soon as I began explaining Carola and the Feldenkrais work, his eyes glazed over. The response of Dr. Lee, Seth's pediatrician, some time later, was even more extreme. She called the treatment "witchcraft."

Every visit to Dr. Lee began and ended the same way. Seth and I arrived, either for a routine checkup or for a visit for a minor sore throat or ear infection or some kind of baby rash. Dr. Lee oohed and ahhed over Seth. He was so handsome. He was so sweet. He had such a wonderful smile. I was such a wonderful mother. I was doing so much for him. It was so amazing. I was the apotheosis of the devoted, searching mother.

My actual response to Dr. Lee and everyone else was always the same. I was doing what any mother would do. I was lucky. I was hopeful. I declined admiration, remaining incredulous that any parent wouldn't do the same.

We visited Dr. Kessler during September. One of my new concerns was how much Seth overheard of our discussions about him, especially when Susan or Peggy or Phyllis came for his sessions. While arriving or leaving, they sometimes wanted to talk, and I wanted to hear their spontaneous reactions. But I was unsure. On the one hand, I didn't want Seth to feel that we had things to say that he shouldn't hear, but, on the other hand, I thought that some conversations should take place without him around. I worried about conversations he overheard between Mayra and the therapists, too. Mayra was young, and though she loved Seth, Seth loved her, and we loved her and valued her enormously, she didn't have the discretion I knew was needed in these circumstances. I wanted professional guidance on how to handle the professionals. I wanted insight about how to protect my child.

I was becoming a juggler and tightrope walker, trying to handle Seth's disability and the legions of professionals involved with it. I was sorting and sifting advice and input, managing the feelings of everyone around me, especially my husband's and son's, but also my family's and helpers'. I was learning to be political. I was trusting my intuitions and not searching out more empirical information, but I was also tuning in to new possible treatments as a result of the body work I was doing for myself.

As I pursued the Feldenkrais work and studied once a week with Carola Speads, I couldn't ignore the remarkable change in my body, in my physical self. I had to acknowledge the value in the work. As September moved into October, I felt more and more that Seth's progress was stymied, that maybe I should be thinking anew about his care. He was still wearing the casts. His therapy sessions continued, but I saw few changes. The routine was comfortable and safe, which was reassuring, but I was nervous.

Robbie's and Annie's words, my visit with Charles Bonner, my own experience gnawed at me. I was primed to plunge into something new when the opportunity presented itself. Then in mid-October Robbie told me that Anat Baniel was coming to New York to live and work.

6

◆

The Plunge

◆

JAY URGED CAUTION, but I jumped to connect with Anat. Jay was open-minded but more prudent in his enthusiasm than I was. I was already benefiting from firsthand experience both in the hands of Robbie and from Anat's seminar in June. My mind was also filled with possibilities that I was gleaning from my work with Carola. It is true that, unlike with Seth, the source of my difficulties was not totally rooted in my nervous system, but my experiences made me believe that there were possibilities for Seth here too.

Because of my relationships with Robbie Ofir and Annie Black, I had personally met Anat during her seminar the prior June. She was quite intimidating, a real star. She is Israeli. Her style is provocative, testy. My own professional life was centered in a celebrity world, but Anat was like no other luminary I had ever met. She possessed confidence and exuded presence only people who are completely comfortable and secure in themselves, physically, mentally, and professionally have. She is striking, with beautiful cascading auburn hair and the lithe body of a dancer. She moves with more ease than anyone I've ever known. She is commanding before a large crowd, very charismatic.

Because of my own celebrity-like life, I was often in the company of movie stars or famous writers. I was traveling every few weeks to my apartment in Los Angeles, and this also attracted Anat to me. In June we had spoken about Seth only in passing. But she was aware of him. Like many people, she was more concentrated on what seemed like my glamorous life.

Jay and I together project a dynamic aura. There is glamour and style about us because of his entertainment practice and my history as an independent producer. But when it came to our son, his struggles and his difficulties, we were innocents and did not feel as capable as we may have seemed. The difference between our public persona and our private one was huge. Bridging this void, using our prominence to attract and maintain what we required socially or for business yet remaining involved in the actual needs of our son, was and is a major challenge. We were always trying to bridge the gap between what we could make happen in the world of Broadway and Hollywood and what we could not make happen for Seth.

Our circumstances played out with Anat on a big stage. We wanted her to be drawn to us, and knew that our social connections would accomplish this. At the same time, we wanted her to recognize us as ordinary parents desperate to do whatever we could to help our child.

Anat was using another therapist's office on the West Side of Manhattan. We played phone tag for some time before I finally reached her. We talked at length about Seth. I knew my participation in the June seminar was a plus. It demonstrated my serious intentions, and Anat is a serious person. I told her everything we were doing for Seth. I described the other therapists, Susan, Peggy, and Phyllis, and their work. I described the casts. She asked me many direct, pertinent questions. She wanted to know only a little about the birth history and about the neurological diagnoses. I told her about the hearing test, his eyesight, his intelligence.

When Anat finished asking all her questions, she said, "You'll have to let everyone else go." I was flabbergasted. "And you'll have to throw away the casts. He will never learn to walk as long as he wears them."

Now I was speechless. She hadn't even seen him! This assessment had taken place by telephone. I made an appointment to bring Seth to see her.

Why did Anat insist on the disposal of the casts when Charles and Robbie hadn't? Because Anat knew more than anyone else and was sure enough of herself and her facts to act on them. Anat taught the teachers. She was at the forefront of the training of new and old Feldenkrais practitioners. She was generally acknowledged as one of the therapy's greatest practitioners and as Feldenkrais's heir. And she was known to be just as difficult and ornery as he had been.

I tempered my nervousness about her for Jay's sake. I wanted us to go to the first appointment with open minds. I told him about the phone conversation, but I was casual. Nothing was written in stone. We were exploring. We were both anxious about Seth. He was two and a half, beautiful, bright, goodnatured, and we doted on him, but he was not walking.

Anat's office was difficult to locate in the labyrinth of a large apartment complex. As we wandered around, I became anxious and frustrated. I didn't want to be late. I knew from the June training that Anat could be late but we couldn't—a carryover of Mr. Feldenkrais's style. Many of the practitioners I met who were students/disciples of Feldenkrais maintained testy, contentious personas. We arrived not a moment too soon at Anat's office. There were two rooms, a small reception room and a very large studio that contained a therapy table, a giant ball, and a huge potted plant. Wonderful big windows made everything bright and airy, but the room was stark, all business.

Anat removed Seth's casts immediately. She said she wanted him to go barefoot as much as possible. The walker was an absolute no-no. She rolled Seth around on the floor, playfully, but with purpose. She picked him up by the back of the neck. She dangled him from his ankles. She put him on the table on his back, rotating his hips, feet, arms. Seth complained loudly during the session. This was work, not play. The session reminded me a lot of what Peggy, the occupational therapist, did with him, but there was new content.

Without fanfare or speeches, when she was done, Anat laid out her treatment plan. Seth was to come to see her three times a week. No casts. We were to pay for all three sessions, at $90 each, every week at the time of the third session. Payment was expected whether Seth attended or not. Except for a death in the immediate family, she expected him to appear. Mayra could bring him to the sessions, but she had to remain outside, and Anat wanted to speak to Jay or me at least once a week. She needed an M.D. who would examine Seth and sanction the therapy in order to be reimbursed by the insurance company. In order to accomplish this, Anat needed to submit forms to the allopathic physician, but she wasn't promising anything. There was no other discussion.

Anat's confidence in herself, her unequivocal presentation of the terms of her involvement left no room for argument. We were either going to do it or not do it. We couldn't equivocate either. We understood without doubt that if we didn't, there were plenty of other people ready to use the time she was allotting for Seth. We accepted her offer and set up appointments for the following week.

We left Anat's office and sent Seth on his way with Mayra. He was animated differently than I had ever remembered seeing him. Jay and I took some big breaths and then talked. The reality of what we were doing began to sink in gradually. What would we tell everyone? We felt awkward about informing Susan Scheer and the other therapists that they were no longer needed after all this time and after all their loyalty and devotion.

There was also the big question of how to explain ourselves in the world. What would we tell the doctors? In addition to Dr. Lee, there were Drs. Grant, Kessler, and Price, as well as the neurologists. Then there were our parents and friends. No mainstream medical community recognized Anat's work. Her work was not acceptable in conventional terms. Feldenkrais work! I could just hear the reactions. Most people couldn't say it, never mind spell it. The insurance company was not going to accept her credentials as valid for reimbursement without the sanction of this doctor she referred us to.

Jay supported my instinct to try Anat. There was plenty to recommend her work, both in my own personal experience and from what I was reading about children with cerebral palsy who had been treated by Feldenkrais. Witnessing Seth in Anat's hands gave us enormous confidence. I wasn't without misgivings and anxiety, but my willingness to be a renegade myself probably encouraged me to try something outside of the mainstream for Seth. Jay's trust in my choices for Seth probably overrode any reluctance he felt. But he was also impressed by what he had seen in Anat's office. And we were both desperate for progress.

In November Robbie informed me that a change in his professional life meant he could no longer treat patients in the city. I was going to need a different therapist. Charles Bonner was still in the neighborhood, so I called him. We planned some sessions. In the meantime, I considered participating in a Feldenkrais training myself. Mia Segal, one of the original thirteen Feldenkrais students, also Israeli, was planning to begin offering a three-year course that would meet in the city.

My conversation with Susan Scheer was difficult. I told her our intentions, what we wanted to try. She wasn't exactly skeptical, but she expressed disappointment and reservations. She was sad about having to say good-bye to Seth, and there was a coolness about her departure. I felt anxious.

My misgivings retreated some when I spoke to Peggy Smith. She was enthusiastic. She knew about Anat, knew her reputation, and believed wholeheartedly in the Feldenkrais work. She expressed optimism about Seth's future.

I spoke to Phyllis by phone. She and I had never stopped struggling over the sign-language issue, and I had remained slightly uncomfortable with her. Seth liked his sessions with Phyllis the least. And there were always those little handwritten notes at the end of every week to influence my state of mind. The power these people had!

As far as the doctors were concerned, I felt no urgency about calling them and announcing my plans. I assumed that the information would come out naturally. Our family and our friends were another matter. I was quiet for the time being.

By November Seth began regular sessions with Anat. We also enrolled him in an early-childhood program at the Studio Elementary School. Serendipity again! When a woman at my gym had overheard me talking about my difficulty finding a mainstream setting appropriate for Seth, she had piped up about the Studio School. What was special about Studio Elementary was that it required that a parent or a baby sitter be present for each child. So Seth would be like all the other children, even though Mayra always had to be there with him.

The Studio Elementary School approached child development in completely psychological terms; it was their primary lens on all issues. I paid attention to this philosophy only later. I chose the school because it met a unique requirement for Seth. Typically, I grabbed onto the aspect that met my primary need, never looking any further. I only did half my research. It was in the neighborhood, Mayra could go, and they wanted him. He remained in the school from the fall of 1985 until the spring of 1987.

For two-year-olds and three-year-olds the school day was 9:00 to 12:00 in the morning, which left plenty of time for him to go to his sessions with Anat. It was wonderful for him to have the daily company of a group of children. They were totally accepting of him, and he was participating in a structured environment of play and learning.

The other monumental change was that Seth now *went* to therapy. Until his work with Anat, everyone had come to the house. His sessions had been in his room, on his turf, so to speak. The change in the therapy environment had a dramatic impact. Mayra was not permitted in the sessions. She waited outside in the reception area, something

Seth resisted ardently at the beginning. He put up a big battle with Anat at every session. He was testing who was in charge, and he didn't like the results. He was as angry, riled, and aroused as I'd never known him to be. Anat's reports in the early weeks focused solely on her power struggles with Seth. These struggles were a centerpiece of their relationship and what she saw as a primary part of his therapy.

Anat's position was that she was in charge, and that Seth needed much more discipline and order. He could not dictate the terms. If he didn't want to cooperate during sessions, Anat simply went about other tasks and made him wait it out in the therapy room until the session was over. Her approach was to treat the whole child, his personality as well as his neurology. She felt that Seth needed to have an ordered, respectful relationship to her and the work they were doing. He needed to see the therapy as work and comprehend the gravity of the effort. At two and a half!

Anat spoke to Seth directly, telling him clearly that she and she alone could teach him to walk. She had rules he was required to obey. She wanted him to do unusual things with his body, things he wasn't used to trying. He was very resistant to start. For example, Anat put a lot of emphasis on Seth's tongue. She wanted him to practice putting the tip of his tongue into each corner of his mouth. She dabbed applesauce, which he loved passionately, on the corners of his mouth to encourage him to practice. When he failed to cooperate, she insisted that we take away applesauce at home. She wasn't kidding. This was not a friendly, chatty relationship. This was professional and demanding work. As much as I respected Anat, even idolized her and knew the value of her work, I worried over my little boy.

We adored Seth. He continued to be outgoing with a twinkle in his blue eyes and an exceptional intelligence. I loved talking about Seth and hearing how wonderful he was. After several sessions with Anat, I called her to talk about Seth. When I got her on the phone, Anat said, "He is a very manipulative, angry, and spoiled young man. Full of expectation." I was in shock, not sure if she knew who she was talking to.

"Seth is a prince," she went on. "He insists on getting his needs gratified immediately. Laura, you and Jay are too doting, too indulgent. He needs to ask clearly for what he wants and to wait, too. He needs to struggle. Helping him in every little way, with his dressing, his feeding, anticipating all his needs, is nothing but disservice."

"But I find him so easy," I replied. "He is such a happy boy, always a pleasure. Easy to take everywhere. He never complains."

"Why should he? You do everything for him. He needs frustration. He needs the experience of his limitations. He needs to become motivated to do what's necessary to overcome his circumstances."

It was very difficult for me to accept these lessons for my child, a child so young, my firstborn, my only baby who was always smiling at me and giving me so much joy. I thought Anat's attitude was harsh. I didn't see Seth in this light. I spoke to Mayra about it.

She agreed with many of Anat's insights. "She's right, Mrs. Kramer. I mean, we all love him very much, but we do everything for him. He doesn't like to wait for anything. Like a big boss. He is very demanding."

Admittedly, I was uncomfortable and not entirely open to these observations. It was hard for me to understand that Seth could be as wonderful as he was and still have these unattractive streaks, traits that were undermining his progress. And traits that would not serve him well in life. Later Seth's other facilitators also perceived these difficulties in him. Dr. Frymann, his osteopath, has told me many times how manipulative Seth is and how little he cooperates. Charles Bonner complained about his power struggles with Seth. Today I often experience for myself the truth of these people's insights. Time has proven all of them correct.

I tended to do less for Seth than Jay did, partly because of the difference in our personalities, but also somewhat owing to our different abilities. My surgery, my small size, my lesser strength made it impossible for me to carry Seth around or lift him from one place to another. I was more inclined to get Seth to do things for himself. And I am more selfish than Jay, lazier. Sometimes I didn't want to get up from the chair to get what Seth needed, a tendency that may actually have benefited Seth without my consciously knowing it. The other reason was psychological. My sadness about Seth's circumstances, the horror of his birth, my anxiety about his future, all were channeled into being responsible for his rehabilitation. I was the prime investigator and instigator of his care. Jay relied on me in this context, although we discussed everything. Jay was very busy making a living and generating the money we needed to meet the enormous financial burdens of Seth's situation.

The therapy Seth had been receiving was only partially covered by the insurance company, and we were always battling with them. Now we were totally insecure about whether they would reimburse us for any of Anat's therapy. Meeting Anat's bills each week put tremendous pressure on our cash flow, but we did it. The strain was enormous, so other bills were sometimes set aside.

The financial burdens were staggering. Jay made a good living by anyone's standards, but not only did we live in Manhattan, the expenses for Seth's treatment continued to be exorbitant. Mayra cost, Anat cost, all the speech therapy was completely out of pocket, none of it reimbursed, and the Studio Elementary School was expensive. There had been the casts, the orthotic devices, Drs. Kessler, Price, and Chutorian. We had been married just five years when Seth was born, and we were trying to establish ourselves in the world. My work was not lucrative, yet there were many expenses associated with it. And we made many business mistakes that had financial consequences.

Jay, too, was silently trying to reconcile his fantasy of a son—the relationship he imagined he was going to have when his boy child was first born—and the undefined reality of Seth's circumstances as it unfolded. Jay was wondering whether he was ever going to play sports with Seth, whether they would ever toss a ball around in a field together. Up to this point, his devotion to Seth was an outlet for his distress. It still is. He has done a lot for Seth. He still does.

Three times a week after school, Mayra took Seth to Anat. On Fridays I sent along money. We sent our money every week, but Anat did not fill out the insurance forms regularly. I was annoyed. I felt I was in my own power struggle with her. By sending Seth and my money regularly I was demonstrating my level of responsibility, my seriousness. I wanted it reciprocated. The physician signing the forms for the benefit of our insurance company needed Anat's paperwork. The lag in her getting forms to him made our insurance claims more tricky.

And I wanted to be part of her inner circle. I knew she thought that my contacts in the entertainment industry could promote the workshops she was planning. I thought that being her special friend would help Seth advance more quickly. A few times we made plans to get together for a coffee in the evening, and every time she canceled, usually at the last minute. Once I went to the appointed place only to have her not show up. Though she had a completely plausible explanation, I was not happy. I tend to be very precise, very organized, and I value my time immensely. I was juggling work, a husband, a son with special needs, a home where three meals a day are planned and served, and I was still almost always on time.

Anat and I finally had lunch together. I lent her some books, and it took a long time to get them back. We both had busy schedules. Aside from her private practice, Anat was teaching several ongoing classes that were heavily subscribed. She was planning an accredited Feldenkrais training to begin the following year and was often committed to speak or teach elsewhere in the world. I was traveling extensively. We communicated mostly by answering machines or by my writing letters.

My work with Charles Bonner was progressing nicely, although it was different from what I had experienced with Robbie. I saw Bonner once a week and attended Carola's classes regularly. I continued to pursue the idea of Mia Segal's training and, when the May segment was announced, I enrolled. In the meantime, my relationship with Anat was strained. Her forgetfulness about the insurance forms irritated me. Some of the time allotted to speaking about Seth each week was absorbed by my going over what forms she needed to send us.

That winter Seth told us, "I am going to learn to walk, and Anat is teaching me." It was February. Seth had been going to Anat since October. Things had been quiet for a while. I had heard no complaints from either Seth or Anat lately, and Anat was away teaching.

It was a Sunday evening, and I was brushing Seth's teeth. I had him propped up on the counter around the bathroom sink in front of the mirror. He made a motion with his tongue into the corners of his mouth, a movement that Anat had been insisting he practice. He grinned at me with his totally ingratiating grin. Then, with a twinkle in his baby-blue eyes, he asked for applesauce. With great sobriety, I told him I needed permission. His persistent lack of cooperation with his tongue during his sessions had meant that Anat had decreed that Seth be given no applesauce at home.

"I have to get permission. Mayra will ask Anat tomorrow," I told him.

"Yes, Anat," he told me. "Where is Anat?" he asked. I told him, and he launched into a discussion about Anat being his teacher and learning to walk. At the end, he sang a song, "Anat, where are you?"

Seth was changing. He was feisty, and he was stronger. He was talking, and his speech was much clearer. I understood everything he said, and Mayra did, too. He was even using his legs to stand. By the spring, he could stand behind his stroller and use it for balance, pushing it as a way of moving. He got tired easily, but it was remarkable to see him upright. Everyone commented about his progress. I knew from my intermittent chats with Anat that she was beginning to be pleased with his progress, too. Their struggles were subsiding. Sometimes she was able to "walk" him around the room, holding him only by the back of the neck. We were very excited.

We were not alone. Others noticed the changes. Up until this point, our decision about the Feldenkrais work had met with extreme skepticism. When I took Seth for a routine pediatric checkup, Dr. Lee was startled by the differences in him. She asked me what we were doing. I saw her eyes glaze over when I began to tell her about the Feldenkrais work. She responded with her typical speech of admiration for all I was doing, but it sounded empty. Our parents, both sets, although informed differently about Seth's circumstances, noticed his progress too. At school the teachers said that they perceived not only increased motor development, but also a psychological change in Seth. We continued to be reassured by what they said about his intelligence.

I took my upcoming training with Mia Segal very seriously and even wrote to the Feldenkrais Guild to check that the classes would count toward accreditation.

At the time of Mia's training there were many political hassles among the various factions of Feldenkrais personnel in the United States, and how accreditation should be accorded was under some dispute. There was a Feldenkrais Guild and a Feldenkrais Association. Who controlled what aspect of Moshe Feldenkrais's heritage was being hotly debated. I wanted to be sure that Mia's training afforded me the best chance of accreditation.

Anat was planning her own training, but it would be taking place at some distance from New York. For the moment, there was nothing definite. However, I know Anat believed that part of the experience of the training was being sequestered. That was fine for some people, but I had a young child and a husband. My intention was not to become a Feldenkrais practitioner, only to be better informed about the work.

As the spring progressed, so did Seth. There was a visible difference in him. All of his upper-body dexterity was improving. His posture and carriage improved. He was not drooling as much unless he was trying hard at something. We were more than encouraged. As we approached his third birthday, our hearts were filled with more hope than we had had for a long time. Anat said he would learn to walk, and I finally knew deep down that this was true.

My relationship with Anat grew even more strained. We weren't getting reimbursements from our insurance company, but we weren't giving up our fight with them. We hoped to prove the efficacy of the therapy, and we wanted the paperwork from Anat for record keeping. The insurance company questioned the allopathic physician about the type of treatment. They took the position that because Feldenkrais therapy was not a recognized orthodox form of treatment that there were only a limited number of sessions they would pay for. The insurance company set an arbitrary cutoff for benefits. The doctor argued with them, but we lost in the end. During this controversy Anat's records were even more essential to us. Then Anat mixed up some appointments, and we argued about whether we were financially responsible for her mistakes. Although I informed her well in advance of a time we would be absent with Seth for a family event in Boston, she forgot and held us responsible for the sessions. She was difficult. I had known this about her, but I was exasperated.

Mia Segal's Feldenkrais training started in early May on a Thursday and ended twelve days later on a Sunday. There was only one day off, and the class began at 9:30 in the morning and ended every day at 5:00 in the afternoon. There was a two-hour break for lunch. About thirty people attended, most of them complete strangers to me, although I had seen some of them at Anat's seminar in June of the previous year. It turned out, of course, that I met people who knew people I knew, and I felt very comfortable.

Among those participating, there were body workers, physical therapists, and Alexander teachers. Alexander teachers are students of the Alexander method, a therapy for changing posture and movement to allow newer, far better physical function. It is a method of adjusting body posture to relieve chronic pain or muscle tension, and to increase range of motion. Through massage and gentle verbal commands, Alexander teachers help students bring about an improved ability to move, to eliminate common problems like slouching and hunching. There were also psychotherapists, marriage counselors, musicians, actors, and teachers. They all wanted training in the Feldenkrais method. A woman named Connie was there, as I was, to do research for her own child. Connie's daughter had been in a car accident and was wheelchair bound, without speech or any chance, as far as the orthodox medical establishment was concerned, of ever resuming a normal life. Connie had come all the way from Ohio to the training and planned to have her daughter join her so that Mia could treat her. I also hoped that Mia would treat Seth once or twice.

Mia was difficult. She was invariably late for class in the morning but was annoyed if anyone arrived later than she did. She played favorites, creating an inner circle of people who got more attention than anyone else. The classes themselves, however, were fascinating and revelatory. I learned something every day about myself and about the body. The work was literally mind expanding. From the first class, I felt different, but not just in my body. I noticed that my memory was expanding. My brain power was different. I concentrated better outside of class, felt more alert, more present. I had some Spanish-speaking people in my life, and I discovered that my Spanish fluency was increasing. I made the mistake of not writing things down during this first segment of the training, but I learned. During the later segments I took copious notes.

As far as my body was concerned, I was experiencing myself anew. I felt my feet on the ground differently. My gait altered. My shoulders relaxed, the neck tension lessened, and I felt my head resting atop my torso differently. My back was soft. I was in an altered physical state. I was also exhausted, not of energy, but of enthusiasm. The days were consuming, and I didn't feel like doing anything after class. Nothing. My mood was good, although I was easily irritated by small, seemingly unimportant things. It was as though I were floating, and the mundane disturbed my equilibrium.

Over the next three years I established strong bonds with a few of the people I met during the training. One, Brian, a physical therapist from New Jersey, specialized in a technique called "Trager." Trager work is the innovation of Dr. Milton Trager. The technique known as Trager Psycho Physical Integration focuses on the subconscious routes of muscle tension. The treatment involves a variety of movements that are meant to promote relaxation and increase range of motion and flexibility. Brian was very interested in Seth, and he was also curious about my back surgery. Neither Seth nor I ever used the Trager technique directly. Brian also spoke often about a body worker from Lithuania who had helped many ballet dancers. He thought that I should go myself and also take Seth to see him. Over time Brian and I became enduring friends.

Then my universe blew up. Two weeks after Mia's workshop ended,

I had an irreparable falling out with Anat. There was another mix-up concerning Seth's appointment. It had to do with a doctor's appointment and a change in time for his session with her. Also, during my week with Mia, I had neglected to send Anat her money on the appointed day. Mind you, I was still not getting my insurance forms from her regularly, if at all.

Anat and I had a very nasty telephone conversation. She told me to find someone else to treat Seth. She didn't care to deal with me anymore. I was devastated. I felt terribly guilty. The shock of her abrupt and severe attitude silenced me. We were through, abandoned. Worse, I didn't know what to tell Seth, how to tell him that the person he pinned his greatest hopes on for learning to walk would no longer be there for him.

It was the end of May. We were going to Cape Cod at the end of June. Where would I begin? What would this mean for Seth? He had come the longest distance in such a short time. Anat had only treated him for seven months, yet there was real hope that he would be walking independently soon. He had matured immensely in a short time. Being in school had benefited him, and the standards Anat had set for his behavior had meant great strides emotionally for him and for us.

I was paralyzed, but only for a day. Then I pushed myself into action. Abandonment is an opportunity for redemption, I decided. I knew Charles Bonner was available and had loved Seth when he first met him. I called him to see what his fall schedule allowed and whether he could see Seth a few times in June. I thought Seth needed a periscope on the autumn. I reassured myself. I had acquired new information from attending the workshop with Mia Segal and had made many contacts, and I knew it would all still be there when we returned from the Cape in the fall.

In September I was planning to resume another leg of the Feldenkrais training. In the meantime, the insights I had gleaned from Mia and the ongoing work with Carola fortified my intentions to work on Seth myself over the summer.

Seth, Jay, Mayra, and I packed ourselves for the Cape. I took with me a renewed, if shaky, faith that I could influence Seth's development and a commitment for Seth to continue the Feldenkrais work when we returned in September. Jay took a sheaf of paperwork. We were initiating a malpractice suit against the doctor who had deliv-

ered (or hadn't delivered) Seth, and against the hospital. Jay was over-
seeing the case with seasoned malpractice attorneys. We left in June.
There were many significant changes that summer. Not the least of
them was that when we returned in September, I was pregnant with
our daughter.

7

◆

The Calm Before the Storm

◆

TOUCHING MY LOVED ONES, my children and Jay, my close friends and family, frequently, casually, seems a natural part of my life. I always held my babies close, carried them around until they were too heavy. To this day, I brush their foreheads lightly or stroke their backs gently as I put them to sleep. A caress is always my response to affectionate feelings. But something happened during the summer of Seth's third birthday, the summer after we were abandoned by Anat. Touching acquired a new dimension. The thoughtfulness I was learning in Carola's classes meant that I put my hands on Seth with new attention. The knowledge I had acquired about stimulating my breathing translated into an awareness of Seth's breathing. The awareness I was acquiring in the Feldenkrais work awakened me to the power of touch.

I became aware of my ability to influence Seth's progress that summer. Every evening, when it was time for him to go to sleep, I would sit on Seth's bed and quietly work on his torso. I would begin at the base of his spine, on one side or the other, and gently gather his soft baby skin into my fingers, lifting it ever so slightly away from his center. Holding it a moment until I witnessed breath filling the space, I would then let the skin fall back toward his body.

These "skin-fold experiments," as Carola called them, facilitate inhalations and exhalations. As she describes in *Ways to Better Breathing,* this technique works the same way as when we loosen a too-tight belt. We immediately feel relief, drawing a big breath of freedom. What you do is grasp a double portion of skin with your thumb and index finger or with your thumb and four other fingers. Or you can grasp a skin fold with both hands simultaneously, but don't pinch. Hold the skin off its base until a deep breath gets through.

The reactions are clearly visible as well as palpable. When I rested my hand on the area where I had just taken a skin fold on Seth, I could feel the softening reactions of his body underneath. I would work over one specific area for a long time before going on to another area. You can grasp the same skin fold several times. I had to skip areas that were too tight to grasp easily. Soon there were fewer of these.

I would work for at least half an hour every evening, always beginning where it was easiest, where there was the least tenderness and the most looseness. I tried to begin at the small of his back then work up from the rim of the pelvis to his shoulders. The reactions were instant and dramatic. Seth wiggled and lengthened his trunk, often yawning widely. He stretched out his entire body along the length of the bed. He inhaled hugely. He loved it.

This was my nighttime experiment. At the end of half an hour his breathing was wide and steady. I could see the sides of his rib cage visibly expand, the breath filling out his entire torso. To this day I can produce this result in Seth and in my daughter, Haya, as well as in myself. Haya's friends, my nieces, and other family members always ask me to "do my back." I have never met anyone who doesn't enjoy this experiment. It feels unbelievably wonderful.

In the daytime I incorporated many of Carola's other lessons into Seth's play. Tapping experiments were the easiest. Tapping influences the condition of the body immediately. I tapped Seth's chest cage with my hand cupped slightly. I never stayed on one part, but covered as much of him as possible.

His breathing responses were remarkable. I tapped his back and his breastbone. I know how this affects me, and he had the same response. He yawned and stretched and took deep breaths. This is the best way to wake a sleeping child. Today when I go to my children's rooms to get them ready for school, I tap them lightly all over. They stretch and yawn, lengthen themselves, and arise with pleasure. Try it.

I did what Carola calls "pressure experiments" on myself and on Seth. These are done very lightly by applying gentle fingertip pressure to the breastbone and the area between the ribs. I did this casually while playing with Seth and tried never to make it "therapy." Especially with the pressure experiments, I limited the time because of the impact I experienced when I did it to myself. Sounds crazy? Try it as you sit and read this. You'll be yawning and gulping breath quickly. In Seth's case, the tightness around his rib cage and abdomen would fade, and an increased elasticity and softness would envelop him. I saw him sleep more calmly. I thought the clarity of his speech improved. These subtle experiments appeared to have profound reverberations. There were no professionals, there was no formal therapy, yet these touches left him in a state of complete well-being.

When we were on the beach, I played many "imagination" games with Seth: we lay on our backs and imagine that we were lying on glass so we could see ourselves from below and above. Then we "painted" ourselves with black paint. We "painted" the length of our bodies, our legs, our arms, in our imaginations. He loved these kinds of mind games, and we did many variations. During this kind of play I also saw changes in his breathing.

We played rolling games. Lying on our backs with our knees up, we rolled our knees from one side to the other. Sometimes we rolled all the way over, sometimes not. Or we counted. I counted all the little knobs (vertebrae) on his back; he counted the knobs on mine. We rolled our eyes. Can you move your right eye to its corner? Back to center? Back and forth? Can you keep your left eye still when you do this? Let's trace our eyebrows with our eyes. Slow and fast. Or make full circles with our eyes, slowly, now quickly. And more. Anyone can experiment with these exercises. We all respond differently and with different abilities, but the actual experiments change us.

All summer I "worked" on his feet and hands using many of the techniques and experiments I had learned in Mia's training. I played with each of his toes, each of his fingers. I knew from the training that if I wanted to learn something, I needed to be comfortable. I reached for this with Seth. I wanted him to be at ease and feeling what he might not have felt before. I was always talking to him, trying, playfully, to bring his consciousness to his body. I still do this today, now more directly, reminding him to soften his tongue, or to think about his big toe. The big toe! Within two years, with my understanding of the importance of the big toe, I could have written a treatise. What I continually learn about the big toe is astonishing. Just wait and see.

I presented these exercises as games, as amusements. Smile, I always told Seth. Be happy in the throat. Smile. Smile. These insights had been gleaned from Mia's training, and they made the summer eventful. Although we didn't witness major steps that summer—Seth didn't suddenly stand up and walk around—we noticed a significantly new freedom of movement, of naturalness. More than anything, I felt connected to him, literally and figuratively. I was experiencing a new capacity in myself and loved my new relationship with Seth.

In September we returned to New York and confirmed that we were going to have another child in late April. I was ecstatic. There was no question that Jay and I wanted another child. We believed in having more than one child. We were both happy we had siblings. We wanted Seth to have a sister or a brother he could turn to when we were no longer around.

But I was also nervous. Seth still wasn't walking, and I worried that we were going to need a double stroller. Everything I knew about cerebral palsy made me feel calm about having another child. I didn't believe that Seth's circumstances were a result of a preexisting condition or a problem with my pregnancy. However, the experience of Seth's delivery put me on alert. This time there were certain unequivocal requirements as far as I was concerned. I wanted a woman doctor. I wanted a doctor who was going to be present during the entire delivery. I did not want Pitocin.

I continued taking classes with Carola and sent Seth to Charles Bonner twice a week. The second section of Mia's training began on September 5. Soon after our return, Seth resumed his days at Studio Elementary School. We had a pattern, a convenient and flowing routine. We were also lucky that Mayra would be staying with us for at least one more year.

There were no major disturbances, except that Charles Bonner also began reporting a struggle for power with Seth. But that was nothing new. I needed a rest from Seth's rehabilitation. I did nothing that fall to pursue other Feldenkrais teachers or other kinds of rehabilitation. I did no research. I made no doctor appointments, consulted no orthopedic people. The casts were long gone. Sometimes Seth was able to stand for a few seconds independently, but he was still using his stroller to walk. He took no steps independently, and he was now over three years old. But Charles was optimistic. I comforted myself with what everyone always told me: Seth would walk independently one day.

My professional life absorbed me. I felt tremendous pressure to accomplish something concrete before the birth of our second child. The nature of independent producing is nebulous, elusive, at least for me. Acquiring a literary property or coming up with an idea is the beginning of a long process of development. I had no financial backing. Jay and I covered all the expenses of traveling and working with writers to prepare our projects. There were meetings with many celebrities, writers, directors, as I tried to attract them to my projects. Sometimes they would say yes one day and no the next day. I often had promising reactions from the motion picture companies and television studios, but up until then I was unable to get any concrete commitments from them.

I was giving the producing one last chance. Two of my projects were of interest to important writers and one movie star. I was commuting to California once a month for ten days to meet with the writers and studio personnel, to do the "Hollywood Shuffle," as I called it. I was making many entries and reentries into the lives of my husband and son because of this coming and going. Early Saturday morning, they would wave as my taxi pulled away from the curb, Seth ensconced in his father's arms. Mayra didn't stay with us on the weekends, so the "boys" would be on their own until Monday morning when she returned to work.

My being away brought about a shift in the relationship between Seth and Jay. Up until then, I had been the central overseer and instigator of Seth's rehabilitation. Jay always spent time with Seth, more quality time than I in many ways, since he had the leisure to just play with Seth without the responsibility of supervising the therapy. But when I was in L.A., he was left to deal with Charles and the Studio School and whatever else cropped up during my absence. And there was another major development that changed Jay's relationship to Seth and profoundly influenced Seth's future. We had initiated a lawsuit regarding the circumstances of Seth's birth. The defendants were the doctor and the hospital. Jay's leadership role in our efforts made him feel as I felt about Seth's rehabilitation: that he was doing something that would help Seth directly and in a practical way.

Two years earlier, my uncle, a malpractice attorney in Boston, had told Jay that the statute of limitations on our right to begin a malpractice case was running out. The statute of limitations was two and a half years. He persuaded Jay to at least explore the merits of a case, reminding us that we needed to keep in mind financial concerns regarding Seth's future. Even if we made enough money to meet Seth's continuing needs, Seth, himself, would need to be independent of us at some point. My uncle wanted us simply to investigate our case.

We had had no contact with the obstetrician after Seth was diagnosed. Although he had taken a cursory, callous, and nonchalant attitude about the events surrounding Seth's birth, I had consulted the doctor routinely during the postpartum period. In April 1984, when Seth was first diagnosed, ten months after his very bumpy arrival into the world, I still owed the doctor a small balance, an insignificant sum, for one of the last visits. His nurse called to remind us. It was in the middle of a busy business day, but Jay took the call. Jay told her to inform the doctor that he was on his way over to the office. As Jay reported to me, he told the doctor about the neurological assessment we had received days earlier. Supposedly, the doctor was shocked. Jay informed the doctor that we planned to take no action against him.

Later, after our preliminary discussions with my uncle, he engaged a reputable New York firm, Fuchsberg and Fuchsberg, to examine the merits of our case. Following Jay's initial contacts and discussions with Fuchsberg, I had several conversations with one of the junior attorneys. At this point I had not yet made any connections between the nightmare of Seth's birth and his present circumstances.

Whenever I had described the events of Seth's birth, usually as part of giving his medical history during the intake process required by the doctors before they examined Seth, I had never put two and two together. Talking about it had always been an emotional experience, nothing more. In the context of the legal setting, while recounting the events of the birth, they acquired new dimensions. Recalling the horror of that night, the concern that the baby was not getting enough oxygen, the doctor's absence, my baby emerging on the labor table in the corridor en route to the delivery room, his blue color, the aspiration of meconium, made me see how all those circumstances were connected to Seth's disabilities.

Ultimately the attorneys counseled us to bring a lawsuit against the doctor and hospital. So we filed the necessary papers. Jay was in the forefront of the lawsuit, supervising and organizing the lawyers. Just as I was able to channel much of my energy into a mission for Seth's rehabilitation, Jay's responsibility to supervise the lawsuit helped him relieve his own sorrow. The momentum of the case was building just as I discovered I was pregnant. Although it had taken almost two years, the lawyers were getting ready to move full speed ahead.

During the fall that Seth started with Charles Bonner, cousins from South Africa sent us an article about a South African neurologist based at UCLA who was doing laser surgery on the spines of children with cerebral palsy. The procedure was called a selective posterior rhizotomy. The traditional surgical procedures for children with cerebral palsy are all orthopedic surgical procedures. However the selective posterior (dorsal) rhizotomy is a method of reducing muscle tone using neurosurgical procedures, operations on the nerves and brain tissue. This new approach involves selective cutting of the nerves of the spine to reduce the spasticity of muscle groups in the upper or lower extremities or trunk.

The success of the surgery depends upon certain neurological factors. Children with spasticity are considered for surgery, but children with low trunk tone or the involuntary, purposeless movements of a certain type of cerebral palsy are not considered good candidates. Although I instinctively recoiled from the idea of surgery, I was instantly energized by the hope of a cure for Seth. With Jay's help I got information from the neurologist at UCLA and the name of a New York neurologist who could assess whether Seth was a good candidate for the procedure. In December we went to see the new neurologist, Dr. Sandra Forem.

As I read Dr. Forem's report today, it is at once informative and amusing. In it she concludes that Seth was not a candidate for a selective posterior rhizotomy at the time. The doctor feared that such a procedure might "unmask" an underlying "dystonic/athetotic" component, bringing on weakness of the hip girdle, and that the operation would offer little functional gain. Dystonia is a slow, rhythmic twisting movement of the trunk or an entire arm or leg. Dystonia may also involve abnormal postures such as severe rotation of the trunk. Athetosis is slow, writhing movements, especially in the wrists, fingers, and face.

We weren't going to take any chances. But the report also makes note of Seth's motor achievements since he "began the Seldencrest [sic] physiotherapy." She attributed his improvements in speech, standing, the initiation of independent locomotion to "Seldencrest therapy." She also noted that although we had previously reported that Seth was hypersensitive in his mouth, now he brushed his teeth and had much less difficulty swallowing foods. "Seldencrest therapy" was responsible, the doctor surmised. But her complete ignorance about Feldenkrais work, her inability even to spell the name properly, alienated me.

More and more I saw my relationship to the orthodox medical world unraveling. I could not imagine telling Dr. Forem about my breathing work and how I practiced with Seth. There was no common ground. She advised us to take Seth to an orthopedist who would follow the development of his bones. She suggested that we consider another orthotic device. I didn't follow through with anything she recommended. I didn't have enough rapport with her to have confidence in anything she told me. Increasingly this was my experience in dealings with doctors.

Seth was going to Charles Bonner twice a week and spending a four-hour morning at Studio Elementary School. I had little direct contact with Charles Bonner, relying on Mayra to tell me about each of Seth's sessions. I consulted with Seth's school routinely, but visited there infrequently, again relying on Mayra for reports. It was as though I had checked out. Lethargy had set in. I was tired after three years of constant vigilance. Jay was busy with the lawsuit. He was helping prepare me for my deposition, which was scheduled for later that winter.

I worked as much as I could, though I was being very careful during my pregnancy. I wanted to stay slim. I went swimming three or four times a week and started race walking, having given up "running" while I was pregnant. My interest in body work did not wane. The third section of Mia's training was planned for December. I was excited about participating. I was attending two of Carola's classes every week. I had faith that Carola's work would enhance my growing child, and Carola was very encouraging, telling me what a wonderful, healthy baby I was going to have. Although I gained only twenty-one pounds during this pregnancy, Carola kept saying that the baby would be very big.

Although I was going to two of Carola's evening classes each week and was diligent about my attendance in Mia's training, I wanted more. Following the December section of Mia's training, I wrote to Anat seeking to enroll in her weekly beginning/continuing classes. Because of my due date I was going to miss the May segment of Mia's classes. I thought that it would be good to fill in with Anat's classes. Anat was also advertising workshops, but I thought a weekly class would be better for me during my pregnancy.

Looking back on this correspondence, it is interesting that apparently I harbored no grudge against Anat, felt no reluctance about studying with her. When it came to increasing my understanding and knowledge, I wanted the best. I knew from attending Anat's June seminar two summers before, and from my summer experience with Seth, that Anat was in a league of her own. I even trusted the "abandonment," believing that things have a way of working out for the best.

What I hadn't counted on when I tried to hook up with Anat was Anat's big personality. While I tried reaching her several times by phone, our busy, divergent schedules prevented us from making contact. I finally wrote to her, enclosing a deposit for a month or two of classes, explaining I was pregnant but still participating fully in Mia's training. Our daughter was due in April. I mentioned in my letter to Anat that I knew Feldenkrais recommended doing the work right up until the day of delivery. Anat's secretary wrote back, returning my check.

In her letter she said that Anat had asked her to write to me because Anat felt that this time in my pregnancy was not a good time to be taking Feldenkrais method classes. Evidently Anat thought that even the beginners class would be uncomfortable for me, requiring agility that would be difficult. The class was almost full, and Anat wanted to offer the place to someone who could get the full benefit from every lesson. I was devastated. I felt rejected and dejected. And angry. It's funny to me that to this day I remain on Anat's mailing list, but this 1987 correspondence finally severed all direct ties to her.

Seth had adjusted to working with Charles Bonner. Over the summer that intervened between Anat and Bonner, I had talked Seth through the separation from Anat. The fact that I was more connected to Seth than ever during that time helped him weather the loss of Anat. I also felt that Anat's separation had made room for me to work with Seth. I asked myself whether I would have used that summer to begin to work with Seth if I had known that Anat was there.

The most important thing was that Seth believe in his potential, that he be secure about his possibilities. I wanted Seth to know Jay and I believed in him, and that we were calm. I wanted him to know that we trusted ourselves to get whatever he needed to help him. What he saw reflected in us would send the most important message.

Through my studying I have learned that the unconscious is central to the Feldenkrais work. Many Feldenkrais practitioners have subscribed closely to the work of Milton Erickson. Both Feldenkrais and Erickson believed that the widening of awareness through movement occurs unconsciously. Learning happens to a large degree through the unconscious functioning of the nervous system. It is the nervous system that has the life experience of the individual available to it, as well as the biological wisdom gained through the process of evolution. The learning process is the important thing; it should be aimless.

Milton H. Erickson was acknowledged as the foremost authority on hypnotherapy and brief strategic psychotherapy. He surmounted enormous health problems throughout his adult life. Confined to a wheelchair, color deficient, practically quadriplegic, he retrained himself in everything. But he believed that it was these very challenges that were the best teachers about human behavior and potentials.

Along with both nonverbal and other verbal techniques, he used stories, especially anecdotes, to suggest, to communicate powerful messages. Erickson believed that our unconscious mind knows more than we do. The conscious mind is our state of immediate awareness. The unconscious mind is made up of all our learning over a lifetime, much of which has been forgotten by the conscious mind but nonetheless serves us in our automatic functioning. In other words, our brain cells are so specialized that we have literally a brain cell for every item of knowledge, and they are all connected.

Erickson believed that the power to change is something that lies dormant within the individual and needs only to be reawakened. He was a proponent of the idea that therapy is anything that changes the habitual pattern of behavior. I try to keep in my conscious mind what I know about Erickson's teachings when I deal with Seth (or anyone, for that matter). I stress the positive as much as possible.

My seriousness about the Feldenkrais work and many other studies including Carola's, the work of the pioneer hypnotherapist Milton Erickson, the anthropologists Ashley Montagu and Gregory Bateson, and the psychotherapist Alexander Lowen still fascinates me as I look back today. I am reminded of how much I invested in the pursuit of greater information and insight into the healing arts. I studied the writings of Alexander; the work of Ida Rolf, the trailblazer of deep tissue therapy; Gestalt therapist Fritz Perls; and many others including the extensive lexicon of B. K. S. Iyengar.

My work in Hollywood felt empty to me now. Producing a movie or television show seemed thin compared to what I was learning about the realms of the mind and the body. I wasn't enjoying much success either. I knew from the workshops and my experience with Seth that I had a wonderful touch. Many people suggested that I consider a career as a body worker. There was a period of time before our daughter was born when I seriously considered changing my career to body work. I began asking myself whether Seth's circumstances were a sign that I should reexamine the purpose of my life. The opportunity to write about my experience with Seth and the Feldenkrais method resulted in an article for *Family Circle* magazine. I finally concluded that my mission is to communicate information to the world with words and to my son with my hands. I would devote myself to writing.

I knew and believed in the power of the mind, the unique and unparalleled capacity of the brain and the human spirit. While I had yet to discover the worlds of cranial osteopathy, homeopathy, and the physical therapist and researcher Glenn Doman's neurosensory therapy, I intuited there was more. I saw that there were many options beyond the mainstream medical establishment. I already understood the innumerable opportunities alternative therapy offered. I knew I was no longer comfortable with the conventional approach to Seth's physical growth. I had crossed over into another sphere. There was no turning back.

The winter before our daughter Haya's birth was calm and routine. Seth went to Charles Bonner twice a week, and I asked nothing except how the sessions were going. Seth was standing alone and unsupported for longer periods of time. He still "walked" on his knees, but he also experimented by taking a step or two independently. Although he was shaky, we were excited and optimistic.

Seth was attending the Studio Elementary School in the mornings, but we hoped to make a change the following autumn. We were committed to sending him to a Jewish day school. The Abraham Joshua Heschel School was a few years old and was in our neighborhood. We visited and liked what we saw. They agreed to enroll Seth in their preschool program for the following September. They accepted his limitations, his not walking, believing, as we did, that the next six months would bring new developments.

Many factors influenced our decision about the Heschel School, not the least of which was that the building had elevators. There were other primary considerations, though. Heschel's academic philosophy and the school's willingness to accept Seth attracted us enormously. The questions we didn't ask would come back to haunt us later. Some of these concerns had to do with class size and groupings, academic objectives, and the phonetic versus the whole-language approach to teaching reading.

In early March I noted in my journal that Seth had gotten himself onto the toilet, cleaned himself afterward, and was able to steady himself while he pulled up his pants. Around this time he also began to pull his sweatshirts and T-shirts on himself. We were overflowing with hope and anticipation.

Haya was born on April 29, 1987, not without incident, but without the same trauma we experienced with Seth. I watched in a mirror as my 9 pound, 10 ounce baby girl came through the birth canal (Carola was so right!). The episiotomy was routine, and I held Haya in my arms, with her sucking at my breast, moments after her arrival. Just my luck, I experienced another go-around with the Neonatal Intensive Care Unit (NICU). The birth was smooth, but there was a scare about an infection from vaginal herpes.

For five weeks before my due date, I had been monitored at the infectious diseases unit of the hospital to see whether I was developing any vaginal herpes, an infection I had contracted years earlier and manifested once before. Vaginal herpes is very dangerous for a newborn. For five weeks the tests were negative. They were administered on Tuesday mornings, and we'd get the results by noon on Wednesday. I went to the hospital at midnight on a Tuesday, and Haya was born at 5:30 on Wednesday morning. The labor was difficult, and I asked for an epidural, but my spinal fusion rendered the epidural ineffective.

A few hours after Haya was born, the doctor came to tell me that Tuesday morning's test for herpes had been positive. Haya was at risk for infection and would have to be quarantined. I was frantic, on the verge of hysteria. I couldn't believe it. Not again! My babies were so hard to bring into this world. The hospital wanted me separated from her entirely. I made a huge fuss, and they eventually capitulated to my demand that I at least be allowed to nurse her inside the NICU. She had to spend a short time there, but this was a different hospital, a different doctor. This doctor was by my side all through labor and delivery and supported me through the ordeal of nursing in the NICU. All in all, Haya's birth was a healing experience.

The irony is that had the doctors known at the time of the delivery that the herpes test was positive, I would have had to have a cesarean section. Because they didn't know, and because the epidural was ineffective, I had a completely natural childbirth with Haya. The experience I had so hoped for with Seth finally was mine.

8

◆

Shifting Currents

◆

THE PLEASURE I TOOK in Haya's birth was immense. It suffused my universe with joy. I loved both my babies wholly, and now I had the perfect two, a boy and a girl. My children and family are the center of my life. They give my life meaning; they inspire all that is good in me. Seth's circumstances have only emphasized this reality more fully.

Like Seth, Haya had a full head of hair and a beautiful face. She was big, just like Seth had been when he was born, with well-formed features and robust color. She was an easy baby, soon sleeping through the night and crying very little, and she sucked readily. I nursed her easily until she was more than a year old. When I stopped nursing, she adapted easily.

Seth was enthusiastic about his sister. While she was still in the NICU, he insisted on watching her from outside the observation window. He came to the hospital daily, and when it was time to take Haya home, he stayed close by, fascinated by her little hands and tiny feet, which he could now see up close. He was incessant with his questions—and advice!

Arriving home, Seth led the way to Haya's nursery. He remained vigilant through the entire settling-in process. He introduced his friends, Kara and her sister, Lia, to his new baby sister. I noticed the proprietary way he had with his new sibling, especially when strangers came calling. This involvement endures even today, although adolescence distracts him more.

The contrast between Seth's development and Haya's "normal development" was unsettling. That feeling was totally unexpected, not anticipated. Perhaps the books I didn't read contained warnings that this could occur, but I was unprepared. Haya's body felt different than Seth's. It was pliable and soft where his was stiff and brittle. Had she been my firstborn and had I touched her first, when he was born, I would have known instantly that something was wrong.

Haya never arched, and the little fists in her hands disappeared by the middle of the summer when she was four months old. Her rolling over, her hand-mouth coordination, her sitting, each milestone filled me with the joy of her achievements. Yet I was tormented by thoughts of Seth's situation. During the next year I finally allowed myself to touch the sorrow I had never given into after Seth's diagnosis.

We went to the Cape in June, Jay and I, both children, and Mayra. It was Mayra's last few months working for us. During the previous two years she had been studying to qualify as a candidate for nursing school. The time had come for her to spread her wings. I worried that summer about the effect her departure would have on Seth. And on me. She had been with us for four years. She had taken Seth swimming at the 92nd Street Y, sat through his therapy sessions, dressed, bathed, and carried him everywhere. She was my link to part of Seth's world, and I didn't want to let go.

All these changes were a lot to accept, particularly for a four-year-old who was still not walking but whose self-awareness was growing. Seth watched others, especially others his age, with new eyes. Although he never articulated his thoughts, I saw in his face the recognition that he was different, although he claims that he didn't recognize or become aware of his differences until later. My observation is that his awareness of his differences began that summer. I saw how he watched other children. Once when we were together we saw a man with lots of involuntary movement walking with two metal crutches. He was trying to maneuver himself onto a boat. Seth was visibly empathic.

That summer Seth attended the Woods Hole Child Center in the morning. It was a three-hour program for children with an emphasis on art, small science projects, and short field trips. There was substantial adult participation. Mayra took him in the morning and went on many of the field trips. Seth made nice friends there, and the program gave him a daily structure.

The Woods Hole Child Center was a "holding station" for the Children's School of Science. The Children's School of Science (CSS) in Woods Hole was a place where older children didn't just study science but did science for six weeks. To be eligible for enrollment, children had to have completed the first grade. Seth was already counting the years until he could go. Many of the children at the Woods Hole Child Center were also waiting to be old enough. Seth's affinity for the ocean, his passion for the sea, the beach, and summer was apparent from the very first summers we spent on the Cape. The Children's School of Science eventually played a significant role in Seth's salvation. And still does.

Of course, the biggest change that summer was Haya, a new baby in the house. And I was nursing her. This took my time, but I tried to be cognizant of Seth and to set aside real time just for him every day. Having decided that I couldn't continue pursuing my career as an independent producer, I was writing my first magazine article that summer. I was reading extensively in the world of physics, anthropology, psychology, and body work. I felt compelled to know more, to educate myself more.

It was ironic that I was immersed in the works of Fritjof Capra, Gary Zukav, Alexander Lowen, Milton Erickson, Gregory Bateson, Margaret Mead, Karl Pribram, Ashley Montagu, and Moshe Feldenkrais but still had not read one book about cerebral palsy. Years later, when I finally did get around to perusing many of the conventional books on the subject that became available, I understood why they weren't of use to me. None of the ways I was thinking about Seth, about his potential or about the options for his rehabilitation, were represented in these books.

As I look over these books today, I am horrified by how irrelevant and how frightening they are. Completely absent from even one book is any discussion of even one of the alternative therapies and medical approaches that currently benefit Seth. There is no mention of the risks of immunization. Glenn Doman's groundbreaking studies, his twenty-five years of success working with brain-damaged children, receives no mention at all. Osteopathy, homeopathy, sensory motor training, Feldenkrais work, Yoga, none of these disciplines is offered as an option. What is especially disturbing for me is the frequent implication that the life expectancy of a child like Seth might be curtailed because of his condition. No doctor has ever corroborated this claim.

Because of Haya's late-April arrival I had missed the fourth segment of Mia's training, but I planned to resume in the fall. Brian photocopied his notes for me, and I read them. I went on practicing Carola's lessons

97

daily. I remembered the work I had done with Seth the previous summer and thought we should continue. If nothing else, it would imbue his progress with that sense of well-being and ease I had witnessed a year before. Of course, Haya's presence made a difference. I had less time and less energy to devote to Seth. While I tried to be diligent, I did less work with him than I had the prior summer, especially at night, because I was tired.

I felt guilty. There were no perceptible developmental gains for Seth. Everything was status quo, and I tended to let that be the fact. I felt incapable of influencing his growth. The optimism and willfulness I had felt in the early years was replaced by languor.

Doubts and misgivings about Charles Bonner plagued me. It had nothing to do with the efficacy of the Feldenkrais method itself. The difficulty was Bonner himself. He didn't have the extensive training of other practitioners I had met, although I hadn't recognized this at the start. Other practitioners never stop studying, taking and offering courses, developing themselves to become more effective, with the constant stimulation of information and exposure. Charles had not pursued additional training beyond his initial course. Then, too, the effectiveness of any direct-handling approach is dependent on the individual treatment skills of the therapist. I was not enthusiastic about Bonner's work. I questioned his effectiveness. Often I felt he spoke to me without appreciating my own increasing knowledge, as though we were strangers. At other times, I was complacent.

The Feldenkrais work appeared to be the best work for Seth, but I wasn't exploring any other alternatives, and I had not done exhaustive research. I believed in the efficacy of the learning, but deep down I suspected that there were other possible routes to explore. And for all my pride in being iconoclastic, the realization that the Feldenkrais work didn't appear in any mainstream lexicon nagged at me. I continued to recommend the treatment to others, but my excitement dwindled.

I did follow through on one intuition, however. Mia had shown us videotapes of Feldenkrais. I saw Feldenkrais bounce children on his knees as though they were riding horseback. The Fieldcrest Farm Horse Stables was two miles from our summer house, so I explored the possibility of putting Seth on a horse. Carolyn Weeks, the owner-director of the stables, was amenable and open-minded. Seth was only four years old, but she worked out an arrangement so he was able to "ride" two or three times a week. While he was at it, I decided it would be good for me, too.

Seth loved being on horseback. Obviously he wasn't able to take lessons in the fullest sense, but his instructor demanded that he sit properly on the horse, keep himself erect, and push his heels down so that his hip flexors stretched. I could see his head and sacrum come into different alignment and his carriage on the horse improve. I experienced a change in my own body while riding. Later we pursued equestrian skills while I was also studying Yoga. The relationship between Yoga and riding was a revelation. In both disciplines, the heels are rooted while the torso remains erect, but at ease. The elbows are bent, but relaxed. The eyes are forward and concentrating. The pelvis/sacrum and head are in alignment.

Seth's relationship with the horses, such big animals, encouraged him to think of himself as more powerful. Riding was good for his self-esteem. He always rode Skippy or Midnight, two very large horses. His teacher kept them on lead lines but had them trot slowly so that Seth bounced up and down rhythmically. I was pleased by Seth's ease around the stables.

In the autumn Seth began at Heschel. We knew they wanted him. He satisfied their requirement to be inclusive without presenting them with the whole range of problems a child with cerebral palsy can have.

Seth's condition, for the most part, appeared relatively benign to the outside world. His was so handsome and intelligent and his movement seemed so regular that it was easy to think that his cerebral palsy was "mild" as Dr. Chutorian had suggested three years earlier. Dr. Chutorian was wrong; Dr. Bresnan had come closer to the truth when he described Seth's condition as "moderate." And we were wrong. His condition turned out to be much more complicated than we had thought, and, as Seth developed, we came to understand his challenges more clearly.

Knee-walking was his basic method of getting around, but he was experimenting with walking independently. He located props nearby to keep himself balanced and steady. He "walked" along the side of the big table in his schoolroom, leaving one hand on the table for balance. Or he stayed along the wall of the classroom. Either he found other supports or he fell back to knee-walking. Building with blocks, drawing, singing, manipulating shapes and forms were done sitting on the floor or at tables, so his clumsiness was a minor issue. The other children were for the most part unconcerned about Seth's differences. The roof playground presented a challenge, however.

When we had first toured Heschel, one of the school's most impressive features was the extraordinary playground on the roof of the building. It had been planned and built at great expense to be one of the most up-to-date versions of a children's playground. Seth went with the class every day to the roof. He didn't exactly run around like the other children, but he found ways to participate fully. There was a huge sandbox, a playhouse that was a duplex, and swings and slides. There were also some high elevations to which he could get himself, but he had limited options for getting down.

He got other children to help him do what he could not do by himself. That was the beginning of an enduring pattern. Seth has an uncanny ability to engage others to assist him. He chooses among the most agile, physically capable boys to be his best friends. He also picks the boys with the most compassionate hearts. His friends at Heschel helped him, and they adapted many of their own games to include him.

Jay worried about the safety of the playground. He was concerned about the extent of the supervision. He felt that there weren't enough adults in attendance during the time the children were playing. I thought he was being overprotective. I've always accused him of being overprotective, and still do. My tendency is to be less heedful about safety issues. Why, I'm not sure. Even today I am surprised by my borderline nonchalance, as though there is something not real about it all for me. For instance, if Seth is sick and might need to get up in the night for water or to call for one of us, Jay immediately thinks about taking precautions: should there be a light on for Seth? How will his balance be affected by a fever? These things rarely occur to me. I'm focused on other aspects of Seth's care. I'm glad Jay is there to remind us.

Eventually one of the older boys suffered a serious injury on this playground, underscoring Jay's general and practical concerns. Seth, too, had some bad falls, although he was never hurt seriously. The parent body was galvanized, and we attended several safety meetings. Jay and I thought about a helmet for Seth once again. We both resisted the idea but considered it an option for playground time. We didn't want Seth to be different from the other children any more than was necessary, but we were worried.

We met with school personnel to discuss the issue of a helmet. I asked Dr. Lee what she thought. I looked at the pictures of the children in helmets in the brochures that came to the house. As with the earlier discussions about the inhibitory casts, we heard arguments on both sides. There were as many opinions as people. We put the decision on hold for the time being.

At home Seth was experimenting more and more with taking two or three independent steps. We were very optimistic. Heschel was six blocks from our house, and one of us strolled him to school every morning and strolled him home at the end of every day. The school day began at 8:30 in the morning and ended in the midafternoon. In the morning when he was fresh, we encouraged Seth to "walk" by pushing his stroller, but by the end of the day, he was much too exhausted physically. But Seth was not different from the other children in this regard. Many of them also continued to need strollers. Outside the classroom there was a pile of folded strollers, particularly at the close of the school day. The children were still babies at four and five, easy as it is to forget, especially in the sophisticated world of New York. I can remember seeing many of Seth's classmates asleep in their strollers while their mothers shopped for dinner in the neighborhood after school.

Seth never slept in his stroller. His intellectual and emotional energy level was at an all-time high. School stimulated him. He was a star. The custodians and doormen, the other teachers, parents, everyone knew who Seth was. That remains true today. When I remember Seth at this time, all I see is the big smile he wore constantly. I remember his finesse in so many complex social situations, a strength he still has. This is one of his strong points, and along with his intelligence it will help him through his adolescence and young adult life, I am sure. My recent concern is that he will rely solely on this magical trait and neglect to cultivate other parts of himself.

Seth's class was a mixed age group. Children ranged in ages from four to five years old, and some of the five-year-olds had their sixth birthday during the school year. So at times during that first year, there was a two-year age difference between Seth and some of the other children. For a child like Seth, the developmental differences between him and the older children were monumental. However, I noticed that he preferred the older children, was drawn to the more mature groups. They were more willing to help him and seemed less frustrated by his limitations.

We noticed no problems with Seth's speech. Nobody complained about having trouble understanding him. I never heard teachers or other children make any disparaging remarks. Not yet. What we did notice was that he wasn't learning his letters or numbers so well. We thought the other children recited the alphabet more easily and had grasped concepts Seth hadn't. He loved "Sesame Street" and sang along with the letter and number games. There was still no question of his innate aptitude. He was also intuitive and socially very skilled, more so than most children. So what was wrong?

I reminded myself that my son was learning to walk. His brain was consumed with processing information other children had mastered long ago. I convinced myself that what seemed like slight delays in letters and numbers were just that, slight delays. Not all the other children were proficient. And the girls seemed to be ahead of the boys. It was a mixed group, I told myself. But I remained watchful. I recalled Dr. Chutorian having said something about "learning problems," but it seemed like a long, long time ago.

What irked me was the complete indifference of the school administration to my concerns. The school was young and still in a formative stage. The current principal was leaving, and a new principal would be beginning the following fall. There was great expectation that with his arrival many of the glitches would be resolved. The early childhood director wanted us to wait until the following year before making any definitive assessments or interventions.

We did discuss which group Seth should be matched with for the next year, the kindergarten year. There were several options, and both of his preschool teachers met with us to explore the best situation. Their diligence was reassuring. Instinctively, I knew something was not quite right, but I set aside my concerns for the moment.

Then, when we least expected it, when we were reconciled to the existing conditions, we were treated to a huge developmental leap. Jay and I went away for an extended weekend in the late fall. At the time Seth was adjusting well to school, and Haya was an easy, cooperative baby just as Seth had been. Mayra's replacement was less capable than we had hoped she would be, but an old friend was willing to help with the children, so Jay and I managed to escape. I couldn't remember having been away and alone with my husband since Seth was born. We spent the entire weekend sharing our deepest worries, fantasies, dreams for our children. We vowed to face the future with a balance of hope and realism.

We returned home early on Monday evening. The house had a long corridor that extended from the front door to the rear of the first floor. As we opened the door, there was an eerie silence. Then we heard "Shhh. Wait. Stand still." We stood quietly. We saw Seth standing at the very far end of the hallway, at the very back of the house. He began walking toward us alone. He was a little unsteady, but one step at a time he came closer and closer. It was a good distance. Jay was quiet. I fell to my knees with my arms outstretched waiting for him. I was crying as he came toward me. He never stumbled once. He was four and a half years old. He was finally walking.

Why? My mind entertains several answers. He was plumb ready. The information the Feldenkrais teachers, Anat, and Charles, had given him was finally integrated. We had been away. He was less inhibited when we weren't around, not needing our approval. He had the space to experiment without our hovering, watching and hoping for every move. Seth and our friend wanted to surprise us. They conspired, so to speak.

Later our friend described the hours Seth had spent practicing, the trial runs. He had been persistent and determined, she said. There was no turning him back. He would get up, take a tentative step or two, "fall" down, and get up again. He had done nothing but practice for days, preparing his ultimate victory. Our joy could not be contained. I think we must have called everyone we knew to tell them.

Seth still tired very easily and still needed the stroller for a long time, of course. I see that I noted in my journal what a great accomplishment it was when, a few months after those first steps, Seth walked from Eighty-sixth Street to Ninety-first Street. Seth expended enormous energy in this effort to do something the rest of us take for granted.

In September, before we went away for that long weekend, I had rejoined Mia's group, having only missed a segment the prior spring. Haya came to the training often during that first year of her life because I was nursing. Our mother's helper brought her at the appointed times. Mia occasionally asked if the group could observe her developmentally. It was fun. When Haya visited one morning, the group sat at a distance and watched her nurse. She was our demonstration.

That September the group was studying various stages of evolution in the human organism. We considered eye-ear organization; how it was connected to the stomach and abdomen. We played with sucking, forming our lips to suck, observing what else was involved, especially the jaws, cheeks, and the space between the upper lip and the nose. (These are all places where Seth makes involuntary movements, but I hadn't made the connection then.) We observed relationships between the ears and sucking by listening and hearing. We asked, What does our tongue do? After lunch one day we each worked with a partner, feeling each other's necks, clavicles, and sternums, the base of our partner's skull as our partner simulated sucking. Haya was my partner.

Because of this work with the training group, I had many thoughts and insights about Seth. I was swept up in the recollection of his initial nursing difficulties and his eventual rejection of my breast. I realized that had I been exposed to these exercises, I would have known there was something wrong with him long before the diagnosis was made.

One fundamental I wish I had understood earlier was how trauma, especially the trauma of being born, is the commonest cause of structural problems in babies. Because so little of a baby's structure is available to assess at birth, sucking and how the baby sucks and swallows is an excellent barometer of problems. These two symptoms of sucking and swallowing indicate how the area at the back of the head, the occipital artery, is affected by the stress or degree of compression it sustains as the baby is pushed through the birth canal during the birth process.

Issues of timing and comfort continually occupied us during the trainings. I realized that an unpleasant learning experience can hamper the learning process. Feldenkrais said, "Learning involves an improvement of the brain function itself. To facilitate such learning it is necessary to divorce the aim to be achieved from the learning process itself. The process is the important thing and should be aimless to the adult learner just as is learning to the baby. The baby is not held to any timetable, nor is there any need to rely on force." These were very important concepts for me to keep in mind as I thought about Seth's progress.

Mia was using Feldenkrais's Awareness through Movement (ATM) technique because it resembles the learning that occurs with human development. We saw that the human infant has everything necessary to maintain life and growth, and that these elements are already connected into the nervous and glandular systems at birth, but that the specific human functions are not wired in at all. As Feldenkrais said, "No baby was ever born who could speak, sing, whistle, crawl, walk upright, make music, count, think mathematically or tell the hour of the day or night. As far as these specifically human functions or activities go, the connections, or the wiring-in, of the neural structures are nonexistent at birth." We are very complex systems interacting with numerous "feedbacks and feedforwards." At birth the organism-environmental link is largely passive. By and by, passivity is replaced by more and more intentional activity. All the mechanisms concerned with movement are incompletely developed in the infant, whereas most other mammals are quite advanced in this respect. On the other hand, behavior in other mammals is primarily reflexive and fixed. Learning new or different responses is slow. However, in humans the brain grows and forms while we adjust to life. The parts of the nervous system that develop after birth are connected with the actual patterns of the cortex. The human motor cortex is very unique. The stages in the programming of the brain are of major neurological significance. Missing stages along this road of development means that a child will not progress normally.

As my studies progressed over the years, I began to recognize that the insights of others matched and enhanced what I had learned during the training with Mia that year. That this information is not more readily available to parents of special needs children astounds me. The relevance and relationship between Feldenkrais's observations and the results of other studies of development is enormous.

At this time I made a memorable discovery about the big toe. Mia insisted that we look at the action of our feet (we were always barefoot) when we rolled over or began to sit up. We played with using the big toe to paw the ground, rubbing it along the carpet in the studio where we were studying. We saw that we could not roll ourselves over from our backs and propel ourselves up to sitting without the action of the big toe.

As luck would have it, during the September training Haya was beginning to sit up. She was almost six months old. I was on our bed at home with her one rainy weekend afternoon when she began stroking her big toe over and over again along the bed's coverlet. The repetition was unceasing. As Feldenkrais wrote and demonstrated: "The tendency to repetition leads, in the end, to repetitive constancy and order." All of a sudden Haya sat up.

Haya's accomplishment flooded me with joy. I was seeing the normal developmental process for the first time. With every one of Haya's milestones, I realized more clearly how Seth was different. I would never see Seth sit up like that. Haya's development telescoped Seth's limitations. The work with Mia underscored time and again the resounding subtleties of the differences of my two children.

Seth had never sat without assistance. He always needed to be set into position or to be propped up. To this day, getting up from a sitting position, especially from the ground, is very difficult for him. I never saw him simulate any action with his big toe. For eighteen months after his diagnosis, his big toes never even felt the ground because he was wearing the inhibitory casts.

Although Seth didn't use his big toe to progress along the normal path of development, other professionals used his big toe in years to come to stimulate him. And I still use his big toe to help him. I learned that through his big toe I could influence Seth when he was tense, or even spastic, in his movements. During the times he "cocks" or "arches" his big toe, I have a clue to his discomfort. I acquired tools from the Feldenkrais work and other body work that helps me put him more at ease, helps him with body tension by relaxing his big toe. When we go to the dentist and Seth has to hold his mouth open, it causes him to gag. He gets very uncomfortable. I sit nearby and say, "Relax the big toe, Seth. Just keep your toes soft." It works. We have to keep at it. I keep reminding him, keep him focusing, recapturing, and the effect is dramatic.

I wouldn't have believed the connection until I discovered it for myself. In all the other body work I've studied, especially Iyengar Yoga, which I began studying in earnest six years ago, the importance of the big toe has come into focus time and again. At the beginning of almost every Yoga class I've been in, "join the big toes" is the first direction. One of my senior Yoga teachers describes the big toe as the conduit to the inner groin, and, therefore, the entire basis of action of the spine. The tongue is the other medium that signals the body. Just as Anat emphasized: bare feet and a limber tongue!

One reason I am involved today in Iyengar Yoga is because of its emphasis on alignment and focus. Like many of the other philosophers, researchers, and body workers I have studied, Iyengar saw the body as a frontier and explored its capacity to achieve balance. In the Iyengar system, postures are explored to penetrate remote anatomical layers of the body. The intelligence of the body and the dignity of the spine are the focus of the work. Active postures in Iyengar Yoga are performed with eyes open, muscles firmly engaged to the bones, and the body lifting, expanding, and stretching with strong internal action. Eventually what I learned in my own Yoga practice enhanced my insights into Seth. Since beginning Iyengar Yoga, I've taken Seth to two senior teachers. I hope Seth will return to this discipline one day.

The links between all the body parts and the body and mind were real for me because I myself was immersed in work where their reality was certain. If someone had come and told me these things, I would have doubted them. But actually experiencing the insights myself, and, in the case of the Feldenkrais work, witnessing them in Haya simultaneously, was astonishing. It changed the way I look at everyone, but mostly it opened my eyes to the magnitude and consequences of Seth's differences. And it gave me ways to help him. I was too busy absorbing the new information to ask why the medical professionals and the physical therapists did not have this information or did not impart it to me if they did know about it.

What the Feldenkrais work showed me was that Seth was learning differently than most of us do. He was learning to sit, stand, walk, and speak using different parts of his brain. His patterns were at variance with ours, but he still had the resources he needed to learn. What these divergences in learning would mean in terms of his schooling worried me.

Seth had completed the first year of preschool, and we were giving a great deal of consideration to his grouping for the second year. I was haunted by all of his academic delays at this point, wary that I lacked the energy to make changes. By late fall of his second year at Heschel, I saw clearly that he was not progressing "academically." He was five and didn't know his alphabet, didn't write or read any letters or numbers. There was no question about his innate ability. I wasn't convinced that his delays were caused solely by the cerebral palsy. I felt that the school should be more attentive and foster a better learning environment for him. My sense was that the school was failing him, not that he was failing. It hadn't yet occurred to me that "special education" might be the answer.

The school was still in the throes of its own growing pains. A new principal had arrived, but he wasn't all they had hoped for. (In fact, one year later he was gone too. His replacement was an extraordinary choice, a visionary woman, whose prior accomplishment had been the founding and building of a nursery school, where we eventually sent Haya. Had I known that she was coming aboard at Heschel, we would have a different story to tell.) The director of the lower school remained aloof and unresponsive to my concerns. It was impossible for me to be focused on Seth because I was distracted by the frustrations of dealing with the school administration. I began to feel hysterical and persuaded Jay that we needed to investigate another school. It never occurred to me that it should be anything but mainstream. Learning differences were not part of my vernacular.

We applied to a secondary school, Rodeph Sholom, which was part of the synagogue with which we were currently affiliated. Despite the fact that their nursery school was where we had first heard the suggestion about a wheelchair for Seth, we were still looking for a Jewish day-school education, and I was ready to forget the past. The nursery school was administered and housed in a separate building from the elementary school.

The subject of Jewish education and the disabled is very much in the center of any discussion of Jewish life and education today. Many people, educators and laypeople, believe that Jewish education does little to address the needs of children with learning differences; that Jewish people would rather ignore or hide special needs children who cannot achieve the pinnacles of academic success associated with Jewish achievement. In the case of Rodeph Sholom, we didn't realize that there was such a debate until much later, when it was too late.

We approached the school directly, communicating openly the problems we were having and what our concerns and goals were, to the degree that they were clear to us at the time. The admissions people at Rodeph Sholom wanted outside testing for Seth to assess his abilities and disabilities accurately. We arranged for testing at the Education Review Board (ERB); they administer standardized tests to the independent schools. Because of Seth's cerebral palsy diagnosis, we were able to arrange an untimed setting for the examination.

The testing was conducted over two sessions. We were not shown the test results. Instead, we went to a formal session where they were described to us. As we expected, Seth tested in the above-average to superior range. Manual tasks brought his test-score averages down.

We were not surprised by this. His verbal ability was extraordinary, as was his ability to make inferences. We were pleased. The test results were compatible with those of Dr. Kessler's two years earlier. Every indication of Seth's intelligence put us at ease.

Based on the ERB results, our interview and Seth's interview, as well as our long, active association with the synagogue, Rodeph agreed to take Seth for their first-grade class in the fall of 1989. There was one requirement. The administration wanted us to commit to a tutor for Seth for the fall. Based on Seth's interview and the report from Heschel, they believed that Seth would need support in academic efforts. They didn't want him to lag behind. We agreed. They suggested that we consult Dr. Betsy Horowitz, an educator and neighborhood resident who tutored other children from the school. We took Seth to see Dr. Horowitz in May for a preliminary evaluation.

Dr. Horowitz also administered a battery of tests over three sessions. Her findings corresponded with those of Dr. Kessler and the Educational Review Board. At the conclusion of the first interview, Dr. Horowitz recommended two or three sessions before we went away for the summer. That way Seth would have an opportunity to get to know her and get used to the routine. I liked the plan, too. Seth was not anxious to prolong the school year, though, and offered some resistance to being tutored at the beginning of his summer vacation. Because I saw myself as being very diligent and responsible, I insisted that Seth attend these sessions.

Like Anat, Dr. Horowitz had a very specific arrangement regarding money. She designated two sessions every week for Seth, and we were to pay for her time whether he came or not. Except for a death in the family, or a serious illness, she expected him to appear for those two sessions every week. If we had to reschedule an appointment in the week, we could count it toward our committed weekly bill. If she didn't have any other time available, we were still billed.

That spring we were also granted an interview with Seth's teachers for the fall. The two teachers met Seth and us in what would be his classroom the following September. We hiked up the six flights of stairs necessary to reach the classroom, not realizing that this would be Seth's trek every day. At the time we believed that the room we were meeting in had been chosen at random. Later we asked ourselves why Rodeph, knowing Seth's situation, had chosen to house the first grade on the top floor. What were they thinking about? Why hadn't I asked them?

One of the teachers was sweet and somewhat interested in Seth. The other, the more senior teacher, was clearly unimpressed. I would go so far as to say that she was put off by Seth. They were discussing Ninja Turtles, all the rage those days. She could have cared less about Seth's interest in them. Seth's speech difficulties came to the fore during the interview. Many times the senior teacher asked me to repeat what Seth said. She was clearly not expending any effort to understand him and was not interested in what he was talking about. She made no attempts to engage him in any other discussion. While Jay and I sat there beaming at our pride and joy, she was glum. The other teacher was only slightly warmer.

Seth always made a wonderful impression. I cannot remember one person who wasn't swept up by the joy he emanated. He was growing even more handsome, and, with his head of blond hair and his twinkling blue eyes, he was striking. While his speech wasn't always perfectly clear and he did drool some, the enthusiasm he exuded more than compensated. The older teacher's lack of verve and her lack of rapport with Seth were signals I wish I had reacted to.

Jay and I left the interview on that spring day, 1989, believing we had made the right decision, hoping that the senior teacher was just having an off day. As I strolled Seth home through Central Park, I silently assessed the situation. For almost three years Seth had been a student of the Feldenkrais method. There were no other rehabilitators or therapists in his life. The only conventional medical care he received was from Dr. Lee, the pediatrician. Seth was walking independently, and after two years of preschool and kindergarten, he would be beginning first grade at a reputable mainstream Jewish day school in September. He was six years old, and his sister was two. I was finishing the second year of the Feldenkrais training and keeping up my work with Carola, but I was doubtful about pursuing Mia's training to its conclusion.

What I didn't know was that I was about to instigate a monumental change. Our lives would shift so radically in the next three months that outsiders considered the change a mutation. By the end of the summer, nothing was the same.

9

◆

Gyrations

◆

IN THE EARLY WINTER OF 1989, I had a fungal infection in my right index finger. Though one of several nagging health issues for me, it was especially nasty. It had persisted since Haya was born. I'd consulted every medical professional I knew including a renowned and expensive dermatologist. Nothing they recommended worked. Finally I went to see Dr. Domenick Masiello, a homeopath who was also an osteopath. His practice was in Queens, an hour ride by subway from home.

Dr. Masiello had been recommended by a close friend who knew me very well. A serious recurring illness had originally led her to another homeopath, Dr. Masiello's mentor, and eventually to him. Admittedly, I was skeptical. Homeopathy? I had only vaguely heard of it. But I was at my wit's end, as I'd been earlier with my back problems. I was game for trying anything. After I scheduled the consultation, a packet arrived in the mail describing what to expect during the intake. There was a detailed pamphlet on how to report symptoms, as well as directions for getting to the doctor's office. I paid attention only to the directions.

The first interview lasted over two hours. The doctor asked me questions no one had ever asked me. Was I thirsty? Did I like hot or cold drinks? Did I object to being hot or cold? Did I like the water? Did I prefer sugar or salt? Did I wake in the night? How often did I urinate? He wanted to know about the onset of my puberty. My family's history was subject to scrutiny, but not just their health. My parent's work, education, their relationship, and my relationship to my siblings was examined.

He probed more areas than had ever been penetrated by a doctor. He provoked recollections of whole parts of my history and my life that were lost to me. I thought about things I hadn't thought about ever before or for a very long time. We discussed Seth and my pregnancy and delivery. He was interested in our course of rehabilitation for Seth.

The doctor gave me a "remedy" to take and asked me to come back in three weeks. He also recommended that I read two books about homeopathy and buy a home health-care guide about homeopathy. When I left his office, I felt genuinely connected to a health-care professional for the first time ever. Dr. Masiello was actually trying to get to know me.

"Doctor" is the appropriate sobriquet because Masiello is, in addition to being a homeopath, an osteopath. At this point I knew nothing about osteopathy, had never heard of it. I knew as little about homeopathy. The only part of the equation I keyed into was that the insurance company would reimburse me because an osteopath is a "doctor." In the months and years to come I learned that osteopathy is the oldest bona fide medical healing art; that osteopaths are primary-care physicians, licensed to practice medicine, perform surgery, and dispense drugs.

While M.D.'s (allopathic physicians) think of the body as a number of discrete systems, doctors of osteopathy (D.O.'s) view the body as an interrelated whole, with each system and organ in constant contact. They believe that the body's structure plays a critical role in its ability to function. Osteopaths use their eyes and a battery of manual techniques to identify structural problems. They focus on the neuromusculoskeletal system (the bones, muscles, tendons, tissues, nerves, spinal column, and brain) and work to support the body's natural tendency toward health and self-healing.

Osteopaths believe that the manipulation of bones, the palpitation of tissue, and the use of osteopathic manipulative therapy (OMT) reestablishes the structural integrity of the body, leading to the free flow of blood. But this is only the beginning of what osteopathy is. It is the belief of the osteopathic physician that once the underlying causes have been diagnosed and treated, the body is then free to repair itself or to respond to other appropriate therapies. For the moment, I had come in search of Dr. Masiello because he was a homeopath.

As explained in the *Family Guide to Natural Medicine,* homeopathy dates formally from the year 1810 and the publication of Samuel

Hahnemann's *Organon of Medicine.* Hahnemann, a German physician and chemist, deplored most popular medical procedures as "heroic," preferring to treat the whole patient instead of the disease. Homeopaths believe that illness is not localized in one organ, but instead involves the entire person, both body and mind. Homeopathy is based on two major principles, the Law of Similars and the Law of Infinitesimals.

Simply put, the Law of Similars states, "Like cures like." A substance that produces a certain set of symptoms in a healthy person has the power to cure a sick person manifesting those same symptoms. The Law of Infinitesimals states that the smaller the dose of a remedy, when properly diluted, the more effective it will be in stimulating the body's vital forces to react against disease. A third principle, the Law of Chronic Disease, states that when disease persists despite treatment, it is the result of one or more conditions that affect many people and have been driven deep inside the body by earlier allopathic therapy.

Three weeks after the visit, my fungal infection had not improved, and I returned to Dr. Masiello. He asked me more questions, but many fewer than before, and he concentrated on the details of the most recent weeks. He gave me another remedy and asked me to return in two weeks. Two weeks later my fungal infection was the same, but there were new symptoms to report. There were other changes in my body. My digestion was different. My energy level was higher. Some of the other small health problems were being transformed.

During our interviews we discussed my back fusion. Dr. Masiello was interested in the history of my back and interested in getting a perspective on my back problems based on my work and my attitudes toward myself and those close to me. He wanted me to describe my daily routine. I was impatient with him. I had come to him for a cure for my finger, and everything else seemed secondary and irrelevant.

Beginning with the third or fourth appointment, the doctor began suggesting that I step into the adjacent room for an osteopathic treatment. I resisted. I still knew nothing about osteopathy. I wanted him to treat the fungus, which I thought was worsening, actually. At this point I wasn't even sure why I was sticking it out with him. It took many years for the finger to heal, but as it did, other fingers manifested the same fungus. The doctor always said that I would heal from the top down, the inside-out, and last things first, first things last. His vision has been proven correct.

In February Dr. Masiello finally convinced me to walk next door to his osteopathic treatment room. I can't remember how he finally prevailed upon me. Maybe I was tired of listening to him extol the benefits he kept insisting I was missing. I lay down on the treatment table, a table exactly like the countless others I knew from my previous physical therapy sessions, from Seth's days with Anat, from both of our sessions with Charles Bonner. After manipulating my whole body, lifting each one of my legs, rotating them in the hip sockets, rocking my pelvis, standing behind me to feel my shoulders, sitting me up and touching my back and neck, the doctor lay me down and stood behind me, placing his hands gently around my head.

How long I "slept" I cannot say for sure. When I awoke I possessed a sense of well-being and openness that I had never known before. The lightness and ease I experienced was empowering, intoxicating. It was a completely unique sense of myself, and the feeling lasted well into the next day and for days afterward. "I have to get this for Seth," was my first thought, my first words. What had this doctor done? I learned that Dr. Masiello was a "cranial osteopath." When I asked him about treating my son, he said, "If you want this for Seth, there is only one place to go, and that's California. Call Dr. Viola Frymann in La Jolla."

Cranial osteopathy is a specialized form of osteopathic medicine that follows the teachings of Dr. William Sutherland. Dr. Sutherland discovered that the bones of the skull are not fixed, but move slightly. Changes in their normal arrangement and motion will affect the brain. Osteopaths who have studied and specialized in this system maintain that because of the linkage in the system of fascial tissue and the vertebral column through the sacrum, palpitation of the skull and sacrum can pick up rhythmic pulsation distinct from the respiratory rhythm or the heartbeat and pulse of the blood. This pulsation is the reverberation of the cerebrospinal fluid, which bathes both the brain and the spinal column.

Restrictions that result from injury or inflexibility in the spine and cranium can cause abnormal motion in the craniosacral system. This abnormal motion leads to stresses that can contribute to poor health, especially in the brain and spinal cord. The purpose of craniosacral therapy is to enhance the functioning of this system. The relationship of one cranial bone to the other is normalized, and the cerebrospinal fluid pressure is adjusted. As a result, the whole physiology of the central nervous system functions more efficiently. Nerve tissue is generally healthier. Common conditions such as earaches, sinus congestion, vomiting, irritability, and hyperactivity have been successfully treated using only craniosacral therapy.

Osteopathic physicians who are trained in craniosacral therapy use their techniques to identify all kinds of disturbed patterns of movement, to diagnose and treat many disorders in a gentle, noninvasive way, and the effects of this treatment can be very far reaching. Children in particular respond well to the gentle approach of this treatment. It is especially helpful in assisting children to attain full recovery after common childhood illnesses, but also after such episodes as falls or traumatic births. Seth was definitely a candidate for this treatment.

The next afternoon I contacted Dr. Frymann's office. They told me that there was a one-year wait to be seen as a new patient. I asked to be put on a waiting list. We were planning to be in Los Angeles for business and to attend a wedding in June. I thought La Jolla was close enough to incorporate a visit into our plans. I couldn't see missing an opportunity like that while we were on the West Coast, and I wouldn't take no for an answer. After the initial phone call, I called every few days. I was very persistent and very pushy. Ultimately, I succeeded in securing an appointment for the first week in June, so the whole family drove from L.A. to La Jolla on June 5. When I arrived, I think the staff at Dr. Frymann's office were expecting the wicked witch of the East.

The Osteopathic Center for Children is in a small, bright yellow clapboard house that sits above the staggeringly beautiful La Jolla Cove. Nestled among the glitzy high-rises and condominiums of downtown La Jolla, the building is an oddity. The blazing yellow color is a symbol of the center's "promise." In that house we discovered everything we needed to know and do for Seth from that day to this.

True to form, as I came to realize and accept, Dr. Frymann was always late. We had a 4:00 appointment, and we were seen at 6:30. By then we were all cranky, hungry, and tired. Except Dr. Frymann. A woman in her late sixties with a head full of white hair secured in a chignon, she was without an iota of hesitancy. She personified forthrightness and frankness then as she continues to do today.

Dr. Frymann interviewed Jay and me while the children played in an adjacent room. She wanted to know about the pregnancy and birth history. Next Dr. Frymann went out to watch Seth. She observed him momentarily and then asked him to crawl to her. She wanted him to stand. She asked him to walk. She shook his hand hello as he approached her. She asked him some friendly questions. After having him weighed and measured, the doctor took Seth to the examination room. Jay and I were not invited. Three quarters of an hour later the doctor met with us again in her office.

Dr. Frymann presented the most succinct assessment of Seth we had ever heard. Although she used medical terms, what she said was totally understandable to us as laypeople. She comprehended his movement patterns, identified his speech anomalies, and described him personally. She summarized his crawling and standing, his relationship to gravity, his teeth and the shape of his head, the movement of his eyes, his general muscular coordination, and his lack of balance. She also told us that she was concerned about an early scoliosis.

The doctor recommended that Seth be treated for one month, twice weekly, in La Jolla. She wanted us to arrange this as soon as possible and to plan to repeat the one-month treatment three times in the course of the next nine months. She wanted Seth to get a CAT scan and an electroencephalogram (EEG) and be evaluated by a neurologist, Eugene Spitz, M.D., at his clinic in Philadelphia. She asked us to read *What to Do about Your Brain-Injured Child* by Glenn Doman and enroll Seth in a neurologic evaluation program. She suggested that we call Dr. Peter Springall, also in La Jolla, and coordinate a program to coincide with her treatments. Without arrogance, she presumed that we were planning to heed her advice and resituate ourselves, our whole life, to fulfill her prescription.

Dr. Frymann told me that the best thing I had ever done was to put Seth on a horse, and that the Feldenkrais work was good too. While acknowledging the worth of his previous treatments, she was unequivocal about what Seth would gain from her. His potential was great. Her program was going to help him realize that potential. I was stunned. Maybe it was the impact of the staggering visual surroundings. Perhaps it was the immediate trust I felt watching the doctor with Seth or the straightforward way she talked to us, but I knew that we had to return to La Jolla for the first month of treatment as soon as possible. We'd come for a wedding in Los Angeles and for an evaluation in La Jolla. We left Dr. Frymann's office and the yellow clapboard house that overlooked the most awesome scenery I'd ever seen with plans to alter the course of our lives.

When we returned to New York, I contacted Rodeph and told them about our plans. Serendipity intervened yet again. The school had a sister school in San Diego, the Beth Israel Day School (BIDS). I called the school in San Diego and succeeded in securing a spot for Seth in the first grade for one month for the coming fall.

Finding the Beth Israel Day School was one of the luckiest occurrences in our lives. We have them to thank for much more than providing a school for Seth, and eventually Haya. In the final analysis, the only positive result of Seth's enrollment in Rodeph was the relationship Rodeph had with the school in San Diego. The first-grade experience at Rodeph turned out to be the worst nightmare we could have imagined for Seth, whereas the Beth Israel Day School in San Diego became a safe haven for years to come.

School personnel at BIDS recommended a place to contact for a preschool setting in La Jolla for Haya. Real estate agents in New York helped us locate agents in La Jolla to find a house. By the time we left for the Cape in June, I knew I was on the verge of a fantastic and risky voyage. Once again I was setting a new course.

Not everyone can afford to seize the opportunities we did for that coming year, and not everyone would have leaped the way I did. I had looked into the eyes of the medical establishment and said to myself, They are not helping Seth. I was taking a risk, thumbing my nose at the conventional, both personally and medically. But Dr. Frymann's competence and her skills were irrefutable. She had been practicing in La Jolla for forty-five years and had been affiliated with the Osteopathic College of the Pacific since 1980. She held the promise of something new, and, in its own way, something very conventional. I knew how I myself felt after a cranial treatment. I saw the doctor with Seth and heard what she said to us. I felt that that was enough to justify my decision. Maybe I should have been more afraid, less daring, considered all the ramifications. Instead I plunged; diving in as I had years ago, going on gut instinct, raw feeling. I was uprooting the family, just at the beginning of Seth and Haya's first year in new schools. I was leaving my husband alone at home for a month and going to live in a new city. With what guarantee?

I called the Spitz clinic in Morton, Pennsylvania, and scheduled a visit two weeks later. Usually the evaluations at the Spitz clinic require an overnight stay in a nearby motel. I didn't want to have to do that because it would mean leaving Haya behind in New York. It would also mean being away overnight only two weeks before we were leaving for the Cape for the summer. I pushed hard to arrange all the testing in one day. I crossed my fingers and got on a train with Seth and Jay early in the morning on June 20.

The experience of visiting Dr. Spitz's clinic was unsettling. The facility was busy with severely disabled people, most of them young. It shook the three of us to our cores. Later I tried to get Seth to talk about his feelings about what he had witnessed in the clinic, but he resisted.

The tests Dr. Frymann requested probably should have been done a long time ago at the time of Seth's initial diagnosis. Dr. Chutorian had not wanted to order them, suggesting that we didn't need them for such a "mild" case. By the time we had seen Dr. Bresnan, who did want to order the tests, we didn't want to pursue anything more. After Seth completed all the tests at the Spitz clinic, the doctor concluded that Seth had a minimal static encephalopathy. Along with his auditory skills, his intellect was preserved. There was no reason to believe that he was at risk for seizures. There were no bony abnormalities, no atrophy, no growths. Dr. Spitz made me feel better about Seth than any doctor, especially any neurologist, we had ever seen before or any we have seen since.

Based on his investigations, Dr. Spitz located precisely all the deviations in Seth's brain and communicated them to Dr. Frymann. Seth would be in the hands—literally—of someone with the most complete medical picture of him ever. We were ecstatic. Dr. Spitz thought that Seth was an ideal candidate for the remediation the Osteopathic Center for Children offered and for an intense sensorimotor-stimulation program. He, too, wanted us to get in touch with Dr. Springall in La Jolla.

I was acquiring a new lexicon. "Osteopathy," "Doman," "sensorimotor"—all of this was new and very exciting. I was also acquiring a number of new responsibilities, not the least of which was explaining to everyone what we intended to do. My parents and Jay's parents were more than doubtful. There was disapproval. We were incurring further financial burdens. I was separating the family from Jay, who couldn't leave his law practice for a month, but was planning to visit for less than a week in the middle of our stay. And who was this Dr. Frymann? What was osteopathy? Cranial osteopathy? My parents remembered that osteopaths were doctors who had treated them in the 1930s and 1940s. If we needed an osteopath, why not find someone who did this in New York, or in the Midwest? Endless questions. I was jittery, but I kept warding off their scrutiny and tried listening to my quiet inner voice that was saying, "It's okay to try."

Rodeph was cooperative, but they were skeptical. I was planning to relocate us for the month of October in La Jolla, judging that the best course was to have the month of September for Seth to get acclimated to his new first-grade class in New York. In the meantime the tutor, Dr. Horowitz, informed us that we would be financially responsible for the eight sessions Seth was going to miss during October. Of course, the school in San Diego expected a portion of tuition. The irony was that the most minuscule aspect of the cost of our expedition was Dr. Frymann's fee. It was $55 a session. (Twenty-five percent of her patients are seen free of charge.) Airline tickets, renting a house, leasing a car, tuitions, tutor's fees for absences: these were the costly items.

The entire summer was devoted to arranging our move to La Jolla for late September. I was immersed in a maze of details about living in the new city. My emphasis was on creating a smooth transition for the children. To that end, I wrote letters of introduction to teachers, to friends of friends, and to distant relatives. I made lists. I consulted museums and libraries, guidebooks and maps. Seth spent the summer at the Woods Hole Child Center again and participated in a few other activities. Haya spent the summer near me. I had a new helper, and she was the best since Mayra. She would be going with us to La Jolla. By the end of August we had finally secured a house in La Jolla, which I would see for the first time when we got there.

That summer resonates with special significance, aside from the responsibilities for arranging our trip. Several events are particularly memorable. During these months I recognized with new clarity and with a new acceptance that Seth had cerebral palsy. One day I was sitting on the floor of my bedroom with Haya in my lap. Seth walked away from me and stood in the frame of the doorway, his back to me. The distortion of his alignment, the abnormality of his spine's shape was unmistakable. It was typical of every cliché about cerebral palsy. The truth of his condition glared at me with new intensity. Denying his circumstances was not possible anymore. I had to be realistic about who he was.

That same summer I became reacquainted with two women I'd

known in high school. One of the women had a son, Michael, with a severe behavior problem. His birth had been traumatic, and the consequences were apparent even though Michael was seven years old. My friend and her husband had consulted many neurologists and tried various forms of rehabilitation, medication, therapy, and schooling. There was a question of his being institutionalized. I wanted us to be friends, his mother and I, believing we shared some of the same disappointments and frustrations in our mothering experiences. I was also eager to share some of the information I had gleaned over the years. I invited her and Michael for dinner.

After dinner we decided to go for a walk to the beach. Until then the children had played well together, needing minimal intervention or supervision. Seth demonstrated compassion and willingness. Haya went along, observant, following Seth's lead. When we got to the beach, Michael began throwing Seth and Haya's collection of small horses and animals into the woods and shrubs. There was no retrieving them.

My children got very excited, crying and asking him to stop. I tried to mediate and downplay the significance of the toys, while remaining sympathetic. We returned to the house, and, as Michael and his mother were leaving, I tried to put my arms around her in a gesture of comfort and reassurance. She spurned me thoroughly. While I have never understood why, from that day to this, she barely acknowledges me when we encounter one another anywhere. She looks right past me as if I don't exist.

From that experience and other later ones, I learned that my developing instinct to open myself, to share my feelings, to embrace the circumstances of Seth's cerebral palsy and my fate as his mother, would not necessarily be welcomed by everyone. Later in my experience I was accused of exploiting Seth. I reassess my emotional stake in his destiny every day, but at the same time I also realize that there is no rest from being attentive, involved, responsible, self-aware.

What is my emotional stake in Seth's circumstances and in his progress? I ask myself this question frequently. My fate as Seth's mother has given me an identity. But I want my selfhood to encompass more than this definition. I do have a high personal stake in outcomes for Seth. While all parents struggle to keep their hopes and expectations for their children distinct from their children's dreams for themselves, the battle for me feels more difficult. Do I gain more importance when good things happen for Seth? Honestly, I believe Seth is special, and his feats are more significant than others because of what he has to overcome. I try to maintain autonomy, but I know when he shines, some of the light falls on me too. I do bask in it. All parents feel enlarged by their children's accomplishments. However, I have to constantly remind myself to be especially aware of who I am and who Seth is.

On the last weekend of the summer, Jay and I took the children to Provincetown for the day, where we intended to spend an afternoon at Race Point Beach and an evening strolling along Commercial Street. We rented a motel room for the day so that we'd have a place to shower and change after the beach. The desk clerk persuaded us to skip Race Point and cross the jetty that extended from the hotel to a very private, pristine beach. He said it would take about fifteen minutes to walk across. It took over an hour.

The jetty started out smooth, and we walked along normally. Then it developed into a craggy congregation of dangerous rocks that had to be navigated very carefully. We were too far out to turn back by the time we realized our situation. For Jay and me it would have been a walk of minimal difficulty, requiring only some caution. But Haya was only two, and for Seth it was an almost-impossible challenge.

Ultimately we reached the beach. True, we could see the whales in the distance, but the beauty of our surroundings was mitigated by the terror I felt when I thought about returning across the jetty. My anxiety spoiled the picnic lunch for me. When it was time to start back, I took a deep breath and told the children, "We'll take it slow."

Haya responded, "We'll go one step at a time." She was learning the lessons of life quickly, I thought.

With Jay supporting Seth every minute, we traversed those rocks at a snail's pace. Anxiously, Seth never flagging, Haya constantly looking behind to watch and encourage him, we made our way across. "One step at a time," Haya repeated over and over. My baby girl demonstrated the wisdom and insight of an adult. I was struck by her concern and her attitude.

Seth smiled a smile of accomplishment and pride when we finally got back. The return walk had taken more than an hour and a half. He seemed undaunted by the ordeal and wanted a dip in the motel pool while Haya and I showered. His energy was high. He knew how great his achievement was. The trip across the jetty felt like a passage to me.

It was the symbol of what and how we do together as a family in the face of unforeseen challenges.

During this same summer I was angry with Seth one morning in a primal way, and my reaction was not wholly warranted given the infraction. I yelled forcibly, so he retreated quickly, but not too far. Almost immediately he tripped and fell, cutting himself badly on the edge of a piece of furniture. I had to take him to the hospital for stitches. Being out of control was not an option for me, but it was less of an option for him. It was too risky. Danger lurked wherever he wasn't on guard. Vigilance was required at every turn.

My adulthood was fully upon me, and there was no escaping my responsibilities to my son. This meant taking charge of my emotional life and learning to respond differently. My anger, which at times feels demonlike, aberrational, would have to be held in check. Self-examination revealed my weaknesses and where emotional growth was necessary. I was committed to behaving as a model for my children to help them in their emotional growth. This realization came none too soon.

School began in September, and so began a nightmare I thought I would never wake from. One week after Seth started in the first grade, he stopped sleeping through the night. He got up and came to me. "When is it going to be morning?" he asked. This was only the beginning. For the entire month of September, until we left for La Jolla, Seth came to me every night and woke me. Sleep deprived, I was a wreck. Night after night I returned him to his bed, firmly, but often I couldn't get back to sleep myself. When I asked him about sleeping, he gave me evasive, nonsensical answers. I didn't recognize that something serious was troubling him.

Was I blind? I thought he was torturing me, but also I felt that I was failing him. I was caught up entirely in how to respond to him without killing him. At one point I considered staying in a hotel for a few nights to get some sleep. At times I believed I was in a power struggle with Seth. Then I thought that the problem was the anxiety of going away, Seth's anticipation about the new school. The children were asking me so many questions about where we were going. I had to give answers but be truthful to some extent about my own ignorance. We were going on an adventure together, and there were unknowns.

That September was very demanding for me. I was settling both children and myself into routines that were going to be disrupted soon. In addition to his new school and his tutoring regime, Seth was taking swimming lessons. Haya was in a part-time program and also had some additional activities. I was trying to make time to write, prepare for La Jolla, spend time with the children, and still be available in the evenings to go to the theater and attend business functions with Jay. The days were long, beginning for me before six and sometimes not ending until late in the evening. My patience with Seth was limited because of my fatigue.

The month passed quickly, however, and suddenly it was time to set off for California. Seth was strangely happy when we got ready to leave. I still didn't recognize the clues to his discomfort. The children and I boarded the flight to San Diego with tons of luggage and with hearts brimming, full of excitement. My sense of adventure took over as I summoned all resources. We were risking, trying, hoping. Our departure coincided with the Jewish New Year. It would be a new year with definite new beginnings.

10

◆

New Directions

◆

ON THE EVE OF THE JEWISH NEW YEAR, we landed at Lindbergh Field in San Diego. I had the two children, ages six and two, and the housekeeper in tow, as I followed directions to a house I had never seen and where we would live for the next five weeks. Accompanying us on a board packed in ice was a whole fish for Rosh Hoshana. The fish is part of the ritual of the holiday, representing the full circle of life.

As a result of meticulous and obsessive planning on my part, just hours after we arrived in La Jolla we sat down in our new home to a holiday dinner, catered by a local Jewish delicatessen. We had an invitation to spend the second night of Rosh Hoshana with a family whose daughter was also in the first grade at the Beth Israel Day School (BIDS). Another invitation to "break the fast" ten days hence was in hand. By the end of the first weekend, I had located the supermarket, the library, and the best place to get fresh-squeezed carrot juice in La Jolla. Sunday afternoon we knew where Seth's new school was. Less than a week later Seth was in a car pool, and I had secured a preschool for Haya within walking distance of the house.

The qualms, doubts, and jitters I harbored evaporated instantly when I saw Seth after his first treatment with Dr. Frymann. He was a changed person. His eyes were set in his head differently. His gait was unencumbered. The next day, when I picked him up at school, he was swinging on a gate outside the school courtyard with freedom and an absence of inhibition I had never thought possible. The change was almost too good to be true.

Seth loved California. We all loved our home there, the setting, the change of pace from New York. We missed Jay, but we were absorbed and distracted with our new surroundings. The astonishing beauty never failed to leave me breathless. To this day the sheer drama of the mountains, La Jolla Cove, and the bend of the seascape captivate me.

The Beth Israel Day School was everything we ever hoped for in a school. Friendly, small classes, housed in a two-story building constructed around a large open courtyard, it combined academic excellence, Jewish learning, and California casual. The first-grade teacher, Ellen Solomon, welcomed Seth into her world. Everyone loved him. He had instant friends. He was a star.

Dr. Frymann's sessions with Seth, as with all her patients, took place behind closed doors. The only other person present in the room with the doctor and her patient is a man playing the piano. The doctor believes in the importance of music. She indicates to the therapist what she wants him to play depending on her assessment of her little patient. As the session progresses, the music changes. Bach is always played at the close of the session, "the perfect blend of science and art," the doctor insists. Sitting outside in her waiting room, parents always know what the doctor thinks of the condition of their child by the music they hear emanating from behind the closed door. Currently art and music therapy enjoy true status as part of rehabilitations, but Dr. Frymann perceived their worth twenty-five years ago.

We had four weeks of relative bliss. Beautiful October weather contributed to our pleasure. Seth was extremely happy at school. Each session with Dr. Frymann brought him new ease. There was only one unsettling episode, and it took place during Jay's time with us in La Jolla. Jay's visit coincided with the Jewish Day of Atonement, a day of fasting and prayer. We arranged for Seth and Haya to take part in the children's activities at Seth's school while Jay and I and the other parents attended the prayer services at synagogue.

At the end of our prayer service, as we came up the hill to the school, we saw an ambulance and paramedics parked outside. My first thought was that this couldn't be about Seth. Jay's first thought was that this was about Seth. He was right. Seth had fallen in the playground during one of the games. He had banged his head hard, and there was lots of blood, as is always the case with head injuries. The paramedics concluded that there was no serious injury just as we arrived. Haya, only two years old, was very disturbed by the incident. It was one more reminder of the reality of Seth's condition.

The coincidence of this event falling on the Day of Atonement, a day of fasting, renewal, and forgiveness, felt significant, too. It made me think even more about my emotional life, about Seth, about my daughter, and about my husband. It challenged and renewed my faith. Frightened and frustrated, I had to tell myself once again how much worse it could have been. In my personal journal I wrote that when Seth was born, I had no idea that being his mother would take me on this kind of journey. More than anything, the spiritual phase of my passage was emerging strongly, clearly.

Jay and I met with Dr. Frymann during Jay's visit. The doctor told us that Seth was struggling for control in his life and struggling with her, too. She wanted us to clearly establish the lines of acceptable behavior for him. She told us that we should constantly orient him to solutions rather than problems. Dr. Frymann also said that it was a mistake for us to discuss Seth's circumstances in his presence, something she had gleaned by sheer observation of him.

The doctor believes that children do not need to be involved in every decision, nor do they need to be privy to every insight. Providing any child with information influences his or her self-perception. If adults discuss the possibility that the child may or may not learn to do something within earshot of the child, the child may doubt his or her ability, and the prophecy will be self-fulfilling. "Interpretation follows the mouth," is a well known Talmudic saying.

She told us that she was interested in hearing from Dr. Springall after he evaluated Seth. Toward the latter part of our stay I was finally able to arrange for an appointment with Dr. Springall and a visit to the Springall Academy.

Dr. Springall is a sensorimotor developmentalist. Here was more jargon, another mouthful. Eventually I discovered that his work was based on the findings of Glenn Doman, the founder and head of the Institute for Human Potential, which were outlined in Dr. Doman's book, *What to Do about Your Brain-Injured Child*. Doman's work emphasizes the brain rather than the body. As I began to study his theories, the philosophy of Moshe Feldenkrais became relevant and pertinent again. The evolutionary stages of a child's development were in the forefront of Doman's research and conclusions, too. In Glenn Doman's world, parents fix their children better than professional people do. This view reinforced something I already knew intuitively, something I had known from the summers when I had worked with Seth myself.

After first working mainly with stroke patients as a physical therapist, Doman realized that the answers to why some people's muscles didn't work properly could be found in the nervous system, and the more complex the individual's system, the more evolved the tasks of learning would be. These insights matched Feldenkrais's exactly.

After years of research and observation Doman was convinced that there were stages on the road to growth. As he explains so wonderfully in his book, the old saying that you have to creep before you can crawl was verified and extended by him and his team of researchers, doctors, and therapists. You have to crawl on your belly before you can creep on your hands and knees; you have to learn to move your arms and legs in the air before you can crawl. Doman explains that crawling and creeping are essential stages in the programming of the brain, stages during which the two hemispheres of the brain learn to work together. If any of the basic stages are slighted, not even wholly skipped, there will be adverse consequences such as poor coordination, failure to develop proper speech, even failures in reading and spelling.

There are five functions that only humans have. They are the ability to walk upright, the ability to oppose thumb and forefinger, the ability to speak and write, the ability to understand speech, and the ability to read. These are all functions of the cortex of the brain. When the cortex is damaged, there is a loss of one or all these functions, the Doman study claimed. Doman and his colleagues set out to "dig a tunnel," or "build a bridge" across an injury to the cortex and/or midbrain. As he describes in his book, they experimented with teaching the hurt brain the function it would have been able to perform had it not been hurt, to awaken its inherited instincts. They developed different ways of putting brain-injured children through motions called "patterning." I hesitate to use this term, especially in such a curtailed explanation of sensorimotor work. Patterning has gotten a bad rap and is often misunderstood. Dr. Springall never called the work Seth did "patterning," but many understand it in this narrow way. The motion the therapist performs mimics the activity the child would have performed if his brain had not been injured.

When Doman's work first came into the public consciousness, there was tremendous excitement about its possibilities. Many saw it as a panacea. The common misperception of the work was that a room of adults in round-the-clock rotations constantly worked on a child in an effort to stimulate the child's brain. In fact, three to five people manipulate the child's head, arms, and legs. However, that is one small aspect of a whole sensory-stimulation program. The problem was understanding that "patterning" refers only to one aspect of the whole therapy program. What is commonly overlooked is how unique patterning is in and of itself. No one had ever employed these techniques with brain-injured children until Doman and his team did. What was most unique was that they were targeting a beginning level of development and function. They were stimulating the sequence of developmental steps as the brain would, providing an opportunity for the brain to program itself. Unfortunately, Doman himself has a very big ego (like Feldenkrais). Because of his larger-than-life persona, it is often difficult for other professionals to listen to his ideas.

Doman understood that no privilege is more important to people than the ability to speak. The same brain injury that stops a child from walking also affects, or stops, his or her talking. Seth was drooling, and his speech was not terribly clear. With Dr. Springall's intervention there was the promise of a treatment that would help Seth in that important sphere, as well as an orientation that would take into account all of Seth's challenges.

Dr. Springall assessed Seth in two respects. He evaluated Seth's functional strengths and used our input to gauge Seth's other capacities. Dr. Springall's lens focused specifically on the academic, educational, and learning aspects of Seth's life, and the doctor related these areas to Seth's sensory and motor functions. He looked at Seth the way I wanted an educator to look at him. He assessed Seth's telebinocular vision, his auditory and visual strengths, his perceptual strengths and deficits. He noted that the weakest links in Seth's abilities arose when cortical resources were needed. This observation corresponded to the deficits that Dr. Spitz had identified in the neurological tests and also to what Doman described in his book. It also harkened back to everything I had learned from the Feldenkrais training. In the Feldenkrais training I learned that high brain development and complexity of life go together. The complexities of our nervous system and of our life are one. To understand human behavior we must look at differences as well as similarities. We must look at the origin of the individual response in order to find a "cure."

Dr. Springall concluded that Seth needed a program of develop-

mental sensorimotor training as a means to overcome his motor dys-
functions and to create strategies so that he would learn more easily.
For instance, we learned that when Seth was presented written words
in the "word-sight" or "whole language" method, or when words were
written very large or supported with auditory reinforcement, Seth was
able to read well. This was my initiation into the debate between phonetics and whole-language approaches to reading. The path to wisdom was endless.

By engaging in a program of exercises designed especially for Seth,
Dr. Springall believed that Seth could stimulate and reorganize his
central nervous system and achieve more. Seth could practice on his
own at home for a few minutes twice a day. The exercises simulated
crawling and cross patterns of creeping. The doctor also believed that
Seth's reading would develop more quickly once he began doing these
exercises. And many of the objectives involved the big toe. Dr. Springall
wanted Seth's big toes to drag on the floor during one part of the simulated crawling exercise.

The doctor's evaluation reassured me I was in the right hands. There
was nothing cursory about his analysis. It was thorough and detailed.
I was at ease with him and knew I was working with another knowl-
edgeable, caring professional.

In the last week of our residence in La Jolla I visited Ellen Solomon,
the first-grade teacher, to discuss Seth's progress. She praised Seth's
social skills, his ability to integrate himself into the classroom, the
pleasure she had in his presence. She thought that the other children
benefited from having Seth in their class, that his courage and forti-
tude set great examples for them. Seth was still having difficulty reading, but he was creating little games for himself as a way to remember
his letters. She thought this was very clever of him. She also said that
there were other children in class who weren't reading yet. She was
confident that Seth's reading and writing skills would develop nicely
as the year progressed.

Mrs. Solomon believed in the "whole-language" approach to reading; whereas in New York the approach to teaching reading was based
on phonetics. She viewed the phonetic approach as outdated, a "di-
nosaur," she called it. She supported Dr. Springall's view that Seth
needed auditory support and large print. (Dr. Horowitz had also said
that Seth would do better if words were written large or in upper case.)
Later Dr. Springall explained to me the physiological and developmental

steps that are needed in order for a child to progress academically. Phonetics, in his view, did not make sense until a child was seven. Seth's struggles academically still seemed out of step with his tested intelligence, and we had yet to figure out how to turn this trend around.

We left La Jolla at the end of October, in time to be home for Halloween. Before we left, I went to talk with Dr. Frymann. She reiterated many of the same things she had told Jay and me when we had met with her earlier in the month. The doctor wanted Seth to have a break from treatment, but she also made a point of noting his progress. She said, "He's much more serene." That was true. There was a new composure about his demeanor. He was a much more tranquil person.

His schoolteachers in New York had no reaction, but everyone else who came into contact with Seth when we returned home perceived the change in him. It was irrefutable. His aura was different. His gait was more steady, open, balanced. There was less spasticity or tension in his body. Even Jay's parents and my parents were quick to acknowledge the improvements.

Seth returned to his class at Rodeph and renewed his friendships immediately. He also remained in touch with many children from the Heschel school. I thought that his social skills were excellent, and I was full of pride about the ways in which he and Haya had integrated themselves into first one routine and then the other. They were flexible and adventurous. I was more focused on Seth and his needs, his schooling and doctors. I hadn't yet read any books about the siblings of special needs children. I bragged about Haya's inclination to go along, fit in, and adapt. A year later, when Haya was four years old, I had a rude awakening, however. I wasn't prepared when Haya demonstrated feelings and fears about her brother that had been brewing and festering all along.

By the middle of December, I was constantly battling with Seth. Every time I asked him to do something, he resisted or gave me an argument. I attributed his behavior to my own failures. My patience was at a low ebb. I was busy house-hunting in New York in contemplation of a move. I was frustrated by the lack of progress we were making and how time consuming finding a new home was. I had been home from La Jolla only a few weeks, and already I needed to think about getting ready to return there in January. I was also busy visiting and applying to nursery schools for Haya. Time for writing and doing things for myself simply slipped away in the face of my other responsibilities. Everything seemed overwhelming. I was sure that my level of tolerance was lower than usual.

Jay and I scheduled a meeting with Seth's teachers. We wanted to get a sense of his progress, especially before our departure for La Jolla in January. They had had no contact with us, nor had we had contact with them since our return at the end of October. When I think about this now, it seems as though my unconscious was telling me to stay away.

The first thing the teachers told us was that Seth was a discipline problem. I was floored. I had never heard Seth described that way. I knew that I was battling with him, but I had been quick to tell myself that the gains he was making from Dr. Frymann's work were probably opening other channels. Maybe it's not so bad that he's finally acting out, I thought. I would have preferred, however, that he not act out in school.

His teachers went on to describe him as aggressive during transitions, full of anxiety and frustration not just in school but in social situations. They said that his academic subjects frustrated him, that concentration was a major issue. They claimed that he did not recognize sight words used in class from ten to fifteen times a day. He didn't know his addition facts and was not good with materials that required manipulation (hardly a surprise). I had difficulty believing their assertions, but I did verify that Seth was behaving poorly in the classroom.

A wave of panic washed over me, and then I let it recede. I just didn't believe all of it. Ellen Solomon in La Jolla had given me such a different picture of Seth. Despite all my struggles with him, and my awareness of the battles Anat, Charles Bonner, and Dr. Frymann had had with him, I still thought of him as a reasonably well-adjusted youngster. What child in his circumstances wouldn't want to have control over some aspects of his life? We were leaving for La Jolla the first of January. Seth would be returning to Dr. Frymann and the Beth Israel Day School. I decided to wait until the end of January before pursuing things further.

Both children made a smooth transition to La Jolla in January. Seth returned to school and resumed his studies and his friendships with great ease. However, he continued to wake almost every night. I rescheduled a visit to the Springall Academy and instead looked forward to my appointments with Dr. Frymann. I was so impressed by her and her results with Seth that I committed myself to attend her Tuesday evening lectures while we were in La Jolla. She offered the talks at the Bishop's School in La Jolla, and the room was always packed. I began taking notes and ended up taping the lectures. I was learning a lot about osteopathy and a lot about the human animal. I knew what she was teaching were wise, sage insights, valuable beyond words.

Seth had excellent sessions with Dr. Frymann the entire month, cooperating without protest during each of his sessions. He instinctively knew that she was giving him exactly what he needed. He came out of every session looking great. He also had enormous energy and a big appetite. I was thrilled to see him at such a pitch and to see him eating so well.

In addition to being an osteopath, Dr. Frymann is a homeopath. She was born, raised, and educated in England. Homeopathy is widely accepted and practiced in England; the Royal family is one of its greatest advocates.

Homeopathy and nutrition are a major component of the doctor's treatment, though her practice of homeopathy is secondary to her osteopathic practice. I believe that Dr. Frymann thinks that the organism has to be liberated and made ready for a remedy through osteopathic medicine first. Many homeopaths, Dr. Masiello among them, believe that homeopathic remedies in and of themselves can liberate the organism.

During our first visit in October, Dr. Frymann had given me a remedy for Seth, his first homeopathic treatment. I was already familiar with the little white pellets from my ongoing care by Dr. Masiello. I had had enough experience myself to trust taking Seth in this direction. Dr. Masiello almost always had told me what he was administering homeopathically, which is not common among most homeopaths. Dr. Frymann did not tell me what the pellets were, but simply instructed me to give them to Seth at bedtime and to use "no other medication."

There are several reasons for this policy of silence among homeopaths. Homeopathic remedies are readily available, usually without a prescription. Even the most potent doses of the most powerful remedies can almost always be bought over the counter. Knowing the name of a remedy could prompt a patient to buy the remedies and take them, and self-medication could prove dangerous. It is not advisable for patients to manage their own case, in other words.

Many of the homeopathic remedies are made from poisons or from pathogenic material, and knowing what he or she was taking could create in a patient's mind a repulsive or worrisome image. The patient might resist taking such a remedy. Or the patient might think about the remedy in a negative way, which would color the patient's response to the remedy. Homeopaths prefer not to influence a patient's case in such a way. They believe that reading information about a remedy and its possible content or purpose could influence the patient's response or the way in which the patient reports symptoms.

Soon after our arrival in La Jolla in January, Dr. Frymann gave me another remedy to give Seth at bedtime. The first night he reacted very violently, waking in a cold sweat two hours after falling asleep, screaming for me. I calmed him down eventually, but he was up later during the night, calling for me as though delirious. He woke again the next evening, but he was easier to put back to sleep.

When we went for our next appointment with the doctor two days later, I told her about Seth's reaction to the remedy and the pattern of waking in the night. I wanted to know about the remedy she had given him. "Let's just say it was directed at the trauma of his birth," she answered.

Soon afterward Seth began sleeping through the night. Throughout the month Seth's energy level remained enormously high. Many months later, when we knew each other much better, Dr. Frymann began telling me which remedies she was administering.

We returned to Dr. Springall for a reevaluation. He was very pleased with Seth's progress and modified Seth's exercise program so that Seth would be "digging in more with the big toe." (I laughed to myself.) The doctor wanted us to get a special keyboard for Seth's computer, a device that he thought would help to further enhance the cooperation between the two hemispheres of Seth's brain. He also wanted us to emphasize skills that did not rely totally on the visual process. He put me in touch with a place that had books on tape. I also got in touch with a library for the blind. The doctor wanted Seth to read large print, but to do his paperwork with an audiotape as additional support. He said that Seth's crawling had become a cross pattern even though the exercises were homolateral. Homolateral exercises used one side of Seth's body at a time, meaning the same arm and leg. Later Seth would do bilateral exercises where the opposite arm and leg were coordinated. He thought that from a developmental standpoint Seth's walking was improving. I was very happy about everything I heard. That month in La Jolla fulfilled all my expectations and then some.

My anxiety about the situation in New York at Rodeph school continued however, festering throughout our month in La Jolla. I thought a powwow with the teachers, the tutor, Dr. Horowitz, the school psychologist, and the lower-school administrator was advisable. While still in California, I asked Jay to help me set up a meeting for when we returned. Because of the number of people involved, it wasn't until February 27 that we got everyone in a room together.

The meeting was devastating. I didn't write down exactly what was said. I didn't have to. I grasped instantly that the school had written Seth off, the teachers had written him off, and the tutor had no influence with the professionals or with Seth. We were at a dead end. Essentially what the school staff members implied was that they had a problem child with learning disabilities on their hands and, although they didn't come out and say so directly, they were completely unprepared to modify or adapt anything on his behalf.

I left the meeting reeling, completely at a loss. I had not been prepared for what I heard that morning. I was frantic. Where should I begin? What was the next step? I thought that the next logical step was special education. Where would I start looking and exploring? Four years earlier the only way I was able to cope was through action. Four years later my response was the same. This time I called a friend who was a social worker. She suggested that I call someone I vaguely knew who worked in the special-education programs at the 92nd Street Y. I didn't really have the tools or information to formulate any questions, but I called immediately.

The acquaintance at the Y gave me the names of several schools for special education in New York and advised me to contact the Board of Education's Committee on Special Education (CSE). She insisted that we contact private education evaluators to secure our own assessment of Seth's education and learning status. I was surprised by the limited options for private special education and nervous about getting involved in the public sector. This was New York City after all, and I was not going to let Seth get lost in the labyrinth of public education, special or otherwise. My own education and initiation into a new world began instantly. The instinct toward advocacy began to brew.

Desperation engulfed me, and the feeling was fueled by our time frame. It was almost March. We would be returning to La Jolla for the month of May. Time was running out. We needed a school setting for Seth for the following September. There was no way we were going to continue at Rodeph. My contact at the Y recommended several people who could conduct the private evaluations. Purely on the basis of location, I chose people in our neighborhood, on our block: the Oldbergs. I wanted as little added inconvenience as possible.

We met with the Oldbergs immediately. They were a husband and wife team. Phyllis Oldberg, Ph.D., would be doing Seth's educational evaluation. Her husband, Julian Oldberg, Ph.D., was a psychologist and would evaluate Seth from an intellectual and psychological standpoint. They both thought that we should hire a special-education advocate to help us navigate the maze we were about to enter at the Board of Education.

It was almost April. As T. S. Eliot said, April is the cruelest month. I knew we were embarking on still another voyage. This time I was much less confident than before. The circumstances felt more pessimistic for some reason. I was entering a land where my instinct for survival would be tested differently. With the physiological issues, I had found a niche, a way to relate, a system for integrating and adapting. And I had been lucky that my own body beamed light on paths helpful to Seth.

The realm of special education was more complex. And my picture of Seth was always colored by my sense of his phenomenal intelligence. I couldn't grasp the idea that he was not going to be an achiever in the intellectual sphere. Up until then I had comforted myself with the idea that although he wouldn't be captain of the basketball team or compete in the Olympics, his intellectual capacity was superior and would develop even further because of his circumstances. I had hypothesized that the Feldenkrais training and the work with Dr. Frymann were enhancing his inherent abilities and providing him with opportunities others didn't have. Whether my idea was true or not would have been hard to measure or ascertain of course, since there was no "control" in the experiment.

Our resistance to accepting the probability of a special-education setting for Seth complicated the process. We were desperate for a school that would address Seth's special needs, but at the same time we were struggling with our disappointment after learning that our son was not a star pupil. Our reconciliation would evolve slowly.

On our expedition to assess Seth and place him in the best education setting we could find, Jay and I were, however, about to encounter denial anew. It had been difficult enough to encounter Seth's diagnosis of cerebral palsy and to cope with many of the consequences. Each time we learned something new about Seth it meant adapting to a new set of circumstances and reassessing our attitudes, being honest with ourselves about our deepest prejudices. Facing Seth's educational challenges meant confronting the core of our own value system. What we discovered ultimately had more to do with us than with Seth.

11

◆

A Whole New World

◆

TOWARD THE END OF THAT WINTER, we scheduled the tests with the Oldbergs and the appointments at the Committee for Special Education. There were eight appointments all together. Our watershed meeting at Rodeph had occurred on February 27. Seth's first evaluation with the Oldbergs was March 3. I had wasted no time. Two more appointments were scheduled with Dr. Phyllis Oldberg toward the end of March, because we were going away on vacation with the children. We also had additional appointments with Dr. Julian Oldberg.

The costs were prohibitive. The first round of tests with the Oldbergs cost $1,900. I don't know how other people meet these financial requirements. I thought that we were very comfortably off, but every time we turned around there was more financial pressure. The first evaluation at the Board of Education was scheduled for April 21. The cost of this meeting would be purely emotional.

On March 26, less than a month after our meeting at Rodeph Sholom, we met with lawyer Marion Katzive, a special-education advocate. Her fee was $2,500. She advised Jay and me about what to expect at the Board of Education and how to prepare. She suggested what our goals should be. Lawyer Katzive informed us that our goal was that Seth be certified by the Board of Education as learning disabled, but that we should also have his intellectual superiority recognized. They—the Board of Education—would be saying "mainstream," she told us, but we would have to say, "no mainstream."

The purpose of the proceedings was to prove to the Board that there was no suitable setting for Seth in the public schools. If the Board sided with us, the city and state would have to provide funding for a private setting. Jay was very conflicted about this. He did not think that we should take money from a city where there were so many in need. We both knew that we could afford private education for Seth if we gave up other things. Ultimately, the conflict was resolved because we chose a school (or they chose Seth) where there was no public funding.

Suddenly I was thrown into the world of Individual Education Plans (IEPs), Public Law 94 (free, appropriate education to handicapped children), mainstreaming, least-restrictive environments, the Parents' Advocacy Network, and so on. New books with new titles were added to my growing library of special-needs literature. It was all very confusing. Marion Katzive was important to us, providing us with ongoing education and an overview. For others who don't have our resources and who are compelled to navigate within the bureaucratic world of New York City's Board of Education, having someone like Marion is especially important. The panoply of information regarding special education is as wide and complex as the issues of special needs. Being an advocate for your child, or having one, is of the utmost importance. Unfortunately, most people cannot afford the services of Marion Katzive or anyone like her. In New York the nonprofit organization Resources for Children with Special Needs fills this gap. They provide advocacy and education services and training. Their staff counsels and/or accompanies families through all the public mazes: special education and entitlements to other public services.

The Oldbergs tested Seth five times, three visits with Dr. Phyllis and two with Dr. Julian. The contrasts between their results and the results of the tests that followed at the Board of Education were substantial. Dr. Julian Oldberg reported that Seth separated from us without hesitation and was well motivated. Six weeks later the tester at the Board of Education reported that Seth "had difficulty separating from his father. His anxieties regarding the evaluation were suggested, and somewhat eased by the reassurance of his father's proximity."

The Special Education Committee went on to write about Seth's "avoidance of material whose anxiety may hamper his adapting to external demands . . . that he appears easily stressed and pressured, quickly overwhelmed." Dr. Julian Oldberg described Seth as "friendly and talkative and easy to engage in the testing situation . . . that he generally did not become frustrated too quickly and tried his best to solve the task. His interest and motivation remained quite high throughout the evaluation. Seth's intellectual potential is, at least, superior."

At the Committee for Special Education the tester described Seth as "feeling isolated from others, concerned with winning approval, with frustration and an ultimate sense that he cannot meet perceived expectations . . . quickly stressed by emotional impact." As with the debate about the inhibitory casts, there was little consensus between the testers, and the disparities worsened when we compared the educational results.

The New York City Board of Education submitted to us their IEP, which described Seth as orthopedically handicapped/impaired and learning disabled. They recommended a special class at a public school with related services like occupational therapy and modified instruction. They recommended two sessions per week of speech and language. In all academic areas they indicated that he was lagging well behind. The only positive result of their testing was a certification that Seth never needs to take timed tests. Timing on standardized tests will always be waived for him.

Dr. Phyllis Oldberg described Seth as tending to drool when he tried to express his thoughts rapidly and as struggling to reproduce his internal language. She wrote in her report that he was "deficient in math; a nonreader with few merging phonic skills although the difficulty was strengthened [*sic*] on the Woodcock Auditory Visual Learning Tests which simulates the whole-word approach to beginning reading." She went on to report that Seth had "excellent listening comprehension with strong verbal and reasoning skills and an underlying desire to succeed, [but] he has a specific learning disability in the area of decoding written language. Deficits in reading will also affect his ability to spell and produce written language. In addition, his performance places him as a nonreader."

Fortunately for us, I sent these reports to Ellen Solomon, who called me immediately to disagree with all the findings. She said that Seth was NOT a nonreader, and that she objected strongly to the label. In fact, soon afterward, when we returned for our next four weeks in La Jolla in May, she helped Seth learn to read and provided us with a resource for "whole language" books so that Seth could practice reading all summer.

Today Seth is one of the best readers among his peers, reading at a grade level way above his present year. He is also tops in spelling in his school, a subject he loves and excels in. Mathematics is his strongest subject; he remains first in his class in this subject. Recently, when the Educational Records Bureau administered the standardized tests for independent schools, Seth tested in the ninety-second percentile in mathematics. Many of these accomplishments were realized with the help and support of the Stephen Gaynor School, the school Seth was to attend for the next five years.

However, if we had been at the mercy of the Board of Education's Committee for Special Education or the independent evaluators, if we hadn't had the insights of Ellen Solomon and eventually the Stephen Gaynor School, where would Seth be today? What happens to other people who do not have the opportunities and backup we have been so lucky to have?

At the same time that we were testing Seth at the Committee for Special Education and with the Oldbergs, we were assembling a list of private special-education schools to visit and decide about applying to. The list was surprisingly short. There were five schools, and one of them, the Stephen Gaynor School, did not accept public funds. Another was in New Jersey, and a third was in Brooklyn.

The need to find a special-education setting for Seth was more daunting than anything that had come before. My anxiety level was at an all-time high. I finally realized why Seth had not been sleeping through the night. His self-esteem had been dwindling because he couldn't keep up in school. He felt he was being left behind. He felt he was failing. I faulted myself for being so slow on the uptake.

My journals from this time are overflowing with information on special education and learning disabilities. There is new terminology, new issues of self-esteem, cognitive and verbal aptitudes, social-emotional adapatations, as well as attention or organization topics. Internal language, auditory blending, adaptive physical therapy, decoding, inferential versus listening comprehension, reversals, and so forth, became part of my lexicon. Each school has a different approach, but I heard this terminology everywhere.

The Gateway School was a place for bright, gifted children with learning disabilities. It felt very "precious" but appealing. It was the first special-education school we visited, and I felt it could solve many problems for us. It was an oasis in the midst of my turmoil and anxiety. Surrounded by experts and specialists and other children who were challenged in their learning, but considered very bright, I was relieved. There was a place in the world for children like my son.

They didn't accept Seth into their program. Although I took reams of notes about our visit, I never wrote down why they didn't take him. However, their presentation, the information they provided, helped me immensely in organizing my thoughts and forming impressions of the schools we later visited. I started to learn which questions to ask.

The Churchill School, which was the best known and which accepted public funds, told us, "We're not interested in children with cerebral palsy."

I was flabbergasted. "What are children with cerebral palsy like?" I asked. Seth was not in a wheelchair, while other children with cerebral palsy were. Seth had no intellectual deficit, but others with this label might. There was no physical reason why Seth should not be a candidate for the Churchill setting. We were searching for a place to minister to his learning challenges. As far as we knew, Churchill had no guidelines that excluded Seth.

Lawyer Katzive, who was a board member at Churchill, was upset that anyone at Churchill had made such a statement to us. Public money means no discrimination. It was a legitimate concern on her part and, had I been inclined, I would have pursued this issue. For the moment, I cared only about what the label "cerebral palsy" meant to others, and what this label would mean to Seth. The Churchill people had never met Seth, yet they ostracized him because of his diagnosis. What would that mean in the future? I was devastated, appalled. This was the all-time low for me.

The McDowell Learning Center was in Brooklyn. We were disappointed in the facility and would not send Seth such a long distance to such a depressing environment. The school's intentions and philosophy were admirable, but the physical surroundings were deplorable. There were only two remaining options. One was the Community School in New Jersey; the other was the Stephen Gaynor School on Seventy-fourth Street in Manhattan.

We made several treks out to New Jersey to the Community School. Seth went for two interviews. It was an appealing place, although its location worked against it. In addition to his education, I worried about Seth's socialization. How would we organize play dates and birthday parties with his schoolmates? How many of them lived in the city? A friendly place in a suburban setting—their program went through grade twelve—the Community School assigned students into small academic groupings. All of the staff were special-education people. The school accepted Seth the week before we left for La Jolla, but because it was located out of the city and a substantial bus ride away, we stalled. Our interview at the Gaynor School was scheduled to take place after our return from La Jolla.

In the late winter, early spring, we had taken the children to a remote and primitive fishing village on the Pacific coast of Costa Rica. It was a wonderful vacation, very different from any of the traveling we had done before with the children. There were no distractions: no television, no hotels, nothing but beach and dirt roads. Walking, swimming, playing on the beach day after day, Seth soon began to open up and share some of his feelings of inadequacy with me. I was very touched and dismayed.

"I'm such a klutz," he told me as we arrived on the beach one day with all our paraphernalia. He was having difficulty maneuvering himself and his buckets.

"Whatever makes you say that?" I inquired, my antennae on alert.

"Well, you know that's what the kids tell me in school. The teachers agree."

"The children tease you about your difficulties? Don't the teachers stop them?"

"The teachers don't like me. They never help me. Mostly they're mad because I'm always the last one. You know, making everyone late."

"What do you mean, Seth?" I asked with a pounding heart.

"There are so many steps. Up six flights in the morning just to get to class. Then right away to the basement for gym or something like art. Down six flights, then up six flights again. I'm slow. That makes me tired too, all day."

As he revealed many of the details about his experiences, his ordeal at Rodeph came into sharp focus. My heart bled. Again I blamed myself for not being wiser, more vigilant.

During our stay, the children met the one other North American family visiting the area. Their daughter, Ingrid, was two years older than Haya and two years younger than Seth. The children played marvelously together. Ingrid's and Haya's abilities in the water and navigating the shoreline increasingly challenged Seth, though.

One day he was left behind during their antics. He sat himself down next to me on the beach. The girls were swimming out over their heads and frolicking in the water. One of the village boys had canoed out to them. The girls were hanging off the small boat, laughing and playing. Seth began to cry, excluded by his limitations in the water. Even though Ingrid was closer in age to Seth, she and Haya were becoming bosom buddies. For Seth, the inclusion of his little sister and his own exclusion was devastating.

He said to me, "I hate my problem. It sticks to me like my skin. I wish I could go far out into that ocean and bury it."

What could I say? I was mute. Here was my beautiful son spilling his tears, letting me in on his grief. I wanted to do the right thing, but I was unsure what that was. I couldn't deny the truth of his circumstances. I couldn't tell him it wasn't so. I summoned all I knew about respecting him and the integrity of his challenge and responded, "It must be very difficult for you. I think you're brave and trying hard. Daddy and I are giving you everything we can to help you. Use it as well as you can."

Alone later, I grieved deeply. Sad for Seth, but while I was sharing with Jay what had happened, I realized the complexity of parenting a special child. I didn't want to deny him his feelings, but I wanted him to know that there was hope. Allowing him to feel that he could talk to me was paramount. I wanted him to know that we, Jay and I, were there for him. At the same time, I had to let him know that I expected him to make good use of his strengths as well as the available therapies.

When we returned from this trip, Seth completed the testing with the Oldbergs and with the Board of Education, and we pursued the school interviews. We were stalling about the Community School but were anxious not to miss out on the best opportunity and only option we had come upon thus far. We also wanted to investigate the Stephen Gaynor School. We knew nothing about it, and neither did the Oldbergs. That was why it wasn't one of our first scheduled visits. We knew that everyone spoke against it because it was a small school and the tuition costs were prohibitive.

In the meantime, we were through with the tutors, the Committee for Special Education, the special-education advocate, and testing. One person remained: Dr. Julian Oldberg. In the Oldbergs's reports, and for that matter in the written information from the Board of Education, Seth's psychological state appeared to be delicate. Both of the Oldberg reports recommended that Seth have ongoing "play therapy." The recurrence of the words "low self-esteem," "isolation," "manipulation," "avoidance," made Jay and me think it would probably be a good idea to engage some outside support for Seth. He continued to exhibit difficult behavior at home: he was challenging, defiant, always negotiating. We signed on with Dr. Julian Oldberg for two sessions a week for Seth, which meant that we signed on for another expense, too.

I was not entirely comfortable with Dr. Oldberg. I like making eye contact with people, especially people involved in the psychological and emotional life of myself or those I love. Dr. Oldberg had an odd anomaly, making it very difficult for me to establish eye contact with him, to feel that I was actually looking into his eyes. I also think that somewhere deep down I didn't really trust that Dr. Oldberg liked Seth or me. He was challenged by us, impressed with Seth's innate intelligence, but not appreciative of Seth's joie de vivre or my forceful personality.

Why did I start with him? Why did I stick it out with him for years to come, despite the fact that I felt completely alienated by him and avoided most contact with him? The truth is I started with him because his office was across the street from where we lived. I was exhausted. I could not face one more demand in our lives. But I also realized that Seth, and Jay and I for that matter, needed some guidelines. At our initial meeting with him, Dr. Oldberg had offered some helpful suggestions.

He helped us sort out how to wake Seth in the morning, especially after a night of many wakings, and given the obvious fact of Seth's not wanting to go to school at Rodeph. Seth was late for school every day. Dr. Oldberg made suggestions to the school, and we asked them to cooperate in the strategies to deal with Seth's lateness. The doctor's involvement legitimized our requests at Rodeph. He helped us with strategies for being consistent. We initiated systems for rule making, which included getting Seth's agreement. We began to see how much Seth was used to having his own way. So in addition to seeing Charles Bonner, Seth began going to Dr. Oldberg twice a week. Finally, in early May, we left for La Jolla.

The trip to La Jolla was very important for me. I went with specific questions for Dr. Frymann and Dr. Springall. I also went with information, and I wanted to talk to the doctors and to Ellen Solomon about the various evaluations Seth had recently undergone. The issues of self-esteem and expressive language were paramount. Dr. Frymann thought the solution to Seth's speech difficulties was improved breathing. Work on his breathing, she told me repeatedly. For all my prior work with Carola Speads, my actual response was to find a speech therapist in New York who would do this, and I scheduled an evaluation for our return.

Dr. Springall thought that Seth was beginning to crawl in a cross pattern, although the movement was not as well organized as he would have hoped. But Seth's creeping had improved, and there was less pronation in Seth's feet. The doctor added new and more challenging exercises including bilateral forms, insisting once again that Seth needed to dig in with his big toe.

Dr. Springall suggested that we purchase a machine called the Execucor. You could stand or lie on it, and it simulated patterns of cross crawling and walking. Athletes use it to strengthen their movement patterns. He also suggested that Seth use a trampoline and monkey bars. I wasn't sure how to make this happen over the summer, but an innovative solution would soon present itself.

The doctor was very patient in describing to me once again the physiological and developmental steps that need to occur in order for a child to progress. He showed me how learning occurs developmentally. Discipline problems, he said, arise when a child is passed by in academics. Again I felt comfortable with all of his assessments.

It was true that Seth was much less challenging in La Jolla than he was at home in New York, but he still had some difficulties sleeping through the night. Dr. Frymann suggested that Seth needed time to unwind and to fantasize, time every day just to be at peace.

Ellen Solomon, Seth's teacher at Beth Israel Day School, said that Seth's writing was improving dramatically and that he was a nonreader only in phonetics. In the whole-language environment Seth was working at grade level. She got me a slew of whole-language books from a special catalog. Seth began to read all the time.

The other observation Ellen made was about how social Seth was, how much of a potential leader he was. Her upbeat assessment of Seth contrasted sharply with the negative observations offered by his teachers in New York as well as Dr. Oldberg. Dr. Oldberg had said that Seth was always expecting things, especially new things, new toys, all the time. He claimed that Seth acted bored during the sessions, pushing and testing and reluctant to talk about some themes, especially his disability.

Dr. Oldberg had also remarked that Seth was living in a fantasy that he was exactly like other children. Dr. Frymann did not seem to think that such a fantasy was so bad. I always felt that Seth was being judged by Dr. Oldberg, whereas Dr. Frymann was simply stating the facts. Seth was six years old, about to turn seven in June, and finishing the first grade. Haya was three years old. Our lives were much more complex than the lives of other families we knew.

Our lives were split. We split our home between New York and La Jolla. The evaluators and the school in New York saw Seth's nature as oppositional. They were pessimistic about him academically. In La Jolla the view of our child was completely different. The doctors and the school noted his progress, academically and socially. The school went so far as to predict his capacities as a leader and guide. In La Jolla his health was ministered osteopathically and homeopathically. In New York we were still using Dr. Lee.

We returned from La Jolla at the end of May and prepared for our visit to the Stephen Gaynor School. Everywhere we had gone for interviews we had been asked to send ahead Seth's test results and school reports. Not at the Stephen Gaynor School. Yvette Siegel, the admissions director, wanted to spend two hours alone with Seth and then meet with us. The entire intake was done on the basis of a written application and her personal evaluation of the child, as well as a meeting with the parents. The interview was one of the high points of our experience.

After two hours Yvette Siegel, much like Dr. Frymann when she did her evaluation of Seth, presented us with the most comprehensive, accurate, and thorough understanding and appreciation of our son we had heard since we had begun the special-education process. Her insights into his learning abilities were awe inspiring and in sync with the results of the most positive testing. When it came to expressive language, inferential and abstract reasoning, she said he was terrific. She thought he was wonderful with sequential picture stories and with size concepts. Her analysis was very different from what we had heard from the Board of Education and from the Oldberg testing. Her appreciation for his humor and life force matched our reactions to him.

Her prescription for his success was grounded in the values we aspired to at home.

Yvette Siegel saw Seth's limitations primarily in terms of dwindling self-esteem, but she also placed his diminishing confidence in himself in the context of the enormous effort required of him. It was the first time that anyone besides Jay and Dr. Frymann and me had recognized this aspect of Seth's life. She perceived Seth's rough cover, his difficulty letting his deficits show.

Once we saw that Seth's psychological, emotional, and academic state were perceived clearly and that Gaynor wanted him, there was no question about enrolling him for the fall. Finally we had a home for Seth in September. I breathed a sigh of relief. Seth did too. Our plan was to enroll Seth at Gaynor and have a month in New York in September before going to La Jolla in October to resume Seth's treatments with Dr. Frymann. Yvette Siegel was concerned about our ongoing commitment to La Jolla, but she said she would reserve judgment until after our first visit in October.

I scheduled a speech evaluation and had Seth's hearing checked once again just to be certain that there were no major changes. Everything about his hearing was fine, which meant that the speech issues were not being influenced by auditory challenges. The speech evaluator described Seth's general lack of precision, his tendency to posture with a tense jaw and stiff upper lip. He said that Seth's tongue was restricted in movement and that breathing was a factor, especially when Seth needed to sustain his voice over a lengthy amount of time. He suggested that we should be working for sound production and recommended that Seth work with a speech therapist at least twice a week. Among those he mentioned was Jackie Morisco. I contacted her about a possible fall slot.

After we settled on the Stephen Gaynor School, there was a marked change in Seth. Our commitment to a new setting, his knowledge that it was going to happen, put us all at ease. I began to prepare for our summer on Cape Cod. Seth was finally enrolled at the Children's School of Science (CSS) in Woods Hole. This was the summer he had been waiting for. After science school he was going to spend afternoons in the older children's program at the Woods Hole Child Center. I planned for Haya to spend her mornings there, too.

The Children's School of Science was Seth's ultimate salvation. At the CSS children come to *do* science projects, not just think about science. The school occupies a historic house in Woods Hole, over-looking Eel Pond. All morning the children from the science school populate the environs of Woods Hole, wandering about in supervised groups with their nets and buckets. Budding scientists, all of them. Seth enrolled in "Seashore Life," the only course for which he was eligible that first summer. He found his niche. He was already investigating which classes he could take the next summer. When he wasn't in class or at the Child Center, he was at the beach with his nose and his net in the ocean.

After the first three weeks, there was a parents' night at the science school. I approached the evening gingerly and alone. Jay was back in the city and not expected until the weekend. I anticipated the evening with some anxiety. The years at Heschel and Rodeph, the ordeal of the previous spring, made me slightly reticent, never sure now about what I would encounter. A minute after introducing myself I heard, "Shoot the moon with this kid," from Seth's teacher and one of the curriculum advisors. "You have a real scientist on your hands."

The teacher, Marion, and the teaching assistant, the son of a prominent local scientist, described Seth as plunging in, raising his hand with answers and questions, fearless and undaunted by challenges. The course demanded several field trips, and although Seth lagged behind slightly, they said that he never lost his sense of humor, his positive outlook and purpose. Seth was an inspiration to them and to the other children, to everyone who came into contact with him.

I saw that evening that everyone in the school knew Seth. His good nature and natural social grace were mentioned by all the people who spoke with me that evening. Later, after returning to the house, and in the exquisite pleasure of my solitude, I cried quietly for a long time. My son was finally out of the darkness.

Seth's exercise program was essential to his ongoing progress, so we purchased the Execucor on Dr. Springall's recommendation. We also planned to bring a small trampoline to the Cape with us. Monkey bars and other paraphernalia were available at local playgrounds, but I knew I would have limited time and inclination to involve myself in these efforts. Jay would be away during the week, so he could devote himself to such activities only on the weekends. Seth needed a regime to engage him in the program that Dr. Springall had outlined.

Serendipity intervened magnificently. The Falmouth Commodores are part of the Cape Cod Baseball League, a serious college league that recruits baseball players from colleges all over the country to compete in a summer-long series. The players are often contenders for the major leagues, whose representatives scout and recruit the players throughout the summer. One of our greatest summer pleasures has been attending Commodore games. A picnic, a blanket, and a folding chair accompany us to Fuller Field in the early evening at least twice a week to cheer our team.

We were very aware of the Commodores because our neighbors, Worthington and Dorothy Campbell, served as a host family every summer, providing housing for at least two boys. The community also takes responsibility for finding employment for the players. Because the boys are only available in the mornings, having practice and games in the afternoons and early evenings, it can be difficult to find them jobs. Some of them work painting local houses or doing odd jobs for residents.

Aware of all this and knowing that two Commodores would occupy the lower half of the Campbell's house, I had called Worth two weeks before we left for the Cape. I had asked him to explore whether there was a player among that summer's crop who would be interested, available, and suitable to work with Seth for three hours every morning before science school. Worth said that he would investigate. A few days later he called to inform me that one of the boys living with him seemed a likely candidate.

A native of Avon, Indiana, Stoney Burke was a physical-education major at Indiana State University. I interviewed him a day or two after we arrived at the Cape. Stoney became not only Seth's "trainer," but his friend and our family friend. He was the catcher for the Commodores.

Together, Stoney and I created a program for Seth that included the monkey bars, the trampoline, and stretching exercises. Working on the monkey bars was very challenging for Seth. Dr. Springall had encouraged it because the exercise involved accomplishing a cross pattern overhead. I wanted Seth running along the beach in the water, doing things to encourage his hand-eye coordination such as hitting a baseball and playing Ping-Pong.

I made one other request. It was intuitive. I asked Stoney to keep a journal of his summer with Seth. I wanted him to make an entry every day describing what he and Seth had done together. My asking Stoney to keep the journal was motivated by a desire to keep track of what actually happened every day, but there was another aspect to it. Stoney was nineteen and focused on college and baseball. I didn't want this job to be just passing the time, the two of them riding around in Stoney's car from the baseball field to the ocean, listening to rock-and-roll, although I saw that that part of it would be good for Seth, too. I wanted it to be a two-way street. I knew from being a writer that committing things to paper in a journal would benefit their relationship. Both Stoney and Seth needed to grow together.

As a surprise for my birthday at the end of July, Stoney presented me with the journal. It remains one of my treasures. In it Stoney wrote about how he took Seth to Woodneck Beach to run on the sand or to the baseball field to run on the track or practice hitting. Gradually he began writing not only about the things they had done, but also about Seth's progress and what had happened to Seth during their workouts. In one entry he noted, "Seth worked up a good sweat, and I told him a good sweat was a really good thing to have."

As the journal progressed, Stoney included his own feelings about watching Seth's struggle. His record of Seth's progress had other dimensions. Reading these entries gave me insight into their relationship and provided me with a record and a lasting memento for Seth. Jay says that to this day Seth has one of the best batting stances of any kid he knows. Stoney went on to play professionally and to complete his college education. We stay in touch by exchanging cards over the holidays, by informing each other of significant events in our lives.

Recently I read over the last entry in Stoney's diary from that summer. It says,

> Dear Laura and Jay,
> I really appreciate all you have done for me. You made my summer worthwhile. I hope that the time I spent with Seth helped. I wish the best for him to succeed in all that he does. I know he will. It makes me feel good to see the expressions on your faces when Seth accomplishes something. The joy I see in you makes me feel like I have accomplished something too. Seth has really taught me a lot about myself, and life in general. He is a great kid. The experiences and moments we shared will last forever.

After spending the summer jumping on the trampoline, working on the monkey bars, running on the beach, playing baseball, Ping-Pong, and soccer, Seth's progress was significant. We were ecstatic. In addition to the mornings with Stoney and the science school, Seth went horseback riding two or three times a week. When I called Dr. Frymann at the end of July, it was to report how happy and cooperative Seth was, how energetic and independent, how self-reliant. At the same time, I thought that Seth was not walking particularly well and that his speech was not improving, although his expressive language was. His progress was always a mixture.

Another significant experience for Seth that summer was that he would go from science school to the Woods Hole Child Center accompanied only by a twelve-year-old girl from science school. I paid her ten dollars a week to walk with Seth each afternoon after science school up the hill to the Child Center. This meant that Seth was not collected by his mother or a babysitter. He was more independent than ever before in his life. Seth and Jennifer Gifford walked the half mile up School Street every afternoon. At the end of the summer, Jennifer wrote Seth a letter about how he had inspired her, and how spending the time with him every day had made her grow in ways she had never imagined. We were incredibly impressed by her feelings about Seth.

Our son's "karma" was touching everyone who had close contact with him. Out of the darkness of the previous year we drew great light during those beautiful summer months. The treasure of Seth was reinforced. It was becoming increasingly clear how special circumstances create special people, and how through recognizing our limitations we strive to know our potential. I redirected my thoughts to how lucky we were. I was fortified for the coming year.

When we returned to New York in September, Seth began at the Stephen Gaynor School. It felt like a safe haven after the experience of the prior year. A small school, founded in 1962 and located in a large, white townhouse on the West Side of Manhattan, the Stephen Gaynor School (SGS) is staffed by special-education teachers and learning specialists and has a devoted administrative staff. Classes are small, at the most six to eight children. The children are grouped on the basis of their social, chronological, and academic compatibilities. Children attend Gaynor from as early as preschool up through the sixth grade or until they are thirteen years old. So we would have to find another school for Seth sometime in the future.

The guiding principle of the Stephen Gaynor School is to create an environment in which children can grow academically, socially, and emotionally. Gaynor's primary goal is to have children return to a mainstream classroom as rapidly as possible. Their success rate is dramatic. Ninety-five percent of Stephen Gaynor students go on to complete their studies at mainstream schools and colleges. For us that was the most significant aspect of the program. We were sure that Seth would eventually be a candidate for the mainstream. We wanted to think of him as a child who was making a temporary stopover to get better prepared.

What we didn't foresee was what it would mean emotionally for us to move into this world of special education, especially since we started out with the attitude that Seth was only at Gaynor temporarily. It took time for Seth and for us to become reconciled to his new school situation.

At first we were so relieved that Seth had a place at Gaynor, we "dumped" him there and had little involvement in the school. I paid little attention to anything I heard that fall at school. I was blotting out all the problems of the previous year, especially the ordeal of the past spring. Of course we attended the parent orientation and other school meetings, but deep down I was in a stupor, totally fatigued. I needed for someone else to deal with Seth. I know now how wonderful the Stephen Gaynor School was for Seth. We could jettison Seth at the Gaynor School, and they took care of him just fine.

We had another child too, and I wanted to turn some attention toward Haya. She always seemed easy and adaptable, going along with all our moves, our sudden changes. Just like the rest of us, she lived in the orbit around Seth. Seth was always the center and the star. I hadn't yet recognized how she was affected by being Seth's sister.

My stupor had its boundaries, however. I called Jack Morisco, the speech therapist, and scheduled appointments. Seth developed an ear infection the first week we were home from the Cape, and I took him to see Dr. Lee. She prescribed amoxicillin, an antibiotic. Seth had not had any allopathic medicine since we began with Dr. Frymann a year earlier.

Like other children, Seth had his share of ear infections early on. My diary documents several routine visits to Dr. Lee for ear infections and follow-up visits. Antibiotics were administered repeatedly, sometimes to no avail. When we adopted a different route to health by pursuing osteopathic and homeopathic care, I concluded that antibiotics were often useless, especially for viral infections. Osteopaths have known for a hundred years that small children are more susceptible to ear infections because their eustachian tubes are shorter. This means that infections reach the middle ear more easily. By the time Haya was born I knew much more about routine ear infections and how viral infections run their course with or without antibiotics. So I decided to ignore Dr. Lee's prescription this time and treat Seth myself with a homeopathic remedy.

While overall self-management is not advisable when a condition is acute, Dr. Masiello always encouraged me, and all his patients, to become competent at deciphering symptoms and choosing remedies to administer for ourselves when there are minor ailments. That is very much a part of practicing homeopathic medicine, learning to analyze, respond to, and report symptoms. The doctor doesn't have to be called for every little ache and pain. Because of my obsessive journal entries, I knew that Seth had had exactly the same kind of cold a year earlier, the same week we left the Cape. I used that information as part of my analysis. I gave the homeopathic remedy a try with Seth, and it worked. I never had to give him the antibiotic. Within a day, he got better. We returned to Dr. Lee ten days later, and there was no infection in his middle ear. I knew it was time to start thinking seriously about a change in our overall medical approach.

In early September, I attended a "Back to School Night for Parents" at Gaynor. There was information about the weekly structure of the children's academic life at Gaynor, classroom instruction, after-school activities, teaching structures, evaluations, and reports. Outwardly I was attentive. Inside I was absent. Gaynor was a salvation, but in my mind it was also just a stopover.

Two weeks into the school year I met with Seth's teachers, and they said he was doing well. I was glad to hear that Seth was participating fully in everything and that he was first in his class in math. As I review my notes, I see that I attended these first two meetings alone. Even more than I, Jay was distancing himself around this time. I remember that later that fall, or perhaps early that winter, I went alone to a forum on life after Gaynor. I was already looking beyond, but Jay was too tired to be involved. Although it took some time and many other developments, eventually our attitude would change.

Seth was very proud of himself and brought home one of his tests.

He was keeping up in reading and didn't need any outside tutoring. We decided to cut back the sessions with Dr. Oldberg to once a week. The doctor did not support this move, but I was determined not to make my son a full-time patient. The big question in everyone's mind was how La Jolla would figure into everything. I was still committed to returning for more treatments for Seth.

In La Jolla that October, when Seth had his first appointment with Dr. Frymann, she said that he had more control over his body and much more energy. Dr. Springall evaluated him and said that Seth was reading 99 percent of all the sight words presented to him, doing more with his left hand, and integrating his creeping and crawling. Seth's speech was definitely inconsistent, but there was more volume in the phrasing. He had more breath. I didn't really know what Seth and Jackie Morisco were doing together during their sessions, but whatever they were doing was obviously working. Before we left for La Jolla she had begun coming to the house twice a week.

I was still completely tuned out. I was exhausted from the traveling back and forth to California, adjusting the kids to their September programs just after returning from the Cape, and then hauling us all to California. Drs. Frymann and Springall would be in charge while we were in La Jolla. That was enough for me. I couldn't think of another thing. Seth did though, and his ability to advocate for himself was about to come into sharp focus.

When Seth went back to the Beth Israel Day School in San Diego, the school recommended that he remain in the first grade with Ellen Solomon. Three days into our first school week, Seth came home and asked to talk to me immediately.

He said, "I've been to see Jill Green." Jill was the principal of the school. "And I've talked to Cindy. She's the second-grade teacher. I want to be with my friends from last year. I told them I can do it."

"Have they decided? Do you want me to call them?" I asked, surprised by his initiative.

"No. I told them I want three days to prove I can be in class with Evan and everyone. I know I can keep up. No problem. I just have to show them."

"What do you want me to do? I can call Jill and talk to her." I kept on the same track, not fully realizing how well he had thought every-thing through.

"I just want you to back me up."

I was astonished. Seth had come up with his objectives and decided on a course of action without discussing the details of his plan with me. Then he had proceeded to find the people who could help him realize his goal. Over the years Seth's ability to advocate for himself has continued to serve him. I want to think that he learned some of this from us, his parents, but I also think that his circumstances offered him two directions. One option was to become a victim, someone not entitled to or not capable of getting what he wanted. The other was to become motivated to get what he needed, knowing that he would have to do extraordinary things to overcome his situation.

At BIDS he knew that he had to act for himself, so he did. He suc-ceeded, too. At the end of the first week of school the teacher and principal called and said that Seth was right. He belonged in the sec-ond grade. He had a wonderful month in school, reaching new aca-demic heights. Sometime in the middle of the month, Cindy, the second-grade teacher, called me. For half an hour I listened to her sing Seth's praises, the joy she had in teaching him. It helped me forget the painful meetings with the teachers at Rodeph a year earlier.

Seth continues to elicit immense satisfaction from his teachers. He loves to learn. He approaches the classroom with excitement and cu-riosity. Time and again, we listen to his teachers say what a wonderful student he is. Now in his teenage years, hormones dominate, and there are more inconsistencies, but one thing remains constant, and that is his sense of responsibility, his eagerness to know more. The key is a friendly environment.

During my last visit with Dr. Frymann before we left La Jolla that fall, she said something very disturbing to me. She thought that some-thing of a psychic nature, some very negative sway, had influenced Seth for a time. I was appalled at the suggestion. It sounded as though she meant that some kind of voodoo had been visited on him. I was shocked and worried.

In retrospect I think what Dr. Frymann was describing was some-thing Seth himself identified years later. So many pairs of hands had touched him. There had been three physical therapists before Seth was eighteen months old. A multitude of other professionals had handled and examined Seth: neurologists, podiatrists, Feldenkrais practitioners, orthopedists. There is enormous power and influence in touch—something you have to experience to know. The sense of touch is the great sense. The whole skin sees and listens, and not only the skin, but the entire body, bones and muscles, heart and mind. Whoever Seth is is a product of a lot of input, the result of the sway of many hands.

12

◆

Anchoring

◆

WHEN WE RETURNED FROM LA JOLLA, the teachers and staff at Gaynor immediately recognized and acknowledged the differences in Seth. However, they remained wary of our ongoing commitment to working with Dr. Frymann because of the interruptions to Seth's schooling. For the time being, I didn't listen to them, only to my own inner voice that told me that we had to return to La Jolla in January. I wasn't listening to anything they said anyway, because I had yet to accept that Seth really needed special education. Gaynor was a way station in my mind. It was only a matter of time and my getting organized before Seth returned to the mainstream. So we thought.

Before we had left La Jolla, Dr. Frymann had prescribed "time out" from treatment. She also wanted me to "stay calm." We were becoming better acquainted, the doctor and I. She was less of a deity to me, which made her more approachable. She respected my seriousness, my strong sense of purpose. Her insights into me were as cogent as her insights into Seth.

Prior to our October trip to La Jolla though, I had begun thinking about access to treatments in New York, or at least in the local environs. Relying on a doctor three thousand miles away unsettled me. Dr. Masiello didn't seem like an option because his practice was not exclusively pediatric. So I began searching for a New York–area cranial osteopath who was also a pediatrician.

Dr. Michael Burrano fit this description. From what I remember, he also practiced homeopathy, although he was not a homeopath. He practiced in Brewster, New York, two hours by train from the city. We went to see him once. I liked him, and I liked his insights into Seth, but Dr. Frymann's admonition in October persuaded me that I shouldn't be in such a hurry to put Seth into any more hands. And Brewster was quite a commute from Manhattan.

The autumn produced many settlings. Seth settled into Gaynor. Haya settled into nursery school at the 92nd Street Y. She had spent two weeks in the classroom before we left for La Jolla, and she adapted splendidly when we returned. "She never misses a beat," I said to her teachers. We were all astonished by the apparent ease with which she slipped into the regime. Everyone was suitably impressed. Little did we know.

In the early winter we settled the lawsuit against the doctor and the hospital out of court. At the eleventh hour, just as a court date for the trial was scheduled, the insurance companies for the doctor and hospital made us an offer. At the time, Jay was preparing me to testify at the scheduled trial right after our January trip to La Jolla.

The lawsuit had been a thorny issue, creating terrible disquiet for me. I had given my deposition in the winter of 1987, while I was pregnant with Haya. The experience had been extremely difficult. The defendants' lawyers were understandably adversarial and made me recount the night of Seth's birth in painstaking detail. They constantly goaded me on, couching their questions with the implication that I should have done more to protect my unborn child. "Didn't the nurse tell you that the baby wasn't getting enough oxygen?" asked the woman interrogator. Such questions only underscored my own sense of guilt and responsibility, which I was already wrestling with constantly.

Another aspect of their inquiry focused on Seth's actual circumstances. The defense lawyers wanted to establish that in fact Seth was highly functional and suffered from little impairment as a result of his birth trauma. I needed to stress the extent and ramifications of Seth's limitations, a task that was painful and arduous for me. Because my entire life is devoted to helping Seth realize his full potential, nothing caused me as much grief as those days I spent giving my deposition, claiming and insisting on the darkest aspects of Seth's challenges.

During the winter of 1990, the defense required us to take Seth to one of their doctors for an examination. I was outraged. With all the medical information, all the reports and diagnoses already available, the idea that still another person was going to examine Seth incensed me. Then our lawyers also wanted someone of their choosing to examine Seth. I felt sick about all of it, offended by the continual probing and the ongoing scrutiny of my son. I raged and ranted. Jay had to calm me down before taking Seth to each of these examinations. I will never forget them. By this time Seth was more aware of his circumstances, so the examinations were difficult for him, too.

The settlement of the case in 1991 meant an end to a nasty legal episode. Although the court set severe restrictions on how Seth's money could be handled until he came of legal age, limiting its growth potential by circumscribing investments, they did grant us an allowance to help meet many of the financial demands we were facing. An appearance before the judge later that spring ultimately closed the door on the legal aspect, although many of the emotional scars remain even today. But we had scored a victory. Because of Jay's hard work with our lawyers, Seth will have resources to help him meet the ongoing challenges and health-care needs throughout his life.

In November and December our life stabilized. Both children were settled in the schools where they would remain for at least another year. Both children had after-school activities. Seth's consisted of one visit with Dr. Oldberg every week and two thirty-minute speech sessions at home every week.

We had one meeting with Dr. Oldberg during this time. He was disappointed that he wasn't seeing more of us. He wanted more input. He felt that Seth had returned in good shape from La Jolla and then had begun to regress. Seth had stopped being creative and had become increasingly secretive, he insisted. I couldn't muster the energy to see Dr. Oldberg again. I had all I could do to contain the relative equilibrium and semblance of a normal life before preparing for our return to La Jolla. I was content that Seth saw Dr. Oldberg once a week, and that there was someone to take him. The doctor's proximity meant that the current babysitter could simply drop Seth off across the street then pick him up at the end of the session.

After twenty-two speech sessions Jackie Morisco wrote in her report that Seth's vocal production was complicated by inadequate loudness owing to the limited neuromuscular control of his respiratory function. Although I was aware that inadequate control of breathing was the obvious impediment, I was still not employing any of Carola's techniques with Seth. Although Dr. Frymann also had told me to work on Seth's breathing as a way of improving his speech, I simply turned Seth's speech issues over to the speech therapist. My own energy was directed elsewhere.

I decided to inform myself as well as I could about osteopathy. Unlike with the other disciplines I was pursuing, I couldn't become an actual practitioner or do a training unless I was prepared to go to medical school. I considered this option, but I quickly realized it was not for me. I knew I could know more though, so I set myself to the task of learning as much as I could as a layperson. The prior spring I had attended all of Dr. Frymann's lectures in La Jolla. In November I asked Dr. Masiello for a bibliography and for some time to study with him. I settled down to work.

Osteopaths use the muscular-skeletal system as a basic approach to treating their patients. They include all body systems, treating tops, bottoms, sides, and fronts. Doctors of osteopathy believe that the body's structure plays a critical role in its ability to function. They use their eyes and hands to identify structural problems and to support the body's natural tendency toward health and self-healing.

Osteopaths are licensed physicians. Fully trained, they can prescribe medication and perform surgery. Doctors of osteopathy (D.O.s) and M.D.s (allopathic physicians) are the only two types of complete physicians. Doctors of osteopathy practice in all branches of medicine and surgery, from psychiatry to obstetrics, from geriatrics to emergency medicine. However, D.O.s are trained to be doctors first, and specialists second.

The osteopathic approach accounts for the entire function of the body, bones being considered the foundation for the body's structure and therefore its function. This is not to say that an orthopedist is not appropriate in other situations, be it cerebral palsy or many other problems as, for instance, in the case of a broken bone. But we think about Seth in terms of his whole body, including his sensory experiences.

Osteopathy's insistence on treating the whole person and not just a disease entity coincided with my growing awareness of somatics. Somatics says that bodies are not different structures, but that through structure we can look at the different ways different bodies function.

The first time I read about somatics was in the work of Thomas Hanna, who writes extensively about how humans function best. Mr. Hanna is the editor of the magazine *Somatics* and is the author of several books. He is now director of the Novato Institute for Somatic Research and Training in California.

The somatic view pays homage to the evolution of the physical life of humans. It sees the Homo sapien as a genetically ancient animal whose physical characteristics are the result of a long series of functional adaptations that have enhanced its survival. The ideas of Carola, of Feldenkrais, of Doman are in perfect sync with this evolutionary concept. Osteopathy is also attuned to this historical view of human function.

Osteopathy recognizes that there is a systematic integrity in each individual, that there is a self-balancing and self-adjusting ability in the human species. But we must be allowed to be self-healing. Osteopathy fosters change in a preventative way, helping us become less suscepti-ble to toxic stimulants in the environment. The manipulative techniques osteopaths use are designed to improve circulation and stimulate the immune system. The theory is that all bodies are in process; they are not static. This view of process is also essential to the somatic vision.

The osteopath's view centers on the patient's constitution and not on one episode of acute illness. Dr. Frymann had said early on that you can't touch someone without influencing his or her whole body. I had seen this for myself in Carola's classes and in the Feldenkrais work. I liked the fact that osteopaths were involved with the structure of the body, not only in their heads but in their hands, because they "listen" with their hands. Osteopathic Manipulative Therapy (OMT) is non-judgmental, a compassionate approach to healing, to resonating, to establishing a link with our structural being.

Osteopaths are not chiropractors. Chiropractors are not physicians and have not had the training of an osteopath. Their objectives are lim-ited to alignment and symmetry. For osteopaths, function and integra-tion are the goal.

In his book, *Osteopathy: The Illustrated Guide,* Stephen Sandler, D.O., describes the cranial osteopath as a highly trained physician who uses refined hands-on techniques to detect and treat subtle dis-turbances in motion patterns of the skull, which are often sympto-matic of certain disorders. Sandler describes how osteopaths who have studied and specialized in cranial work maintain that palpitation on the skull and sacrum picks up a rhythmic pulsation distinct from the respiratory rhythm or the heartbeat and pulse of the blood. This pulsation is the reverberation of the cerebrospinal fluid, which bathes both the brain and the spinal column. Cranial osteopaths explain that the brain is suspended inside the skull by sheets of tissue known as the meninges. These meninges extend all the way down the vertebral column to the sacrum. This linkage connects the movement of the skull bones and the movement of the pelvis. Cranial work tries to balance the rhythmical forces at work in the body by gently guiding and releasing the tensions within the reciprocal tension of these tissues.

Osteopathy can be especially valuable in helping to diagnose and treat developmental problems in children. Dr. Frymann claimed that only ten percent of children have normal body structure. Ten percent of children have distortion that is visible to the naked eye. Eighty percent of children's structural distortions are not visible. Eighty percent of children with learning problems had suffered difficult births. Dr. Frymann thought that all children should have an osteopathic evaluation at three months.

A young child's nervous system is still forming, still in flux. There is a plasticity in a child's central nervous system, an ability to recover completely or partially after an insult to the brain. As I mentioned earlier, the brains of very young children have a greater capacity to repair themselves than do adult brains. A child's central nervous system produces many more brain cells and connections than are eventually used for complex motor tasks. As long as a child's nervous system has not yet matured, there is still a chance that the child can make at least a partial recovery from early movement problems.

An osteopath would have known immediately what Seth's circumstances were. When I think back to all the routine physical examinations Seth had with our pediatrician, I realize that an osteopath, trained to know what the "norm" *feels* like, would have recognized Seth's anomalies immediately. If only I had known to take him to one. There is no doubt that earlier intervention for Seth would have made an enormous difference. Cranial work at an early stage would certainly have been significant for Seth and for his future. My hope is that I can use what I know to persuade others to act and intervene early.

Settling in at home during those eleven weeks felt good, but then we were off again, back to La Jolla in January for almost five weeks. Seth's adjustment was immediate. He loved our life in La Jolla, his school in San Diego. And everyone at Beth Israel Day School loved him. California was his milieu. Haya's adjustment to La Jolla was not as easy. She didn't like her school program as much as Seth liked his. She missed her nursery school at the 92nd Street Y, a superb program without peer. La Jolla offered a day-care environment, but it would be another year before she would be able to participate fully in the principal school at BIDS. Nonetheless, she adapted, rode to school in the car pool, and made a few friends.

Dr. Frymann thought that Seth was in better shape in January than he had been in October. She maintained, however, that he had a deep conflict about taking control of his body. Dr. Springall thought that there had been an improvement in the clarity of Seth's speech and in his writing. Seth's reading was excellent, including the phonics, the approach that was emphasized at Gaynor. The drooling had subsided, the walking had improved, and Seth's creeping and crawling were better organized, but he still needed to dig in more with the big toe during his exercises.

During Jay's visit to La Jolla in January, we went together to see Dr. Frymann. The doctor described Seth as having a violent, opposing nature. We were both surprised to hear her say this. And sad. This was a departure from her ususal positive outlook. I knew she had been disappointed when he was not cooperative, but I had never detected this strong criticism before. She emphasized that this characteristic was a result of the rage Seth feels deep down, a rage he does not often express.

When I questioned Seth about his rage, he avoided the discussion. Except in the few instances I've described, it was rare for Seth to be forthcoming about his deepest feelings. Mostly I had to divine what was happening beneath the surface. Sometimes his behavior did betray anger at his situation, but he was not frustrated easily or often. What had occurred occasionally was anguish, demonstrated by his breaking down into tears and expressing profound sadness about his circumstances. These days there is even more of this. It's a sadness he contains for a long time but that eventually overflows.

The doctor went on to say that Seth could and would eventually do better. He was motivated and sometimes very cooperative, but he still offered a lot of resistance. His aggressive attitude toward issues with his body persisted and was making him disrespectful of the work. She wondered whether we should elicit his input about the treatments. She suggested that Seth needed to mix in a more casual way with other children with disabilities. We had never sought out such opportunities.

Dr. Frymann still believed that Seth required discipline and limits, but she also thought that many of his problems had to do with his possessiveness about me and not having me all to himself. This observation echoed some of the insights Dr. Oldberg had passed along earlier in the year. Dr. Oldberg had made me aware of the heightened competition Seth felt with Haya concerning me. My reaction was that it was typical for siblings to compete for attention. Then I began to wonder, why me? Why not Jay? I chalked it up to being the mother, not fully able to grasp my responsibilities. There were always too many responsibilities, too many distractions, for me to have time to explore how better to handle this tension between the children. Later I probed the parts of myself that contributed to their stress. As I dealt with my own anxiety and my feelings of inadequacy, the darker disagreements faded between Seth and Haya.

During our visit to La Jolla, Dr. Springall and Dr. Frymann together presented a lecture entitled "The Developmental Process of Children with Special Needs" in which they pointed out the strong correlation between how much a child progresses in individual stages and a child's intellectual development. They emphasized what happens to children who do not pass through normal developmental processes. These children do not function as well as other children who do pass through normal stages of development. Sensation and motor ability are vital to the programming of function. Each stage in children's development is essential to the development of the next stage. Each stage in the human individual, even on the cellular level, recapitulates the prior stage. Development can be viewed as an ever-expanding spiral. As the child moves along the widening turns of the spiral, there occurs a return to various developmental themes, but each time they are experienced, it is with a broader perspective, with new knowledge, new skills, and greater independence. They also stressed the importance of leaving the future wide open, of removing the obstacles, especially by not listening to typical prognoses. They said that providing a child with the opportunities to evolve was the most important job of parents. That encouraged me enormously. I was ready to be open-minded and assess things as we progressed without any prescription for the future. As Carola had suggested years earlier, I wanted to remain open-minded about the developmental possibilities. I intended to continue pursuing new possibilities to enhance Seth's potential.

We returned to New York in February, knowing that in May we would go back to La Jolla for the last time that year. My focus was on two things: seeing whether I could find a setting or an opportunity for Seth to mix casually with other children with some disabilities and getting Seth's eyes fully examined. I never succeeded in finding the casual setting Dr. Frymann had recommended—an opportunity for Seth to encounter other children with disabilities. Everything I investigated was extreme. I only accomplished the eye examination.

Seth had complained about headaches. I was aware that visual acuity and visual constancy are paramount for learning, and that any visual impairment interferes with development. In *Children with Cerebral Palsy: A Parents' Guide,* I am reminded, there is mention of very common vision problems among children with cerebral palsy. The symptoms can be indicative of underlying disorders including sensory delays that affect balance and body awareness, trouble discerning background from foreground, and so on.

Seth's auditory skills had always tested better than his visual ones. However, I had never taken him for anything more than a routine eye examination. I consulted Dr. Richard Kavner, a vision specialist and behavioral optometrist. His specialty is "vision training." Dr. Kavner believes that vision skills can be improved through exercise and nutrition geared to the eyes.

In his book, *Total Vision,* Dr. Kavner defines behavioral optometry as the combined knowledge of psychology, neurology, biology, child development, and other related fields. He writes that our eyes are receptors of the brain. The eye is not just a camera, but a part of the entire visual apparatus, which begins and ends at the back of the brain. The eyes take in the data and channel it along neural impulses to the cortex, where the central control makes sense out of the information.

Case studies demonstrate that enhancing or expanding vision changes personality and behavior. That theory melded perfectly with the information I had gleaned from working with Feldenkrais's teachings, studying Doman, and with my increasing interest in and understanding of somatics. As vision changes, so may personality and behavior. As Dr. Kavner explains, our eyes are active seekers of the essence of life. They are constantly searching, scanning, and selecting from the environment. The eye is a living organ that is always in communication with other vital centers of the body. What we think and how we feel are constant companions of the images we pay attention to.

The basic premise of vision therapy is that vision is not a passive occurrence but a learned process. Vision therapy teaches a person to use his nerve and muscle systems better and put them at the command of the mind. Good vision involves a whole spectrum of skills. How do you use both eyes together? How quickly can you judge left from right? How well do you see objects in space? Can you shift focus from near to far quickly and easily? How good is your visual memory?

Dr. Frymann and Dr. Springall explain development based on the stages of growth. Similarly, Dr. Kavner understands vision. If certain behavioral patterns are not acquired in the usual sequence, more advanced patterns may be damaged. To repair them, therapy may have to begin at the base level. Then that level opens a path to the next level. In vision therapy, body balancing skills which are learned in the first few years of life, often must be rehearsed and perfected as a way of reaching the specific problem that is interfering with eye-body coordination. The actual therapy a person receives depends on age and the exact nature of the problem. This is a highly individualized program of assessment and treatment. Dr. Kavner says the ability to use the eyes and actively examine the environment is so intimately connected to growth and development that without it, normal development could actually cease to occur.

Dr. Kavner discovered that Seth had some focusing difficulty, that Seth was not always able to hold focus. He identified premigraine symptoms and the possibility that Seth would develop vascular headaches, a symptom of a problem with the reactive nervous system. Otherwise, he thought that Seth had the best visual ability of any child with cerebral palsy he had ever seen. We all agreed that the Feldenkrais training and the cranial work was the reason. The doctor recommended some vision training, exercises Seth could do at home (along with the Springall exercises). We also planned a course of biofeedback for the near future.

Biofeedback is not a medical treatment, but a learning process that helps patients develop their own ability to achieve relief from symptoms. In biofeedback, sensors measure muscle tension, skin temperature, or other bodily processes. The sensor readings are then amplified and translated into signals that you can see or hear—or both. As you become accustomed to sensing certain of your body's processes, you can gradually gain some control over them.

Eventually we did have Seth participate in a program of biofeedback with Dr. Kavner. Seth reported how good he felt after each session. I was pleased with the results and with Seth's reaction to the sessions. At the same time, I felt the gnawing of the warning "too much therapy, too many hands, too much being a child with cerebral palsy" for Seth. I wanted to deemphasize the therapeutic in his life.

Seth no longer participates in biofeedback sessions, but I still take him for regular eye examinations with Dr. Kavner. During a recent visit Dr. Kavner suggested that Seth could benefit from more sessions. Seth resisted ardently, already overwhelmed with his academic responsibilities and some of the other rehabilitation work we insist on. He admits, however, how good the other sessions of biofeedback made him feel. I have surrendered to my son's adolescent howls momentarily, but I know that one day he will return to this work and benefit from it enormously.

The most significant recollection I have of our return to La Jolla that May was the welcome Seth received from his classmates and from the school, especially from the teacher, the very teacher who had been cautious about admitting him into her second-grade class. Cindy Cohen called me shortly after we arrived to say, "Thank you for bringing your beautiful son back to me." No wonder Seth loved California. He made an incredible transition, slipping right into the routine without a misstep. He was sleeping through the night and was generally cooperative. There were continuing instances of manipulation and deception, but nothing extreme or out of the ordinary—the regular testing of limits. Bedtimes, how much television or junk food: these were the issues (and still are).

Things had been going just as well in New York. Before we left for La Jolla his teacher at the Stephen Gaynor School had reported that Seth was doing well academically, reading with good comprehension and progressing in math. I was happy to hear the reports, but I was devoid of any energy, so I doubt I would have done anything if the reports hadn't been encouraging. I also knew that Seth was happier in California, and I was more comfortable with the Beth Israel children and their parents. The difference, of course, was that the Beth Israel Day School was a mainstream school. The Stephen Gaynor School was a place for children with special needs.

This contrast was especially noticeable among Seth's classmates at the two schools. At Gaynor some of the children had severe behavior problems, a facet of learning disabilities we hadn't anticipated when we had first applied to the school.

Seth told me, "I'm more comfortable in my chair in San Diego. At the Gaynor School I feel like throwing my chair out the window. My ideas are always accepted at BIDS, even just part of them. Everything at Gaynor is black and white."

I encouraged him to tell me more, even though my heart was sinking. What kind of a place was Gaynor? I knew many of the children had to be kept in check, that their difficulties were being treated with medications such as Ritalin.

Seth told me, "We are a group in San Diego. We're together. Nobody puts anybody else down. There is more acceptance of my ideas. I like the cooperation in San Diego. All of us share answers and information. At Gaynor the kids taunt each other when someone is wrong."

"But why is that? Why doesn't everyone cooperate in New York?" I wanted to know specifically.

"Because the whole class can be punished at Gaynor for one kid's misbehavior. They're all too out of control."

Seth went on to say, "If I tell someone at BIDS to stop, it's like having a key to open a door. At Gaynor I can shout 'stop' forever, and it's like a key that doesn't fit."

He described a sense of feeling welcomed in San Diego by teachers who didn't even have him for a student. This was not true at Gaynor, with its strict discipline.

"But we live in New York, sweetie," I had to tell him. "This is where your daddy works and Haya goes to school. It's here that we have family."

"Everyone else in my family has more of a life in New York than I do," he replied. "My life is here in San Diego, where I want to stay, where I intend to return to study, where I have real friends with whom I really feel safe."

When I recounted to Jay my conversation with Seth, he became very uncomfortable. Neither of us knew exactly how to respond.

Suddenly I realized that we had a monkey on our backs. There were problems with returning time and again to La Jolla. It was true that at Gaynor there were many rules and regulations. Some of these were responses to the behavior of the students; some were part of an overall philosophical approach. On the other hand, Seth was not a full-time student at BIDS, but a "star" who came and went, enjoying a certain status and occupying a unique position. It was easy to romanticize his San Diego school life, a transient, temporal existence, set in the mesmerizing grandeur of the scenery.

I was alert to this phenomena. At the same time I wondered whether Gaynor was the right alternative, given that so many of Seth's fellow students were battling emotional and behavioral problems. In my mind, Seth didn't have those types of issues, not, at least, to that extent. I suggested to Jay that in the autumn we should explore some other schools, mainstream settings that could support some of Seth's special needs. Seth's San Diego experience had been so good, I forgot that other educational settings had not been as successful.

Once Seth got wind of our doubts and some of our dissatisfaction, he adopted our attitude. The message Seth got was that Gaynor was a temporary situation, that he didn't belong there and didn't have to give it his all. It did not help him in the classroom or in other school activities. He felt that he had one foot out the door, and he even went so far as to tell the administration that he would be leaving anyway.

In retrospect, it was a major mistake for Seth to have so much access to our opinions about his school. As Dr. Frymann had so astutely pointed out two years earlier, it wasn't a good idea to allow Seth to be privy to the decision-making process. It was better not to discuss his circumstances within his earshot. Now that we've learned our lesson, Jay and I thrash things out between us first, then we invite Seth to participate in selected aspects of decision making.

We almost let ourselves be flung out of Gaynor, and at one point, Gaynor was willing to let us go. It took more than a year for us to repair our mistakes. Once we took hold and hauled ourselves up onto sure footing, we sent a different message to Seth. Afterward, his experience at Gaynor metamorphosed him and us, and as a result a mainstream setting became a real possibility.

Meanwhile, I began getting us ready for the summer. Seth was to spend his second year at the Children's School of Science, this year taking three courses instead of one. He also hoped to learn to play tennis. I had to find someone to replace Stoney, who would not be returning to play with the Commodores. Eventually I found a great college student who was spending his summer in Falmouth.

Haya was going to the Woods Hole Child Center in the mornings, and I planned to use the free time to do some writing. Everything "fell" into place. (I was exhausted from all the careful planning. I wrote in one of my essays that once I had managed touring theatrical shows, and now I felt that I was one.)

That summer I became acquainted with a woman who was an associate professor and director for learning-disabled students at a small college on Long Island. I talked with her over several cups of tea and began thinking about learning disabilities and other kinds of disabilities in a new light. She encouraged me to consider whether there is a valid way to measure innate potential, and what it means. In the core of my being, my values were challenged.

She and I talked about what we mean when we speak of a brain injury and a disability. At the instant of conception we were all intended to have a good brain. At some time after that instant, if something happened that hurt the good brain—something that may have occurred a minute, an hour, a day, a week, a month or a year or more after conception—a good quality brain is hurt. It may be severely hurt or it may be mildly hurt. It may be hurt in a way that limits walking or talking or hearing or seeing or feeling, but it is a good quality brain nonetheless, and not an inferior brain. We talked about what terms and labels mean. Too often she felt that the trouble with all the names and labels is that it mistakes the symptoms for the disease.

I was forced to confront my deepest prejudices. I had grown up in a home where intellectual, athletic, and social achievements had an objective standard. My brother and sister had both gone to Ivy League colleges. We had all been encouraged to be competitive, especially intellectually. When I thought of my children's future, I wanted nothing less than the best for them, the pinnacle.

It was dawning on me that these gifts of nature, bequests of intellect, of grace, these favors, abilities we so easily take for granted, are simply that, gifts. People with disabilities are not really essentially different from the rest of us. We are all "temporarily able-bodied." We are each of us only seconds, only a fall or an accident away, from disability, from incapacity. All types of disabilities reside in us. Seth already knew what he needed to confront in himself in his life. Some of us wait an eternity to find out, and then we must start over. Who among us doesn't have special needs?

Another enlightening incident occurred at the annual summer picnic for the Children's School of Science. Seth and Haya and I went with much anticipation, knowing that it was quite a shindig. Everyone brings their own supper, and CSS supplies the drinks and the watermelon and, more important, the volleyball game. Seth was very much part of the community of CSS now and committed to being a student for as long as he could be. The picnic was emotional, since it signaled that three weeks of classes were all that remained of the summer.

That evening, when we were happily sharing our repast with a New York family we had gotten to know over that summer, their daughter, Anna, asked her mother why Seth talked like he did, why he was so difficult to understand.

Immediately I began to give Anna an explanation. "Everyone has things that challenge them, Anna," I began. "Seth has some differences that make it hard for him to do many things you and Haya and I do very easily. Talking is one of them."

Seth put his hand on my arm to stop me. He turned to Anna and said, as clearly as he has ever spoken anything, "I have a friend in San Diego named Evan. He listens to me even in the noisiest room. He understands everything I say. When he isn't sure, he asks me to say it again."

That was the last time I felt I needed to answer for Seth. The implications of his answer, that it was the responsibility of others to make the effort to understand him, were enough to silence my crude attempts at a response.

Returning to Gaynor in the fall was not easy for Seth. His enrollment that school year was postponed, however, because we went directly from the Cape to La Jolla. Dr. Frymann's schedule demanded that we be there in early September if Seth was to get all ten treatments. I scheduled private testing in New York for our return. Jay and I wanted objective advice about applying to mainstream schools for Seth. It would be a busy year of school visits since Haya was "graduating" from nursery school and needed a kindergarten for the following September.

We were also buying a house in New York and would be moving in

November. Given the mammoth responsibility of the move and the financial demands, we could no longer maintain long sojourns in another house in San Diego. The constant instability was taking a toll on Haya, too, because I was so tense, so torn by the demands of our commuting life.

Jay and I rethought our plans and decided that I would take Seth alone to San Diego in January and March for shorter but more frequent visits and stay in an apartment-hotel. I didn't love the idea of being separated from Haya, but the new plan seemed like a good compromise. We agreed that in June, after the school year was finished, I would take both children to La Jolla for a more extended stay before going on to the Cape for the summer. I was beginning to think that I would never get out of a suitcase.

We had an excellent visit in La Jolla that fall, although I was busy packing up the houses in La Jolla and New York for the move to our new residence in New York. Dr. Springall reported that Seth had made a two-year leap forward in reading. He said that Seth's focus was significantly better and always improved when he was interested, engaged. Seth was demonstrating persistence in tasks and greater strength and accuracy. His hand-eye coordination had improved also. His sessions with Dr. Frymann proceeded without major incident.

Both Seth and Haya were to be given standardized tests that October and November. When I had scheduled the appointments for Seth's testing in New York in early October, the psychologist-evaluator reassured me that she would make recommendations about schools once the test results were known. The tester for Seth didn't want Seth to be too tired, since the tests were taking place after school, so Seth's testing sessions were short and the tests untimed. Haya also would need to take standardized tests, which were routinely administered to children her age at the 92nd Street Y Nursery School. These tests were necessary for application to a kindergarten. I was sanguine about Haya. Her self-possession, her lovely presence, prompted others, strangers and intimates, to comment constantly about her intelligence and her demeanor.

Our research persuaded us that girls succeed more easily in an all-girls school. In Haya's case, since she was so tall and so beautiful, I wanted to emphasize academic subjects. I believed that at an all-girls school she would encounter fewer social distractions. She would wear a uniform, too. With an older brother at home and with other social environments such as our synagogue, I wasn't worried that Haya would want for a social life. I scheduled visits and the necessary interviews for the five top girls' schools in the city. The autumn was about evaluations, visits, interviews, and applications. It was also about my fantasies and expectations for my children.

In early December we met with Seth's teacher at the Gaynor School. She reported that he was happy in the class; his group was made up of boys he knew, and there were only two new students in the class. Seth loved the social aspect of his school day, she observed. Of course the speech issues remained. But Seth was reading beyond his grade level and had good comprehension and decoding skills. In math there were some memory problems when it came to facts. In receptive language he needed simple directions because he jumped in before all the directions were completed, going off on a stream of consciousness, or going off on a tangent. Her strategy was to give him information in parts. Because of his impulsive nature, he would blurt out answers, jumping in, feeling pressure to get it out. We all agreed that this behavior indicated how much he was constantly comparing himself to others and finding himself inadequate. His teacher said that Seth demonstrated a tremendous love of learning, a love of being taught. That is something we hear often, and it acts as a flag for me. If I don't hear this from Seth's teachers, then I know something is wrong.

An occupational therapist routinely saw Seth as part of the Gaynor curriculum. She said that he hated working with her. Their sessions challenged him on the most fundamental levels of motor skills, so he avoided the work, resisting and struggling. The old patterns of manipulation were at play in a big way. This information reinforced my belief that Seth needed one place where he could be absolutely comfortable, even if it was in front of the television.

There were accomplishments and progress, but the gains seemed to be accompanied by immense anxiety on his part. I wanted him to relax more and put some emphasis on pleasure. While I felt committed to finding occasions for him to unwind, I recognized that he was busy with speech therapy, Dr. Oldberg, and more testing. Summer is Seth's balm. In the summer Seth recharges and rejuvenates. Fortunately, there is no television in our summer house. Seth reads voraciously every summer and relaxes with his books, fishing, and the beach.

The test results repeated what we had heard from the beginning. Seth is very bright, with a superior intelligence and excellent reasoning skills. He was ahead of his second-grade standing in reading. In math and spelling he scored in the high third-grade range. He worked hard but needed tricks to remember things, especially facts. The psychologist who administered the tests recommended three possible mainstream schools to consider moving Seth into the following year, when he would be in the fourth grade. I sent for the applications and scheduled visits.

The entire first six months of that school year were spent looking at mainstream schools for Haya and planning which ones we would investigate for Seth. Again, I was challenged to meet my inner expectations head-on. In terms of finding appropriate school placements for the children, my hopes were hanging in the balance. There were some ironic and enlightening twists.

Because Seth and I were away in La Jolla when Haya's test results were delivered, I didn't learn about Haya's miserable performance on the standardized tests for almost two weeks. The expectations I had of her matriculating at one of the two best girls' schools were dashed. I was devastated and confused. My child who was without a flaw suddenly had only a marginal chance of going on to one of the better schools. The daughter I thought was untouched by the demons that haunted my parenting experience with Seth suddenly presented the biggest challenge of all in my agenda.

New York parents are nuts on the subject of the best schools. I was a New York parent, and I discovered that I was just as batty as everyone else. I had thought I was immune to the concerns that plagued the other parents, but I was far from it. Questioning everyone and every possible reason for Haya's poor performance, I even wondered about her intelligence. How I could doubt her abilities is ludicrous to me now, but I was ignorant about what was really troubling her.

Over the following few weeks and well into the next eighteen months, I learned much more about Haya and even more about myself—what kind of mother I was, what values motivated and informed me. I got a new grasp of "special needs" and who had them. I was embarking on another voyage. Except this time the path wound solely into my very visceral self.

13

◆

Haya

◆

"Is this going to happen to me? Why did it happen to Seth and not to me? Will Seth die from cerebral palsy?"

Suddenly I was hearing questions I had never heard Haya ask before. Of course, I had never invited questions. When she finally verbalized them, I was shocked at how blind I had been to her deepest, unspoken fears. What had I been thinking about? Obviously, not Haya.

Haya was big, beautiful, and poised. Her size alone made it difficult for me to think of her as a baby, but it was her maturity that made me forget what a little girl she actually was. The first few years of Haya's life had been very peripatetic. We had spent one Halloween in California and another one in New York. We would leave New York in the midst of a snowstorm and arrive in San Diego where it was eighty degrees and sunny. Our apartment in New York had a small terrace, but in La Jolla the Pacific Ocean was our backyard. Here we were traveling back and forth to California, with Haya switching schools, switching homes. We trekked around New York in strollers and on buses, and then we lived in an automobile in California. Things were always changing. We spent our summers on Cape Cod, so she was sleeping in three different bedrooms during the year. Sometimes she lived with her daddy and sometimes not. Haya never made a peep. She went along cheerfully, anticipating each move with nonstop questions, and with plenty of enthusiasm.

Haya has always been very affectionate and very sweet, but she has a stubborn streak. There is a strong-mindedness about her that is always a surprise. I always can trust her to hold her own with her brother. As children, they had a secret language between them that I thought very extraordinary. Even today I am impressed by how they understand one another.

Haya's standardized test results tested me more than they tested Haya. Eventually I had these evaluations to thank for the wake-up call they provided. But first I had to recover my equilibrium and confront my disappointment that my little girl was probably not going to the elementary school I had dreamed about for her. In the final analysis, she turns out to be more perfect than anyone could ever wish a child to be and is attending a wonderful school that is perfect for her.

When I got the results of the Educational Review Board tests (ERBs), I just got caught up in an empty syndrome. Years earlier I had stood in the elevators of the 92nd Street Y and quietly criticized the mothers who were competing for places in the best secondary schools for their children. Here I was doing exactly the same thing. Worse.

Instead of immediately asking what had gone on during the testing that could have made my very intelligent child perform so badly, I worried about the status of Haya's future. Haya's scores made me wonder whether there was something lacking in her intellectual abilities. I thought about the other children who had performed better, children who still used a bottle, weren't as socially adept, or whose behavior made it hard to have them around. Yet these children, especially the girls, had performed better than Haya on these tests and would go on to the better schools.

No wilting wallflower, Haya could more than hold her own in an environment and an atmosphere where Seth was the star attraction. Or at least I assumed that she could. At home she spoke her mind and stood up for herself. She asserted her independence by tying her own shoes, selecting her clothes independently. She asserted her individual preferences for food, for movies. During the years of our commute to La Jolla, she went along happily, making all the adjustments with good spirit. The assertiveness we witnessed at home, however, was often absent in the public arena. She was quieter, more shy outside of the house until she was familiar with the people and the surroundings. Still, that felt normal.

After we received the results of the tests, we immediately consulted the school psychologists. How could such a focused, well-adjusted child, always described as being so smart, perform so poorly? The answers provided insights into our daughter and into ourselves. They also set us on a course of family conduct that serves us incredibly well today.

The psychologist described Haya as concerned about what "testers" wanted from her. Haya seemed uncomfortable when asked to perform or to assert herself. And her behavior was skewed. Either she was wearing the clothes and taking on the attitudes of a teenager, or she was sucking her thumb and talking like a two-year-old. There was no middle ground. Haya felt that she had to pay special attention to Seth. Did she think he was our favorite child? I don't think so.

Our inquiry didn't stop with the school psychologists. We also consulted the evaluator who was testing Seth for the mainstream school placement. The psychologist described Haya as extremely bright with an astonishing memory, but not forthcoming during the testing period. She found a real disparity between Haya's behavior with her friends, in her classroom, and Haya's behavior in her adult world, the world of her family and their friends. Haya was not using the skills she had and was very cautious and anxious. The most striking observation the psychologist made was how often Haya brought Seth into the conversation, how excessively worried about her brother she was.

I had often witnessed Haya's obsessive concern for Seth but had never intervened. So I became more attuned. Although the children had normal sibling rivalries, the typical name calling and fights, if there was anything amiss with Seth, Haya always assumed responsibility for setting things right even when she was just three and four years old. If Seth had a cold, she tended to him and administered all remedies. If he was hurt or disappointed, especially as a consequence of his disability, she was there to reassure him. This pattern acquired many hues and persists today in some other guises. The need to tend, to be helpful, is a behavior characteristic in any family where there is a need. Think of the families of alcoholics. Recognizing this tendency, I had to be more cognizant, more aware.

We saw that Haya had a sense of Seth needing a lot. She was also very focused on people's feet, their bones. Because of Haya's size and her physical beauty, her inner strength, our expectations were always that she could handle the demands we placed on her. What we had overlooked was her fear of the unknown, her desire to please, to compensate for Seth. We didn't want her to feel guilty about stealing attention for herself when she did perform well. Issues of self-esteem I so obsessed about in Seth's case I never ever considered in light of Haya's circumstances. As a result of her lack of confidence, her ability to take risks was being stifled. Her natural sense of reserve, her retiring instinct, were fully revealed when she was tested.

We had failed to take account of Haya while we were working out the family equation. When a member of the family suffers from a disability or from an illness, the entire family experiences the stress. Each family member feels he or she isn't getting enough attention. I was concerned at the time of Seth's diagnosis with my husband's feelings. My parents and my in-laws got "special handling." Later it seemed normal for Haya to have intense feelings about her brother's disability. I do. But I neglected to address those feelings with her.

When a child is young, he or she is less able to understand the conditions involved in a brother's or sister's problems. I was long overdo in providing Haya with explanations that were clear, honest, and age appropriate. She needed a forum to develop the language for expressing herself. We needed to start by bringing her into the equation in a conscious way.

I had never considered the problems a sibling of a special needs child has. I hadn't considered Haya's emotional life. I hadn't been diligent enough to investigate the literature. And is there literature! Where was I? Asleep? My research shows that the majority of the studies on the effects of a special needs child on siblings was done in the late 1970s and the 1980s, although there were also some studies in the late 1960s. As a result of these studies, there is now a Siblings Information Network that assists people and professionals interested in serving the needs of the families of individuals with disabilities. This network disseminates bibliographic material and directories, places people in touch with each other, and publishes a newsletter written for and by siblings and parents.

Debra J. Lobato's book *Brothers, Sisters, and Special Needs* was published in 1990. (Haya was three by then.) Her book provides concrete strategies for dealing with the sibling of a special needs child. It also has a companion packet for developing a workshop. I saw an advertisement for the book in *Exceptional Parent* magazine.

Each sibling of a child with a disability is unique. However, all of them have similar needs and concerns. These change with age and circumstances, but most need information on their sibling's disabilities, including how such problems can be treated. Knowing when to communicate this information is one of the great challenges. Lobato reports in *Brothers, Sisters, and Special Needs* that one of the most positive outcomes of the sibling support groups is learning to identify when the nondisabled sibling is ready for conversation.

Studies also show that a child with a disability has a positive influence on the lives of other children in the family. Children involved with a brother or sister with a disability often seem to have better relationships with one another and other people. They must know that they have to be especially agreeable and pleasing. But they also learn that difficulties can be surmounted.

Since my sorrow about Seth is recurring, I imagine that Haya experiences this too. When I talk to Haya, hearing my own words helps me. I feel less isolated. As she grows up, her feelings will change, so will her friends' questions about her brother. I always maintain with her that it is okay to have strong emotions about Seth.

We try never to deny Seth his feelings about his problem. We try to support the integrity of his experience by not confusing it with our own. The same holds true for Haya. I encourage Haya to express her negative feelings so that they won't fester or build up inside of her. I don't emphasize only strengths. I like to acknowledge differences. Her teenage years will bring changing emotions about her brother, also.

I have read that resentment and bad feelings toward a brother or sister with a disability are highest when a sibling has a lot of child-care responsibility. When Haya concerns herself greatly with Seth's well-being, I thank her and offer the reassurance that I or another adult can be responsible for him. I deliberately try to free her of responsibility. I don't want her to have an extra caregiving burden.

Until recently Seth needed help tying his shoelaces and regularly asked Haya for assistance. This skill is still difficult and tedious for him, and when he's in a hurry, as often occurs at breakfast time when everyone is rushing to get to school and to work, he needs help. That used to mean that Haya would begin her day by helping Seth. Now no matter how busy I am, whether I'm getting the food on the table or into our stomachs, getting the children out the door or ready for the school bus, I make it a point to help Seth myself or call on another adult. Seth has learned not to ask Haya anymore.

I am also encouraging Haya to risk more by sharing her concerns. If she says she doesn't want to go somewhere or try something, I support her. For instance, if she's not sure she wants to participate in the ballet school's performance of *The Nutcracker,* I say, "Maybe you're right. You can be in it when you feel like it. Maybe next year." When it came time for her to participate in her first horse show and she was unsure, I didn't force her. Often I leave it to others, especially her peers, to do the encouraging. My emphasis instead is always on expressing my confidence in her. At the same time, I keep the pressure to perform to a minimum, letting her find her own time.

If she complains about something, I don't contradict her. I express sympathy in appropriate proportion, always careful not to encourage self-pity. Sure, things hurt, are frustrating and difficult. Failure is important in developing self-esteem. We all struggle with issues of self-worth. Knowing our feelings are acceptable is important. Learning that everyone is special and coming to terms with our own inner strengths and weaknesses are the keys to maturity.

After I had investigated more about the siblings of special needs children, I decided we needed an at-home, weekly family meeting. The emphasis is on listening, on simply hearing one another. To begin, each of us has ten minutes to voice his or her anger, frustration, pleasure with each other or in life in general. There is no rebuttal or response, just an audience of three.

Conflicts and feelings get ample ventilation during these sessions. Nuances of the children's interaction are revealed, and this is helpful to me. I grasp more of their struggles with themselves and each other, as well as with Jay and me. I find that I am able to interpret their behavior more realistically. After we go around once, and each of us has had his or her say, there's a response time for each of us. The rule is to preface each response with a repetition of what the other person has said, just to be sure that we all understand one another.

In one family meeting Seth complained, "Haya helps me just to show off what she can do that I can't."

Haya claimed, "Seth only asks me for help when he is lazy about doing it himself. When he wants to be on the jungle gym alone and make it his house, he doesn't need me. And he never gives back."

"You only want to help when you can do it better. Like on the cross bars."

"That's not what I think," Haya responded. "And you want to sit at the table next to me on my birthday, but you don't want me to even come to your party. I had to come with Mommy." Then Haya got very quiet and wouldn't say anything for a long time. She only nodded or shook her head when Jay and I prodded her.

"Cluck. Cluck. Haya's in an egg," prompted Seth.

"What does Seth mean?" I asked.

"That I'm like an unborn chicken. That's why I'm not talking. You can't talk if you're not born," announced Haya.

I was aghast. How these two understand one another. Obviously, it is better for them to work things out without my interfering. They need to engage one another in their differences. Haya says that her friends' questions about Seth, his speech, his gait, disconcert her. Seth demonstrates remarkable insights and resilience and self-identity in response. She expresses embarrassment and hesitation about performing tasks of her own. His reaction reassures her. These meetings are a source of revelation. I realize that two children have special needs in our family. I feel especially responsible for addressing these issues because Haya is not involved in a sibling support network. As she gets older, if it is something she desires, I will encourage her to join such a group.

Lobato also reports in her book that studies show that one of the most powerful influences siblings have on one another is their ability to affect each others' relationships with other people. Many researchers and scholars believe that brothers and sisters actively shape one another's lives and prepare each other for the experiences they will have with their peers when they grow up. Characteristic of the interactions between younger brothers and sisters are intense, uninhibited expressions of the full range of human emotion—from love, affection, and loyalty to hatred, hostility, and resentment. Experiences of both positive and negative feelings and behaviors are a guaranteed reality of siblings' relationships, and an enduring bond. Although the young siblings of disabled children share emotions and experience their disabled brothers and sisters in the same ways that other children experience their "normal" siblings, in the family of a special needs child there are stressful factors unique to the special circumstances. Open communication within the family about the problems and sharing the negative and positive experiences of all family members, both seem important. Strategies for coping with stressful events, and especially peer and public reactions as well as extra responsibilities at home, need to be developed.

There are some positive effects to growing up with a sibling with special needs. Maturity, responsibility, tolerance, compassion are found in great supply in my daughter. Some of the potential negative effects are embarrassment, resentment, and restrictions in social activity. I see how the questions about Seth are changing now that Haya and her friends are older. Her friends observe Seth differently.

Haya's acceptance of Seth's disability is an ongoing process, just as it is for me. Naturally, when Haya was little, she wanted to do many of the things for Seth that we were doing. Her response to Seth is different now that she is in school. I think she may worry about how to tell friends that her brother is different. She obviously worried that the something "wrong" with Seth might mean there was something "wrong" with her.

What I anticipate in adolescence is many of the same concerns Haya has now, especially her fear and guilt and her increased sense of needing to perform for us, as though to make up for Seth or to get attention. I also know that teenagers are working on their own identity. Appearance and body image are increasingly important, so is the appearance of family members. Having a sibling like Seth may make Haya feel embarrassed as an adolescent. Or she may worry that if she gets married she will have a child like Seth. She may worry about caring for Seth in the future. By providing her with clear and honest information, Haya should be able to deal with these questions.

As I mentioned, in the winter of 1992 when Haya was in kindergarten, I began traveling alone with Seth to La Jolla for his treatments. She was left behind, and I recognized the possibility that Haya might resent Seth's having special time with me that she didn't. I made it a point to carve out similar time with Haya during the year. We went away for three days together soon after I returned with Seth from our first trip. It meant a lot to both of us. Since the winter of 1993, our trips to La Jolla occur annually, and I schedule them so that we can all go together as a family. During the intervening months, I find time away alone with each child.

Awakening to Haya's needs changed us. It intensified our family bonds and helped to make us as close as we are today. Haya's challenge provided the opportunity for us to change our behavior, not just in dealing with each other but in coping generally. Recognizing Haya's needs meant strengthening our love for each other, and it also propelled us toward an understanding of each other that might not otherwise have occurred. My own identity remains more intact as a result.

Listening to the children and Jay during these family meetings enhances my understanding and appreciation of members of my family while allowing me to keep myself separate. I hope that by being all I can be I will be an example to the children and inspire them to be all they can be.

14

◆

Ashore

◆

As THE NEW YEAR OF 1992 BEGAN, we had moved into our new home. It was also a time of evaluations, school visits, applications, and interviews for both children. By the spring, we had happily accepted a place offered to Haya in a private girls' school we thought was great. Seth's situation was different.

After considering the results of the private testing in the fall, Jay and I had taken the recommendations of the evaluator and gone to visit several mainstream private schools. We determined that a co-educational school was the best setting for Seth. The emphasis on athletics in the all-boys schools would be too challenging. We wanted a setting where he could thrive. We needed Gaynor's cooperation in forwarding transcripts and school reports as requested. The staff seemed relatively indifferent to our requests.

Seth was received graciously everywhere, but ultimately we seriously considered only one school, and that was the only school that seriously considered offering Seth a place. The conundrum with this school was logistical. The school housed the fourth-grade class on the top floor, but all the "specials" including drama, music, physical education, and lunch took place in the basement, six floors below. The stairways were narrow and steep and double height between some floors. As at Rodeph, Seth would always be the last to arrive everywhere, and he'd always be tired. Neither Jay, nor I, nor the staff at the school thought all that stair climbing was a good idea. Jay and I decided to wait. We went back to Gaynor for a meeting.

That was the turning point. It was obvious to the administration that we had no great stake in Gaynor. In our minds Gaynor was only a stopgap. However, we were without options and wanted to explore Gaynor's view of Seth and to discuss the coming year and possible student groupings.

We met with the director of curriculum, the director of the school, and Seth's current teacher. While the teacher was emphatic about Seth's progress, she also stressed the support and the work she thought Seth required. The director of the school was quiet, recognizing, I believe, that we were in an abyss. The director of curriculum, however, was tired of us and tired of our indecision. She was willing to let us go, and to send Seth packing. Even without serious alternatives, I was ready to capitulate and was on the verge of accepting this impasse.

Fortunately, Jay had the courage and foresight to jump in and say, "Wait a minute. We don't have an alternative for Seth next year. What can we do for the time being to realize a good year for him here?" Jay was not ready to write off the school so quickly. The discussion changed from that moment, and ultimately so did Seth's relationship to Gaynor and our relationship to Gaynor.

By the end of the meeting, we knew that Seth would return to Gaynor for the fourth grade and would probably remain for one or two more years after that. Recognizing Gaynor as Seth's best alternative, we became reconciled, recommitted, and ready to help Seth realize that Gaynor was his best chance to get ready for the mainstream. We already knew that trips to La Jolla would take place only during vacation time or just before school let out in June of each year. We no longer had the energy or the money to keep enrolling Seth in school in San Diego. It was too much for everyone. The academic interruptions were also a strain.

We left for the Cape with the sense that both children had the right school waiting for them in September and with no expectation of going to La Jolla until the winter recess. Seth was angry at first, but as the summer wore on he forgot his frustration, absorbed as he was in science school and fishing. We also sent him a clear message about our own satisfaction regarding the decision and were unwavering in our equanimity about Gaynor.

Fortune reigned. In the fall, after another spectacular summer, the children thrived. Seth's fourth-grade teacher, Mrs. Virginia Melnick, was a perfect match for Seth, an inspiration and a whiz. The class was an excellent mix of boys. Some of Seth's program was now departmentalized, meaning that he was grouped for reading, math, spelling, and computer with others at his level. That was very good for Seth.

His homeroom, history, and social studies were taught by Mrs. Melnick. She ran a tight ship but was a motivator. She focused on the students' writing and long-term projects as well as on behavior. Her own son was learning disabled, so she was extremely sensitive and astute about children with learning challenges. She was also highly perceptive about Seth, and she had enormous affection for him. At the end of the year she gave him the award for "Best Manipulator: May you use it in the service of humankind." It was a watershed year for Seth and for us. We knew we were lucky that fate had intervened, so that with no other alternatives, Seth had stayed put at Gaynor.

In June 1993 Mrs. Melnick suggested that Seth progress into "Team" the following fall. This was an enormous step for Seth and a reward for a year of hard, diligent work. "Team" was the one- or two-year program the children participated in before going on into the mainstream. It was a rigorous academic program that required another level of maturity and commitment. Two male teachers, Mr. Warren Jacobson and Mr. Doug O'Hare, famous in the annals of Gaynor lore, along with Ms. Laura Kennedy, taught the Team. In Gaynor's terms, it was the big time.

Our own promise to ourselves was to pledge to Gaynor some of our financial resources and the use of our new home. We became active in fundraising, the annual auction, and social activities. For three years we hosted the New Parents' Evening in September to welcome new families to Gaynor. Who understood better than us the anxieties and disappointments that came with enrolling a child at Gaynor? Who knew better the possible rewards? We opened our home to the families, the staff, and the administration, always inviting Seth (who wouldn't have missed it for the world anyway) to welcome our guests.

The message to our son was loud and clear: we were committed to his school. It was a lesson for us with Haya, too. We immediately got involved at her school, recognizing that our children would take our lead and follow our example. If we cared, if we were committed, then they would be too. The other dividend was our increased intimacy with the staff, and other parents, often the parents of our children's friends. It made Seth feel he had access to people who had once seemed very distant. Once a year his teachers and the school directors were eating cake and drinking coffee in his home.

Seth spent two years in Team, proudly graduating in June 1995 with an acceptance for the seventh grade at a top secondary school in New York, a school of his own choosing. Gaynor had prepared him exceptionally well in several areas. They had coached him and readied him for the ERBs, the standardized tests. They had taught him the subjects he needed so he could feel comfortable about meeting his peers in a new surrounding upon graduation. They had spent time helping him with school interviews. The Team members who were graduating had met once a week to talk about their feelings, their anxieties about leaving the Gaynor haven. Looking back, we couldn't have asked for anything more.

We were also lucky that we could afford Gaynor, a school with a large tuition; lucky, too, that circumstances prevented us from leaving Gaynor when we thought we should. Ours was purely an emotional reaction to having to face the fact that our son has special needs. Without Gaynor, Seth would not have the opportunities he has today. We were lucky that at the time of our indifference and fatigue, Gaynor was there for him anyway. I think they must fulfill this role for many parents, as we all struggle with the disappointments and denials we have to face.

In the fall of 1992, as we were beginning to commit ourselves to Gaynor in a substantial and conscious way and as Seth found himself so fortunately in the hands of Mrs. Melnick, we made another radical decision. We decided to eliminate Dr. Oldberg from the equation. Our weekly family meetings were consistent and extremely productive. By then we were living on the other side of the city, and the doctor's office was no longer convenient. Seth had complained that he had too much to do and didn't like going to Dr. Oldberg.

Seth also was in very good shape emotionally. He was happy. He performed his school work diligently. Except for routine issues, typical conflicts about television, bedtime, controls, and such, there were no problems of cooperation with Seth. For more than a year now he'd been sleeping through the night. At the same time I was a little anxious, feeling many of the same fears I had experienced years earlier when Anat insisted that I cut off all the therapists.

Admittedly, Seth complained about the time-consuming demands of his various treatments. From time to time he would let us know his personal feelings about a practitioner. But Seth had never said, "I don't need this treatment," except with Dr. Oldberg. Seth was adamant. He consistently voiced his displeasure about having to go to Dr. Oldberg each week. I could not see the point of his continuing. While I didn't want Seth calling all the shots, I also didn't want to make him a patient for life. But I didn't want to cut off Dr. Oldberg in such a way that Seth couldn't call him if something difficult came up, if he wanted to work something through with the doctor.

Jay and I discussed the situation between ourselves and then talked with Seth about the best way to terminate the relationship. Seth didn't care if he ever spoke with or saw the doctor again, but I did not agree. I insisted that Seth visit with the doctor one more time after I called to say we would not be continuing. I asked Dr. Oldberg if he was willing to speak or meet with Seth from time to time if it proved necessary. While he was not enthusiastic about our decision, he agreed to be available on an ad hoc basis should it be needed. The truth is Seth has never seen or asked to speak with or see Dr. Oldberg again.

In the last year, Seth asked for a way to learn how to do some of the daily tasks that challenge him enormously, such as tying his shoes, buttoning his buttons, cutting up his meat, pouring from a pitcher. We found Kirsten DeBear, an occupational therapist, who took Seth on as a student for a limited number of sessions. Seth can now tie his own shoes, cut his food with a knife alone, not easily, but successfully, and has acquired a small tool to help him with buttons. Occasionally he asks for some extra lessons with Kirsten.

Once Dr. Oldberg was no longer part of our New York life, I realized that we had no real medical care in the city outside of the speech therapist and Dr. Lee. I was not happy depending solely on Dr. Frymann three thousand miles away. And I was not happy with Dr. Lee.

Each time I took Seth and Haya to see Dr. Lee—which by this time was only once a year for an annual checkup—she exclaimed loudly about how incredibly well Seth was doing. She remarked on how little I required her services for the children. They were never sick. (This wasn't exactly true. They had their share of colds, but I treated them with osteopathy and homeopathy.) She asked me what I was doing for them. When I started to tell her about the cranial osteopathy and the homeopathy, she declared that it was "witchcraft." I decided I'd heard that for the last time. I wanted a pediatrician in New York who accepted what I was doing for the children, for Seth especially, outside of the allopathic world. I wanted a doctor with an open mind.

I found a new pediatrician (who is only slightly more accepting of my methods, although time is wearing her down). Haya insisted that I choose a woman doctor; this requirement narrowed the field immediately. And I decided that both children needed osteopathic and cranial treatments on a consistent basis. I phoned Dr. Masiello to discuss treatments with him. He made the most sense as our family practitioner. He agreed to take Seth and Haya on as patients, but he wanted to talk to Dr. Frymann about Seth. That was no problem for me. By then Jay was seeing Dr. Masiello on a regular basis. Nothing suited me more than having a doctor who knew the whole family and knew us intimately.

Dr. Masiello sees all of us on a regular basis, Seth more often than everyone else. In between Seth's now annual visits to Dr. Frymann, Seth sees Dr. Masiello about every three or four weeks for an osteopathic and cranial treatment and for a homeopathic evaluation. Haya goes once or twice a year for a general treatment or when I think she needs to be seen. Both children visit the pediatrician annually to be weighed and measured and to get all the health forms signed for school. She remarks each time how she sees us only once a year.

For acute problems I call Dr. Masiello first. Colds, flu, coughs, falls—we consult by phone. This requires a clear report of symptoms. It's not good enough to say that one or the other of us has a sore throat. I report which side of the throat hurts more, whether hot or cold makes it feel better, when it began, if there is a change in appetite, if there has been a recent emotional trauma, and so on. I administer the remedy the doctor recommends and keep an ongoing watch on the symptoms. If they change, we often rethink the remedy.

In the case of sore throats, Dr. Masiello always does a test for strep. If we ever have strep throat (so far so good), then an antibiotic will be prescribed. Dr. Masiello is licensed to write prescriptions. If the children are sick, the doctor usually makes time that same day to see them in case of any anomaly. Then they get an osteopathic or cranial treatment if he thinks it is warranted.

Dr. Masiello has been treating me for more than six years. Seth and Haya have been under homeopathic and osteopathic care for almost as long. During this entire time I have never filled a prescription for an antibiotic. I have only administered an aspirin occasionally. Seth did not miss one day of school last year as a result of illness. Haya missed four days when she was sick with a cold or sore throat twice.

The funniest morning was the day after Haya's seventh birthday. Four of her friends had slept over as part of her planned birthday celebration. They all came with medication. The bottles of liquid anti-biotic occupied the entire first shelf of our refrigerator. It was up to me to dispense the girls' medication at breakfast time. For one thing, I couldn't get the caps off the bottles. What a struggle! The potions are offensively colored, sticky fluids that require pouring measured amounts on to spoons and then into the child's open mouth. I administered this charge as Haya sat by with her own mouth agape. In the meantime, the irony was that all four girls were hacking away with terrible coughs and noses running. One of them had already been taking the anti-biotic for three weeks.

There is nothing "kooky" about the path I have chosen for my family's medical care. Osteopaths are fully qualified physicians, licensed to practice in all fifty states. Osteopaths, like M.D.'s, diagnose diseases, prescribe drugs, refer patients to hospitals, and perform surgery. D.O.'s are represented in all the practice specialties. There are osteopathic hospitals, some of which include large academic centers. There are seventeen schools of osteopathic medicine in the United States. The fact that Dr. Masiello is also a classic homeopath adds simply another dimension to our health care, which is drug free. The remedies are easy to administer (no bottle tops, no gooey masses of offensively colored syrup) and are cheap. A few dollars often buys a lifetime's supply of a remedy.

We had a terrible scare with Seth when he was eleven, however. On the day of his birthday party, he was listless, without good color, and generally not looking well. We proceeded with our plans on his insistence. By nightfall he was running a very high fever of 102 degrees. I consulted with Dr. Masiello throughout the evening, reporting Seth's symptoms as best I could. The overriding symptom was a severe, unrelenting headache, so that he could not bear any light or even open his eyes. The doctor prescribed one remedy and then another and even another.

The cycle continued for four days, his fever climbing or staying the same, the violent headache persisting. He had no appetite. I was beside myself with anxiety. I was fatigued from the all-night vigils. I was constantly sponging him down with cold water in an effort to keep his fever from rising and to help make him more comfortable, and applying cold packs to his head and around one of his ears, which was aching. Dr. Masiello was on the phone with me constantly.

Seth seemed to be fading away before my eyes. Never one to gain a lot of weight, although he can eat as much as the biggest man (especially these days), he was eating nothing. He was so thin I could carry him easily back and forth to the bathtub for his sponge baths. I rubbed him down with oil. He was dehydrated from the fever. I just about force-fed him liquids.

After Dr. Masiello first examined Seth, we consulted him incessantly, trying to decide what to do. We considered taking Seth to an emergency room, although there was nothing that could be done there. He didn't have a strep throat or an ear infection. Finally on the fifth day his fever began to diminish, his interest in fluids returned, and his headache subsided. By then I was a wreck.

As soon as his temperature returned to normal, I took Seth to see Dr. Masiello again. The doctor examined him thoroughly and gave him a cranial treatment. He also prescribed a course of homeopathic remedies to administer over the following two months. Two weeks later we left for California to see Dr. Frymann. At the same time we noticed a remarkable change in Seth.

Up until then Seth's one absolute personal characteristic was his lack of stamina. He was intelligent, enthusiastic, sociable, irascible, but he fatigued rapidly. He always required twelve hours of sleep every night. Suddenly, that was no longer the case. Not only was he more energetic than ever before, he was vigorous. He no longer slept as much. He stopped complaining about being tired. During that summer following his illness, he went to science school, sailed, played tennis, trained with a local athlete, and had energy left over. We were amazed. (In adolescence, sleep again seems to be his favorite pastime.)

Dr. Frymann examined Seth and told us that she believed he had "shed an old skin" during the terrible illness that had gripped him only weeks earlier. She remarked that children often experience an extreme malady prior to a significant neurological and/or physiological and/or emotional transformation. She also suggested that it was possible that Seth had suffered some degree of meningeal infection. I flew to the dictionary to learn that anything "meningeal" refers to an inflammation in the brain often caused by a bacterial or viral infection. I was beside myself with anxiety and fear.

Asking myself whether the course I had chosen was sanguine or whether I had just been stubborn in my resistance to medical care different from what we were presently doing, I thought through all the care Dr. Masiello had offered during Seth's trauma. On reflection, I decided that administering an antibiotic probably would not have made much of a difference. Viruses have to run their courses. But I faltered in my beliefs and gave some thought to reconsidering our future decisions.

In the fall of 1993, after another wonderful summer during which Seth demonstrated this phenomenal surge of energy, we made another change. Dr. Frymann had always encouraged me to think of Seth's speech difficulties, his inarticulation, as a problem with proper breathing. I was seriously studying and practicing Iyengar Yoga and met a fellow student who studied with a breath coach, Carl Stough, known as "Dr. Breath."

Carl Stough had acquired his sobriquet during the Olympics in Mexico City when he prepared the United States Olympic track team. Mexico City's high altitude alters breathing, making more demands on a runner's lung power. Carl Stough came to the rescue, coaching the team in breathing techniques that helped them to win many gold medals.

Opera singers, trumpeters, pop vocalists, musicians, and body workers are students of Carl Stough. His students also include people suffering from serious emphysema. Getting an appointment with "Dr." Stough is probably equivalent to trying to be seen initially by Dr. Frymann. It took time and persistence. I engaged everyone I knew who knew Carl Stough to help me. My efforts finally paid off, and he agreed to meet Seth. Once Carl had agreed to take Seth on as a student, I let the speech therapist go.

Much of the work Carl Stough does with Seth relates to what I learned in Carola's studio years ago. The lessons revitalize Seth, change his carriage, his voice, and his alignment. Seth sees Carl once a week, and he has made friends with many celebrities whose lessons either precede or follow his own. I think their presence and their commitment to the breathing work helps Seth recognize its worth. It's not easy for a young boy to do this kind of work consistently and comprehend its value.

We feel content, usually, about the course of "treatment" Seth is receiving as he prepares to enter the seventh grade. Dr. Frymann and Dr. Masiello oversee his primary care, augmented by annual trips to the pediatrician. Carl Stough sees him weekly. Seth swims every week. In the summer he plays tennis often and goes to science school and sails. When he graduated from Gaynor this past spring, the director of physical education made a special presentation to Seth for "courage and persistence on the playing fields." He said that he had learned as much from Seth as he ever could teach anyone.

There are those who dispute our choices, and think that Seth needs a rigorous, orthodox physical-therapy program. It makes me wonder whether I'm doing everything I can to help my son. Eighteen months ago Seth twisted his ankle, and Dr. Masiello wanted X rays. The pictures showed no broken bones, but there were bony spurs growing on his ankle bones.

We consulted a highly recommended mainstream pediatric orthopedic doctor, but not Dr. Grant. The new doctor faulted us for not having Seth enrolled in a more strenuous program of physical and occupational therapy, pronouncing that Seth was far from his potential. He recommended the program he supervised at the hospital. This shook me at first, but after I looked into the program and discussed it with Dr. Masiello, I saw its limitations and decided to proceed on the course we've elected.

This question of the mainstream verses alternative treatment is at the heart of my story. There is continuing tension. In both areas the responsibility is actually put on the consumer, but that role doesn't feel as clear in the orthodox world. In the world of alternative medicine, the imperative to question the practitioner's qualifications, to ask all the right questions is ever present. And we must do this. Individuals who present themselves as healers, homeopaths, naturopaths, nutrition counselors, Feldenkrais teachers, and so on should be questioned closely as to their qualifications and training. In some of these areas standards are different in different states.

When being treated in the orthodox world of medicine, we tend to accept the license of our doctors as a sanction for almost anything. In England, where there is no regulation or licensing, it is up to the patient to ask physicians what they are qualified to administer. That would be a good skill for us to learn. We need to be sure that our doctors are really listening to us, answering our questions, and practicing their medicine responsibly.

We must become better consumers. What should compel us is the need to investigate all our choices when it comes to our health and the health of our children. We must be vigilant, discriminating, unflappable. We cannot make gods out of men. We must prepare ourselves to ask the right questions. We must not hesitate to ask every question we think we must have an answer for. We must be open-minded. Breathing, Yoga, nutrition, meditation—all are now proven aids to our well-being. We must learn not to look for quick fixes. We need to evolve into people who have an influence in our own progress.

AFTERWORD

◆

Wandering

◆

THERE IS NO END TO MY JOURNEY. I am still roaming the paths that Seth's circumstances have created. Because of Seth I am writing this book, work that gives my life definition and meaning it would not otherwise have. I have much to be thankful for. Seth is not in a wheelchair. He will not die from his condition. He is intelligent and handsome and sociable. We have had all sorts of resources, financial and otherwise. Our family is close, and we have drawn closer through the years. Haya is a wonderful and healthy daughter and sister. My husband, Jay, and my daughter Haya have made special contributions to my journey, and Seth's.

Recently at a ballgame as I watched Seth walk away with a friend to seek some players' autographs, I felt my usual pang. Seth's alignment is distorted, his gait awkward. He will never have that strapping, fulsome physique the boys I had crushes on had. I wondered about him asking for the autograph. His speech is a giveaway. Strangers watch him disconcertedly or get confused when he starts to speak, not sure of what is wrong, straining to understand him.

Still Seth never hesitates to repeat himself when asked or when he feels he has not been understood. He performs this task cheerfully and without frustration. But I watch him struggle, especially when he is excited and hurrying to communicate his thoughts and ideas. Because I am his mother, because I love him in all the ways I do, I hate to be witness to this struggle. I wish I could change it.

Seth has so much to say. One wishes it were easier for him, but he remains determined to express himself. Now entering adolescence, he insists on ordering for himself in restaurants and requesting what he needs independently of me. He prefers to make his own phone calls, although the telephone further distorts his speech. Even holding the phone requires so much effort that it depletes his speaking strength. Yet he seems to have no embarrassment and is very determined and very upbeat.

My instinct is to jump in and say it for him, jump in and do it for him. I am consciously trying not to do this. My maternal instinct to protect and nurture is hard at work. I have much to learn from the birds who nudge their little ones out of the nest and let them fall so that they'll learn to fly. The whole purpose of falling is to rise up, to use our wings. This is the lesson I repeat to myself and to Seth over and over. So that no matter how far we fall, we may never be discouraged.

Recently I began to document the numerous times I had explained Seth's circumstances unnecessarily to explain myself or our circumstances. I was appalled. I realized that there was nothing pure in my motives, and the accusation of exploitation or overprotectiveness probably held more truth than I wanted to admit.

That insight provided me with abundant opportunities for self-growth. There is no escaping the imperative of self-examination. It benefited me and benefited my relationship with Seth. Seth and I needed to talk about where we both exploit his situation. We needed to discuss when this was appropriate and when it was not. The discussion is ongoing.

Reminders are important. I never really forget the challenges of Seth's circumstances, but sometimes I need to step back and reconsider my expectations. This is especially true in regards to Seth's physical capacities. I have to remind myself how difficult, taxing, and tiring it is for Seth to do certain things that we do unconsciously, especially speaking, walking, sitting down, and getting up. When he needs to collapse in front of the television, I need to make allowances.

As we continue on our voyage parenting Seth, there are doubts, moments without faith. There is pride, there are times of frustration and fear. There are tears of joy and tears of sorrow. And then there are the hard facts of my relationship to my son's condition. The biggest question I face each day is who and where I am in all of this. Sometimes the answer is terrifying. At other times I thank the power greater than myself for sending me Seth. Seth continually leads me along on my path. I wouldn't have it any other way for myself, but what about him? I benefit from Seth's situation, but what does he feel every day? My hope is that he feels good about himself, about what he has accomplished, about what he can look forward to in his life, and about how much we love him and believe in him.

There are times when I am caught off guard by Seth's deepest feelings. When he was writing his chapter for this book, I knew that there were topics he didn't want to talk about. It must be very hard to be adolescent and have cerebral palsy, on top of the pimples and the teenage insecurities. I think that Seth is doing a remarkable job of keeping up his spirits and his self-esteem. I want nothing more than to encourage this. On the other hand, I would be fooling myself not to acknowledge his rage, disappointment, and frustration, even if he doesn't want to share it with me now.

In his introduction Seth says he knows that having cerebral palsy makes him special. I know that being the mother of a child with cerebral palsy makes me special. We all use what life offers to help define us and give us purpose. I think knowing this and admitting it enriches my life, a life already blessed, and blessed again because Seth is my son.

Resource Guide

ASSOCIATIONS AND ORGANIZATIONS

American Academy of Osteopathy and the Cranial Academy
3500 De Paul Boulevard, Suite 1080
Indianapolis, IN 46268-1139
(317) 879-1881

American Association of University Affiliated Programs for Persons with Developmental Disabilities
8605 Cameron Street, Suite 406
Silver Springs, MD 20910
(301) 588-8252
Fax (301) 588-2842

American Osteopathic Association (AOA)
300 Fifth Street N.E.
Washington, DC 20002
(800) 962-9008
(800) 560-6229 (legislative hotline)

142 East Ontario Street
Chicago, IL 60611
(800) 621-1773

Ayurvedic Medicine of New York
Director: Scott Gerson, M.D.
13 West Ninth Street,
New York, NY 10011
(212) 505-8971

Children's Defense Fund
122 C Street N.W.
Washington, DC 20001
(202) 628-8787

Office of Special Education and Rehabilitative Services (OSERS)
U.S. Department of Education
Room 3006, Shwitzer Building
Washington, DC 20202-2524
(202) 7205-5465

The Cranial Academy (see American Academy of Osteopathy)
3500 De Paul Boulevard, Suite 1080
Indianapolis, IN 46268-1139
(317) 879-1881

Disabilities Rights Education and
Defense Fund (DREDF)
2212 Sixth Street
Berkeley, CA 94710
(510) 644-2555 (Voice/TDD)
Fax (510) 841-8645

Execeptional Parent
209 Harvard Street, Suite 303
Brookline, MA 02146
(617) 730-5800
Fax (617) 730-8742
TDD (617) 730-9856

The Feldenkrais Guild
524 Ellsworth Street S.W.
P.O. Box 489
Albany, OR 97321
(800) 775-2118

Homeopathic Education Service
2124 Kittredge Street
Berkeley, CA 94704
(800) 359-9051

Iyengar Yoga
Iynaus News
P.O. Box 583
Austin, TX 78767

The New York League for the Hard
of Hearing
71 West 23rd Street, 18th Floor
New York, NY 10010
(212) 741-7650
Fax (212) 255-4413

Learning Disability Association
of America
4156 Library Road
Pittsburgh, PA 15234
(412) 341-1515

National Center for Homeopathy
801 North Fairfax Street, Suite 306
Alexandria, VA 22314
(703) 548-7790

National Information Center for
Children and Youth with Handicaps
(NICHCY)
P.O. Box 1492
Washington, DC 20013
(703) 893-6061
(800) 999-5599

National Vaccine Information
Center/ Dissatisfied Parents Together
(NVIC/DPT)
512 W. Maple Avenue, Suite #206
Vienna, VA 22180
(800) 909-SHOT
(703) 938-DPT3
Fax (703) 938-5768

Neuro-Developmental Treatment
Association (NDTA)
(Berta Bobath Method)
P.O. Box 14613
Chicago, IL 60614

Resources for Children with Special
Needs, Inc.
200 Park Avenue South, Suite 816
New York, NY 10003
(212) 677-4650
Fax (212) 254-4070

Sibling Information Network
Connecticut University Affiliated
Program
991 Main Street, Suite 3a
East Hartford, CT 06108
(203) 282-7050

The Somatics Society
1516 Grant Avenue, Suite 212
Navato, CA 94945
(415) 892-0617
Fax (415) 892-4380

Resource Guide

Alfred Grant, M.D.
301 East 17th Street
New York, NY 10003
(212) 598-6605

Marion Katzive
(advocate for special education)
230 Park Avenue
New York, NY 10017
(212) 557-0040

Richard Kavner, O.D., F.A.A.O.
(behavioral optometry)
245 East 54th Street
New York, NY 10022
(212) 752-6930

Domenick Masiello, D.O.
333 East 49th Street
New York, NY 10017
(212) 688-4818

Susan Scheer, P.T.
173 Riverside Drive
New York, NY 10024
(212) 799-8221

Joseph Shapiro, M.D. (optometrist
specializing in vision therapy)
Center for Unlimited Vision
80 Fifth Avenue, Suite 1105
New York, NY 10011
(212) 255-2240

Carola H. Speads
Miss Speads' Studio
of Physical Re-education
251 Central Park West
New York, NY 10023
(212) 787-6610

Peter Springall, M.D.
The Springall Academy
6550 Soledad Mountain Road
La Jolla, California 92037
(619) 459-9047

Carl Stough
Institute of Breathing Coordination
200 East 66th Street,
New York, NY 10021
(212) 308-7138
(212) 861-9000

Bibliography

*A Shot in the Dark: Why the P
In The DPT Vaccination May Be
Hazardous to Your Child's Health.*
Coulter, Harris L. and Barbara Loe
    Fisher. (Copyright 1991)
    Avery Publishing Group, Inc.,
    New York:
Avery Publishing Groups, Inc.
    120 Old Broadway
    Garden City Park, NY 11040

*A Teaching Seminar with
Milton H. Erickson.*
Zeig, Jeffrey K., ed.
    Brunner/Mazel, Publishers, New
    York: (Published 1980)
Brunner/Mazel, Publishers
    19 Union Square West, 8th floor
    New York, NY 10003

Brothers, Sisters, and Special Needs.
Lobato, Debra L. With a foreword
    by Eunice Kennedy Shriver.
    (Copyright 1990)
    Paul H. Brookes Publishing Co.,
    Baltimore:
Paul H. Brookes Publishing Co.
    P.O. Box 10624
    Baltimore, MD 21285-0624

*Children with Cerebral Palsy:
A Parents' Guide.*
Geralis, Elaine, ed. With a foreword
    by Tom Ritter. (Copyright 1991)
    Woodbine House, Inc., Maryland:
Woodbine House, Inc.
    5615 Fishers Lane
    Rockville, MD 20852

*Children with Disabilities:
A Medical Primer. (3rd ed.)*
Batshaw, Mark L. and Yvonne M.
    Perret. (Copyright 1992)
    Paul H. Brookes Publishing Co.,
    Baltimore:
Paul H. Brookes Publishing Co.
    P.O. Box 10624
    Baltimore, MD 21285-0624

Explorers of Humankind.
Hanna, Thomas, ed. (Copyright 1979)
    Harper & Row, New York:
Harper & Row, Publishers, Inc.
    10 East 53rd Street
    New York, NY 10022

Family Guide to Natural Medicine: How to Stay Healthy the Natural Way.
Guinness, Alma E., ed. (Copyright 1993)
Reader's Digest, New York:
Reader's Digest Association, Inc.
Medical Department
Reader's Digest Road
Pleasantville, NY 10570

Health and Healing: A New Look at Medical Practices from Herbal Remedies to Biotechnology and What They Tell us About.
Weil, Andrew. Houghton Mifflin Co., Boston: (Copyright 1983)
Houghton Mifflin Co.
2 Park Street
Boston, MA 02108

Organon of Medicine
Hahnemann, Samuel. Translated by Alain Naude et al. (Published 1980) St. Martins Press:
St. Martins Press, Inc.
175 Fifth Avenue
New York, NY 10010

Osteopathy: The Illustrated Guide.
Sandler, Stephen. With a preface by John E. Upledger, and a foreword by Domenick Masiello. (Copyright 1989)
Harmony Books, New York:
Harmony Books, div. of
Crown Publishers, Inc.
225 Park Avenue South
New York, NY 10003

Somatics: Magazine-Journal of the Bodily Parts and Sciences, 5 No. 3.
Autumn / Winter 1985/86.
The Somatics Society, Navato, CA:
The Somatics Society
1516 Grant Avenue, Suite 212
Navato, CA 94945

The Case of Nora
Feldenkrais, Moshe (Published 1977) Harper & Row:
Harper & Row, Publishers, Inc.
10 East 53rd Street
New York, NY 10022

The Child Who Never Grew.
Buck, Pearl S. With a foreword by James A. Michener. (2nd ed. 1992)
Woodbine House, Inc., Maryland:
Woodbine House, Inc.
5615 Fishers Lane
Rockville, MD 20852

The Magic of Touch: Revolutionary Ways to Use Your Most Powerful Sense.
Cohen, Sherry Suib. With a foreword by Delores Krieger. (Copyright 1987)
Harper & Row, New York:
Harper & Row, Publishers, Inc.
10 East 53rd Street
New York, NY 10022

Total Vision.
Richard S. Kavner, Richard S. and Lorraine Dusky. (Copyright 1978)
Kavner Books, New York:
Kavner Books
P.O. Box 297
Millwood, NY 10546

Vaccination, Social Violence and Criminality: the Medical Assault on the American Brain.
Coulter, Harris L. (Copyright 1990)
North Atlantic Books, Berkeley, CA:
North Atlantic Books
P.O. Box 12327
Berkeley, CA 94701
Center for Empirical Medicine
4221 45th Street, N.W.
Washington, DC 20016

Bibliography

Ways to Better Breathing.
Speads, Carola H. (Copyright 1978,
   1st ed.) Healing Arts Press,
   Rochester, VT:
Healing Arts Press
   1 Park Street
   Rochester, VT 05767

What to Do about Your Brain-
Injured Child.
Doman, Glenn. Better Baby Press,
   Philadelphia, PA. (Copyright
   1974. This ed. 1988)
The Institute for Achievement of
   Human Potential
   Philadelphia, PA
   (215) 233-2050

What to Expect When You're
Expecting
Eisenberg, Arlene (Published 1984)
   Workman Publishing:
Workman Publishing
   708 Broadway
   New York, NY 10003